Fair Winds and Far Places

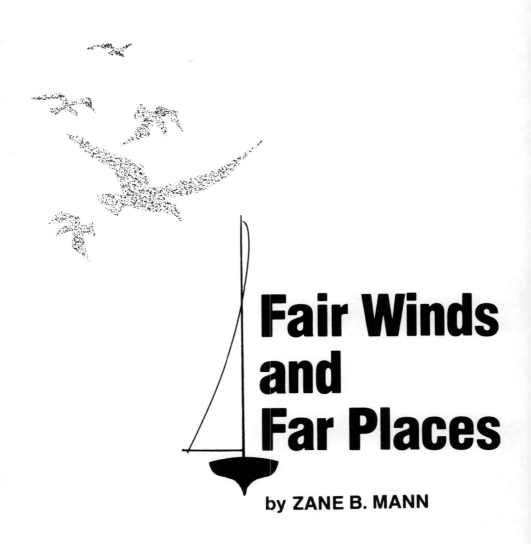

Fair Winds
and
Far Places

by ZANE B. MANN

DILLON PRESS / MINNEAPOLIS, MINNESOTA / 55415

©1978 by Dillon Press, Inc. All rights reserved

Dillon Press, Inc., 500 South Third Street
Minneapolis, Minnesota 55415

Printed in the United States of America

Library of Congress Cataloging in Publication Data

Mann, Zane B.   1924-
  Fair winds and far places.

  Autobiographical.
  Includes index.
  1. West Indies—Description and travel—1951-   2. Yachts
and yachting—West Indies. 3. Mann, Zane B., 1924-
I. Title.
F1612.M34   917.29'04'50924   78-543
ISBN 0-87518-159-7

Contents

It is customary to dedicate a first book to your wife. But in my case, Es was an equal participant and, indeed, practically co-author of the book. Such a dedication would be presumptuous and minimize her role in its publication.

Instead, I would respectfully dedicate it to my sister, Betty, and her husband, Irwin Rinnig. It was at their home in Palm Springs, California, that the manuscript was written.

Betty insisted on locking me in their poolside compound every morning. Eight hours later, I was allowed to come into the house and submit my day's writing. Betty received every word reverently and compared the offering favorably with Hemingway, Mailer, and Bellow. Irwin, less impressed, corrected my spelling and punctuation and researched every location and fact. Only when he was satisfied did he allow the manuscript to be sent on to the publishers.

It is to both of them, in appreciation of their hospitality, encouragement, and contributions, that I fondly dedicate this book.

Introduction

I grew to have a recurring vision of my epitaph:

> Here lies a nice guy. He waited
> until he solved all the world's
> problems before doing what he
> really wanted to do.
> It's too late now.

We decided sailing was our way to go. Freedom was bounded only by the horizon. The physical and mental effort of sailing was the stimulus. The new places and the new friends were the reward. If you think you might like to follow us, then it is our hope that this book might reinforce, even precipitate, your decision.

If the book is anything, it is an "If we did it, you can too" guide to dropping in—not dropping out. That doesn't necessarily mean you should give up everything and go sailing. There may be too many people out there now. I am urging you to examine your life honestly and decide if you are satisfied with the way things have worked out. If you are content —great. You are lucky. If you find, as I did, a restlessness, a disenchantment, a feeling of unfulfillment, then it is time to think about yourself for a bit.

Fair Winds and Far Places is an account of what we did,

how we did it, and how much we enjoyed our new way of life.

In fairness, it should be stated what this book is not. It is not a cruising guide, a how-to-do-it book for sailors, or sailing directions for the Caribbean. There are already several books written on those subjects.

If you have no interest in taking a little boat out into a great big ocean, then maybe this book will inspire you to do whatever that secret desire is that you have locked away.

Whatever you decide, remember the last lines of *Huckleberry Finn*.

> I reckon I got to light out for the territory ahead of the rest because Aunt Sally says she's going to sivilize me, and I can't stand it—I've been *there* before.

1 In Which We Buy a Boat and Take Off

This trip began a long time ago—years ago, really. Very few people have the courage to make a sudden decision. In my case it wasn't even a decision but a slowly growing awareness that I wanted to do something different. It began on a whole series of Minnesota winter mornings: twenty degrees below, the car wouldn't start, the snowplow didn't arrive, and the boys missed the bus to school. It began on five thousand exhausted drives home on monoxide-choked evenings, a thousand business conferences where everyone said the same thing over and over again, and hundreds of martini lunches where everyone said the same thing over and over again.

That lack of access to other people was truly troubling me. I wasn't hearing what others had to say, and certainly no one was listening to me. My sons said it was proper that I go to work every day because I enjoyed it so much. They should be allowed to "do their own thing." No one ever said it was proper for parents to "do their own thing."

Yet, with it all, I wasn't mad at anyone—well, maybe just a few. We had a good share of what passes for happiness these days. We led pleasant, active lives. I raced cars, skied, and flew my own plane. We had a beautiful home at Lake Minnetonka, a Minneapolis suburban area. We had lots of toys—snowmobiles, sports cars, sailboats, and ski boats. Es and I had been married during World War II and shared a warm, friendly companionship that seemed a great deal more secure than most of our neighbors' marriages. Our two sons were neither better nor worse than others of the "alienated generation." At least they participated in the endless debates that comprise family life today.

In short, we had the kind of life all achievers are promised if they work hard, pay their taxes, don't drink too much, and don't think too hard. But if I wasn't dodging the rocks of life's irritations, I was certainly in a hail of tiny pebbles—pebbles that were piling up slowly into a very high wall.

That a Minnesotan should choose to go to sea has always been difficult to explain. To begin with, it was more to find the warm sun than the sea. We found both while visiting Nassau several times. The Bahamian Tourist Board used to sponsor something called Speed Week, and sports car race drivers were invited to spend the last week in November as the guests of the government for a series of races held at the old Oakes Airfield. We were first introduced to scuba diving at the Fort Montague Beach Hotel in the late fifties, and during the next few years we spent more time diving on the reefs off Nassau Bay than at the races. I was really hooked. The warm, clear waters, the beauty of the teeming life on the reefs, the hot sun, and the blue, blue skies were a long way from Minnesota.

It was because of diving that we chartered our first boat, the *Tiercel*. At that time, Carl and Sumi Powell had the only scuba gear on a sailboat in the Virgin Islands. We had a perfect vacation and repeated the trip the next year. We had our first experience sailing on the ocean, if the protected waters of Sir Francis Drake Passage can be called the ocean, and we took our first deep dive on the wreck of the *Roan,* lying in about 125 feet of water. We had our first shark scare and took hundreds of photographs. The hook was being set deeper.

To this day, some of my fondest memories are of our two

weeks on a twenty-eight foot plastic boat we rented at Hope Town in the Abacos. Never before had I experienced the peace of lying quietly at anchor in calm little bays at nightfall. The brilliant sun turned from orange to a huge red disk and dropped suddenly behind the low scrub of a distant cay. In the east, the moon gathered up the light and became iridescent; a silver path formed on the still waters of the bay. And then silence, a heavy blanket of soundlessness that even the sea birds would not disturb. As we sat in the cockpit, still warm from the departed sun, we talked in hushed voices, not wanting to interrupt the overwhelming silence. It was in this ideal setting that we first talked about spending our future life aboard a boat in the tropics. It seemed a simple decision in those surroundings.

Another set of circumstances helped to push us toward a decision. After our boys were graduated from college, the big house in the distant suburb began to lose its appeal. Es found an old triplex town house in the city and spent a year remodeling what was to be our income property. We never moved in. We did rent two of the apartments and started getting phone calls in the middle of the night.

"The light in the kitchen burned out."

"Here's what you do lady. You grasp the light bulb, turn it in a counterclockwise direction, and it will come out of the socket. Screw in a new bulb and flick the switch. The light will go on. Good night, lady."

It turned out that property management was another profession I was not suited for.

We listed both houses for sale and took off on another bare boat charter, this time aboard a fine old Abaco ketch. When we returned, *both* houses were sold. I was all for having the world's largest used furniture sale and heading for the South Seas. Es, as usual, had a more sensible plan. We moved into a small apartment and signed a one-year lease. We promised ourselves that at the end of the year, we would be ready to begin a new life.

We bought all of the Hiscock books, read Slocum, and sub-scribed to *Yachting, Sail* and *Soundings.* The Minneapolis Public Library never had such a run on sailing books as it had that year. My total celestial knowledge was how to locate the North Star, and that was only because my high school student newspaper was named *Polaris* and I once wrote an article on the subject. We signed up for two courses in astronomy at the University of Minnesota. The first, called "Galaxies, Quasar, Super Novas," turned out to be an esoteric explanation of the formation of the universe. The second, "The Solar System," did teach the names of the planets and where tides come from, but very little else useful in navigation. Since I had a private pilot's license, I did know how to read a chart and make com-pass conversions, but my idea of getting a fix was to switch on the radio and locate a couple of Omni stations. We bought a plastic sextant and sent away for a "celestial navigation in ten easy lessons" type of book. I practiced faithfully on the rooftop of the apartment building, but the closest I ever got to determining my position was a point just south of Sioux Falls, South Dakota.

We began corresponding with several yacht brokers on the east coast and transcribed their listings to file cards, cross-indexed by location, price, length, and type. Yacht brokers will tell you that every day some nut walks in and wants all of his listings on a wooden ketch, shallow draft, wide beam, thirty-five to forty feet, diesel engine, in "sailaway" condition for about $12,000. By coincidence that was exactly the boat we were looking for. Admittedly, none of the hundred listings we received came close to those specifications, but we were committed to buy a sailboat—some kind, somewhere.

In March, armed with my careful filing system and a road map, we set out on a trip. I planned to start in Camden, Maine, and end in Miami with stops at every seaport in between. You have to think big if you are going to find your boat!

Our first appointment was in Greenville, Connecticut, to

see a 36-foot Rhodes yawl. The broker was sorry. It was sold, but he had a 105-foot schooner he'd like to show us. No thanks.

In Stamford, there was a 34-foot Garden ketch. It, too, was sold, but the broker had a $100,000 flying-bridge trawler. Pass.

In Southport, the boat we wanted was sold, but there was a 1903 gaff-rigged cutter that was in our price range. The broker called the owner and reported,

"You'll have to come back next week. He'll have it pumped out by then." Yeah, sure, we'll be back next week.

That night in the motel I was discouraged. We had driven halfway across the country and not only hadn't we bought a boat yet, we hadn't even seen one. Obviously, all of the good boats were already sold.

Early the next morning we were at the Bruce and Johnson boat yard in Branford to see a thirty-five foot Alden yawl. The yawl was there, but the broker wasn't and he had the key. There were hundreds of boats in the yard for winter storage, all without their masts and all covered with dark tarps. As we walked among them on that cold, gray morning, they looked like giant misshapen mushrooms growing out of the mud.

Back at the office the broker was still out, but we met Seth Houk. He had sold out the brokerage business and retired, but he still dropped in occasionally. It wasn't the first time Seth heard a story like ours, and he was sympathetic. He flipped through the loose-leaf notebooks full of listings.

"There is a boat here that you could see. The owner has been working on it, and it's uncovered. It's not *exactly* what you want. She's forty-five feet long and a sloop, and they're asking quite a bit more than you want to pay, but she's a Hinckley designed by Aage Nielsen, and a beauty."

"Anything. I just want to look at a boat."

Seth walked us down the rows of stored boats and there, rising slim and graceful among her ugly covered neighbors, was the most beautiful boat I had ever seen. Long, delicate lines swept back to a small transom where her name appeared in gold letters—*Serenity*. Sitting on a full straight keel in her cradle, her toe rail seemed twenty feet off the ground.

"How deep is she?"

"Seven foot draft."

"That's too deep."

"She needs it. Wait until you see her mast."

Seth swung up a ladder, and we climbed aboard. The decks, cockpit, and cabin sides were teak. There were bronze winches all around the cockpit. The wheel was bright mahogany inlaid with maple. On the cabin top there was a teak gabled hatch as a proper yacht should have. I sat behind the wheel and gave it a spin, looking off to the heavy clouds over the sound. I was sailing already.

"It's too big," Es said.

We climbed down the ladder into the saloon. More teak—drawers, lockers, shelves, doors—all shiny teak. The sole was teak, too. There was a pilot berth and two settees. Forward was a galley. The bulkheads, sink, icebox—everything was stainless steel. Forward of the galley, the V berths had been removed, and the area was filled with shelves, lockers, and storage racks. Aft, opposite the ladder, was the head, and aft of this was the owner's cabin, two large quarter berths, a dresser, navigator's table, and the access to the engine.

"The owner just installed a new Perkins diesel. It hasn't ten hours on it."

"It's too big," Es said.

Seth walked us over to the pole shed.

"The mast is too long for the racks in the shed. They keep it on the side." He pointed to the longest varnished piece of wood I had ever seen, wrapped in a web of stainless shrouds.

"My God, how long is it?"

"About seventy feet. It's a tall one. There's the boom and the spinnaker pole over there."

The spinnaker pole was about ten inches in diameter and

had huge bronze fittings at each end. I tried to lift it, and it didn't move.

"It's too big," Es said.

She was right about that.

We settled around a table in the coffee shop.

"It's too big," I said. "We are looking for something that is easily handled by the two of us. A split rig so I won't be overpowered by the size of the sails. A shallow draft because we know the Bahamas and want to spend time there. We have lots of other listings to check out, and I think we'll stop and see you on our way back. Keep us in mind."

"You could always cut off the mast and shorten the boom. You'd still carry plenty of sail." One last try from Seth.

We left for Camden, Maine. The next day, parked in front of the broker's office, I summoned the courage to say what I had been thinking all night.

"*Serenity* is just not what we're looking for," said Es.

"I want to go back and buy *Serenity*."

"You're crazy, you haven't even looked at another boat. Did you see that mast? It looked like the Eiffel Tower."

"We could always cut it off and shorten the boom. We'd still carry plenty of sail."

"You can say that again!"

We drove all night to arrive back at Branford, Connecticut, early in the morning. After all, someone else might buy *Serenity* before we got there. The broker still wasn't in, but *Serenity* hadn't been sold in the intervening twenty-four hours. Seth met us at the coffee shop. He didn't seem surprised— he knew a buyer when he saw one.

"Why is the owner selling?" Es asked.

"He hurt his back and feels he can't sail any more."

"He probably broke it trying to lift that spinnaker pole."

It turned out that Brad Limbert, the owner, had made an offer on an Egg Harbor power boat in the yard and was willing to accept our offer and check subject to survey.

Seth arranged for our surveyor. I had confidence immediately. He was about seventy and looked like one of those little wood carvings of seamen they sell at Mystic Seaport. He arrived with a leather pouch filled with picks, screwdrivers, and mallets and began tapping and digging from stem to stern. He pointed out some dry rot in the after cabin and delaminated plywood under the teak deck, and he pulled fastenings in the hull, but in the end he wrote a reasonably clean survey for a twenty-six-year-old wooden boat.

Es finally gave in.

"OK, we'll buy it. But you have to promise me one thing. You're not going to spend the rest of your life with that silly grin on your face. I don't think I'd be able to stand that."

The next day we met Brad Limbert at our new office table in the coffee shop. He was buying a power boat from a guy at the next table who was buying a bigger power boat from another man at still another table. The first one offered the second a thousand-dollar discount if he would pay cash, the second called Brad over and offered him the same discount for cash, and Brad returned to our table and offered to sell *Serenity* for one thousand less. Since I had planned to pay for the boat in full anyway, the deal around the tables was completed. At this point I still hadn't seen the broker who had the listing on my boat. Seth finally located him, he filled out the appropriate papers, collected his 10 percent, and left.

And so it came to pass that we bought *Serenity,* the first yacht we ever seriously looked at.

We never regretted it.

My first task when we returned to Minneapolis was to quit my job. For many years I had been a municipal bond consultant and underwriter and was a vice-president at Piper, Jaffray and Hopwood, the Northwest's leading investment banking firm. When I announced to my partners and senior officers that I was leaving, nobody even looked up from his work. Whether they didn't believe me, or didn't care, I can't

say. But I am sure of one thing. If you are delaying the fulfill-
ment of your dream because you think your business can't
survive without you, forget it! It's only embarrassing to learn
how dispensable you really are.

I finally had to resort to stopping friends on the street to
show them pictures of our beautiful new boat and tell them
of our extraordinary plans. They weren't impressed.

"Yeah, sure. But if it's a sailboat, how come there aren't
any of those poles sticking up there?"

"Well, at least you're picking a good time, business stinks."

"I'm going to do the same thing—when business gets better."

It was April, and we decided that I would go to Branford
and work on the boat. Es would stay at the apartment and dispose of the possessions we had accumulated through the years.

I arrived with my tools and old clothes, rented a one-room
apartment near the yard, and went to work. From early
morning to sundown, seven days a week for two months, I
sanded, scraped, painted, fixed—I learned every square inch
of *Serenity*. I was very fortunate that Brad Limbert was working on his power boat on weekends and could guide me
through the tangle of wiring, plumbing, fuel lines, switches,
and valves. I spent a week carving two solid maple blocks
into compound curves to hold our new dinghy. The workers in
the yard started calling me Michelangelo. Maybe it was because of my skill as a bottom painter. I asked questions of
every boat owner who would stand still, but I didn't take most
of their advice, just as you won't take most of mine. It is a
boat owner's inalienable right to make his own mistakes.

I was later to learn that there are at least 100 things in the
Manhattan Marine Catalogue that you don't have to have. In
those days I fell for every gimmick in the book. I installed a
wind speed and relative wind indicator, and because airplanes
have remote compasses, I had to have one on the boat. It
didn't work the day I put it in, and after a dozen service calls,
it still doesn't work. Coming from the north country, I

couldn't picture life without hot water, so I replumbed the lines and installed a heater. A year later, just as it was about to rust through, I threw it overboard and we lived very well without it. I had to have an electric anchor windlass and once installed, I never used it. It finally rusted into a solid block, and I threw it overboard, too. I bought a VHF transceiver which worked fine within twenty-five miles of the U.S. coast, but once we left, it was never turned on again. We were lucky the boat came with an illegal AM radiotelephone because it is the standard means of communication in the West Indies. I have no idea where you could buy a new one in the U.S. today, but if you are planning a long-distance cruise, it's worth the effort to locate a used one and get a bootlegged installation and checkout. In addition to 2182 Khz, the standard crystal frequency south of the Virgin Islands is 2527 Khz. When you're sinking off Kick'em Jenny or trying to get a hurricane warning out of English Harbour, you won't care what the FCC has to say about this illegal suggestion.

Serenity, under a different name, was built in Hinckley's yard in Maine during 1946 for a former Connecticut yachtsman, Clarence Wimpfheimer, who sailed and raced her for many years. She then had five different owners in rapid succession. At one time she was donated to Saint George's School in Newport, Rhode Island. With the exception of some long-distance races, she spent most of her life on Long Island Sound as a day sailer, and no one felt it important to have her documented. This registration and proof of ownership is a standard requirement in foreign countries. Since we were leaving the United States, it seemed a necessity and as soon as we received title, we began what was to become a very long process. We received instructions and a ream of forms to be filled out. We had to locate all of the former owners, determine all previous state registration, and get a certificate of construction from the builder. The boat had to be officially measured. All of this, together with various affidavits, declarations, certifications, and vows of various kinds were delivered to the Coast Guard office in Bridgeport. The work on *Serenity* continued while we awaited our official documentation papers.

Serenity was finally ready for the water. It's a frightening sight to see your greatest possession hoisted up in slings and trundled off to the waterfront. She was lowered into the water and towed around to a slip at the dock, and I climbed aboard to look around. My beauty was sinking! Water poured into every seam. There was two feet of water in the bilge. Before I had time to have a heart attack, the yard foreman was alongside with a huge pump.

"It happens to all wooden boats. They dry out every winter, and they leak until the water swells the planking," he explained calmly. "You go home and have a drink—by morning she'll be fine."

In a pig's eye! I sat all night peering into the bilge with a flashlight and listening to the pump cycle. The foreman was right. By morning the flow had reduced to a trickle, and in two or three days, the hull was tight and the bilge dry. At every haul out since then, I go into shock each time the boat is returned to the water. In New England most boats spend more time wrapped up in their cradle than in the water—I can't believe that does them much good.

I must have walked five miles while sanding and varnishing that long mast and boom. (I gave Brad back the spinnaker pole and I think it's planted in front of his house as a flag pole.) I checked all of the standing rigging and mast fittings. I found a crack on one jumper strut and replaced it. It was fastened to its mast plate with fifteen 1½-inch copper rivets. When Hinckley builds something, he doesn't plan to have it replaced. Because the mast was so tall, we had to wait for extreme low tide to allow clearance as the crane lowered the big spar into place. Naturally, low tide was at 6:30 P.M., so I had to pay six men overtime for the job.

At least now she looked like a sailboat.

It was June, and time to go back for Es and prepare for our first sail. By the time I arrived, all of the furniture, china, silver, and most of our paintings and other valuables had been sold. I had a very sad lady to comfort. While I had been working and thoroughly enjoying myself, she had watched the bits and pieces of her life walk out the door. I tried to convince her they were just "things" and not worthy of such affection, but I don't think I ever really succeeded.

All our old race car buddies and their wives threw one last goodbye party and presented us with a beautiful brass ship's bell engraved "For *Serenity* from the Liars Club." The club was nonexistent, but the name was given to the drivers by the wives in honor of our endless re-telling of our exploits. It was time to leave—my liver couldn't take any more parties.

The very absolute, bare minimum possessions that we had to take with us to Connecticut filled an eight-foot U-haul trailer. Remarkably, everything was eventually stowed in our many lockers. As I continued outfitting, Es made daily trips to the grocery and discount stores, and *Serenity* slowly settled another six inches in the water. My last job was to install a self-steering device. Since we had wheel steering and didn't want lines and blocks cluttering up the cockpit, we decided on an auxiliary rudder type, the Reibandt RVG. With its V-shaped cloth vane and heavy, noncorrosive construction, it was our most satisfying purchase. It usually steered better than I did and worked well on all points of sail. Our trip would have been much more difficult without it.

Serenity had come with ten sails—too many to carry on a cruise. After having them checked and reworked by a sail-maker, we settled on the best main, a No. 2 jenny, two working jibs, and a drifter. We had a wire luff sewn in the jenny and one jib and bought the largest Schaeffer furling reel and swivel. The plan was to use the furling jib and the hanked-on jib winged out for downwind work and leave the spinnakers and all the accompanying gear behind. The twin jib idea never really worked out well. I grew disenchanted with the whole idea of self-furling jibs, stowed the expensive gear, and went back to the old-fashioned way.

Whenever we could take a break in our chores, we would go out to the sound for a practice sail. The first time Brad Limbert took us out was not only to show us how everything was rigged, but also to steer us in and out of the river. As it turned out, we never had a more complicated entry or exit. As expected, *Serenity* sailed like a dream.

The reality of what we were about to do began to sink in. Soon there would be no more easy day sails, and no more going back to the marina each night. We would be out in the ocean, and all of the unknown fears that fact conjured up caused Es to believe we needed a crew. I'd never considered a crew. The whole idea had been to do this thing alone—to test ourselves and to learn. I didn't relish the idea of anyone less tolerant than Es watching me make mistakes. I didn't want to give orders; I wanted to do things myself. And I didn't want to share the experience with anyone else. It was to be our private dream, not suitable for an onlooker.

I gave in for two reasons. The first was the understanding that Es had made the only real sacrifices for our trip. Women's lib be damned—she loved her life, her work, her possessions. She enjoyed her comfort, too, and the pleasure of familiar places and friends. I guess I have always had the philosophy of a bum, but Es had agreed to all of this in order to share the experience with me rather than from any overwhelming desire to go roaming. The second reason was that she was right. It was foolish to jeopardize years of adventure because of my ego trip.

We didn't have to look very far. James Bruce, the former owner of the yard we were living in, stopped by the boat and volunteered the information that he would like to see his son crew a boat. The boy would have the summer free and while he wasn't much of a sailor, the experience would do him good.

So it happened. We signed on our first crew member, Jim Bruce—eighteen, strong, eager, inexperienced, and more than a little accident prone.

It was time to cut the dock lines and leave. I went to say goodbye to our broker, but he was out. Seth came by the dock and bought our old Chevy over a bon voyage drink. Most touching, our landlord at the apartment, who had overheard our planning during the weeks we rented from him, drove over to see us off. This wonderful old Italian's only voyage had been the one that brought him to this country, and he never forgot it. His wave was the last thing we saw as we rounded the river's bend and sailed out into the sound.

An easy sail in light winds brought us to City Island, New York, for the night. The next morning, timing our passage through Hell's Gate at slack tide, we were on the East River. I don't believe any sail we ever made has so enthralled Es. As we passed Gracie Mansion, she insisted she saw Mayor Lindsay, a pretty fair sailor himself, waving to us. Then we glided by the UN, that towering monument to futile debate; River Drive, where the skyscrapers rose brilliant and sparkling in the clear sky above the heavy fumes; Wall Street, where I had worried away so many years; and the Battery, where we dodged sightseeing boats and float planes.

It was all so corny and emotional. I insisted on sailing by the Statue of Liberty. As we worked our way across the busy harbor, our tiny boat was dwarfed by the giant tankers, freighters, ferryboats, and gleaming white ocean liners with their swarm of tugboats hooting around them. Let all the modern sophisticates and the super cool turn away. We sailed *Serenity* by Ms. Liberty, glowing green and orange in the declining sun. If you don't like parades or marching bands, you won't understand the emotions that filled us as we sailed our first yacht past the lady with the torch and through the lower harbor. Manhattan settled in the blanket of haze behind us, and the sharp smell of the ocean blew in over the bow.

2 Down the Intracoastal Waterway to Florida

Considering the inexperience of the crew, the four-day sail down the coast was uneventful. The weather gods were kind, the breeze slight and off the quarter, the seas easy. We set up a sea routine and began to practice our new chores. Once we learned to set up the self-steering vane, we could sail for several hours without touching the wheel. Es had prepared several meals in advance, which we froze in dry ice, so except for an occasional trip below to heat up soup or our morning coffee, she sat curled up in the corner of the cockpit that was to become "her" spot. Jim spent his days eating peanut butter and jelly sandwiches, and reading Chapman's *Piloting, Seamanship, and Small Boat Handling.* I was in my glory playing captain. I kept a running fix every inch of the way, which didn't require much skill since the landmarks and the cities of the east coast were less than a mile off to starboard. At night it took hours to sail by incandescent Atlantic City, then Cape May and the wide expanse of Delaware Bay, Cape Henlopen, and that wonderfully named Harbor of Refuge Light.

The only incident of the trip took place the next night. A rain squall blew out from the land, and the eye splice in the wire jib halyard let go with a loud bang. The jib whipped and snapped in the rain. I jury rigged a new thimble in the halyard with bulldog clamps and got the jib back up. All was peaceful and serene by the time we saw Cape Charles blinking in the distance.

As we rounded the cape in the early morning, I pulled one of my dumber stunts. I went below for a Chesapeake Bay—Norfolk Harbor chart, and when I climbed up the hatch, it blew out of my hand. The only thing we had to direct us into that busy place was a four-by-four-inch drawing in the *Waterway Guide*. We spent the entire day trailing freighters and naval vessels into the bay. We were damned lucky none of them was headed for Baltimore. It was 2030 when we tied up to a marina in Norfolk. Our first ocean cruise was at an end.

A word about charts. Because we didn't know how much of the trip would be outside or how much on the Intracoastal Waterway, I had bought a full set of coastal and harbor charts from Connecticut to Miami and a full set of strip maps of the waterway, along with three *Waterway Guides*. The bill was more than $135. Before we finished our voyage 3½ years later, there would be more than 200 charts filed away on *Serenity*. Norfolk was the last time I needed one and didn't have it.

We spent a couple of days getting the halyard fixed, took on more food and fuel, and set off down the waterway. The Intracoastal is a fantastic trip. Linking canals, rivers, and broad shallow bays, it winds down through the tidewaters of the southeastern coast. We passed through agricultural lands, where cows grazed to the water's edge and tractors worked the green fields just over the banks. In other places sturdy old trees overlooked the stream, deer drank undisturbed, and flocks of water birds exploded upward as we motored slowly by. Sometimes we went by the front yards of lovely old homes. I'd like to take four months and a shallow draft houseboat on the waterway someday. I'd start in New Jersey and drift down to Miami. What a trip that would be!

The bridges came along every few miles in all sizes, shapes, and means of opening. You blow your horn three times and then hope for the best. The bridge tenders, understandably, wait until the last second to open the bridge in order to minimize the interruption of auto traffic, but their concern for cars can lead to tense moments for migrating sailboats.

You are constantly reminded of the reason the waterway was constructed in the first place—barge traffic. These behemoths, two abreast and as many as six in a line, are towed or pushed up and down the waterway during the daylight hours. Their momentum and lack of maneuverability give them the right of way wherever they go. The barge captains are professionals, and within their obvious limits, they are considerate.

The real menace of the narrow waterway is the power boat maniacs. The same nuts who water-ski through a crowded anchorage leap into their sixty-foot "pleasure" boats and roar down the channel, trying to knock down the "No Wake" signs and collapse the banks with their stern waves. Their favorite pastime is to charge up on an unsuspecting sailboat and set her rocking. Extra points are scored if the spreaders touch the bank. I don't know where these crude bastards are headed for in such a hurry, but I hope they get there—and they stay there.

We came out of the locks just north of Great Bridge, Virginia, (that's the name of the town—the bridge isn't so great) in company with another sailboat, *Marakesh,* and two houseboats. As we approached the bridge, Es stationed herself on the bow, blew the horn, and waited for the bridge to open. As we moved closer and closer still, there was no movement on the bridge. At the last second someone ran to the center of the bridge, waving a red flag and shouting something undiscernible. The four boats circled awkwardly and tied up to the town dock parallel to the canal. It turned out that the opening mechanism was broken, and no one had any idea when it would be fixed. There was a big sign saying that the dock and the adjoining park were town property and off limits to transient yachts, but we figured if they couldn't open the bridge, we could take advantage of their inhospitableness.

By the time the bridge was repaired the following day, there were at least twenty boats and barges on either side, waiting their turn through the opening. For this and other reasons, progress down the waterway was slow. Even early risers seldom averaged forty miles a day. It was necessary to pick out an anchorage or marina downstream well in advance, and sometimes this meant quitting by 1500. We alternated watches on the wheel. Someone would check off the day markers as we motored by and read aloud from the *Waterway Guide* to describe what was around the next bend or warn of the approaching bridges. We all worked on our suntans and soon lost our New England pallor.

After a few days the routine became pretty settled, but tempers were getting a little frayed after a couple of near misses at the bridges.

At Coinjock, North Carolina, the bridge did not open until the last instant, despite Es's repeated blasts on the horn. As we passed through the split span, Es saluted the bridge keeper with a fist and arm gesture that, in Italy at least, is considered obscene. Since each keeper records the time, name, and description of any vessel that passes, I hid my face and pointed to my offending crew on the bow. The bridge snapped shut behind us with what seemed like a little more force than usual.

About an hour later, we pulled off the waterway into Broad Creek, an attractive anchorage described in the guide. We were barely moving as we inched our way out of the channel and up the narrow creek in what the map reported to be twelve feet of water. The bow slid upward with a shudder, and we stopped dead. Aground again. I went overboard and found we were wedged into a gooey bank of mud about the same consistency as potter's clay. We tried everything I ever heard of. We dropped two anchors 100 yards astern and drew them tight as guitar strings on the big jenny winches—nothing. I swung the boom out, and Jim and I climbed on it and tried rocking as Es reversed the engine—nothing. I pumped out our 120 gallons of water and repeated the process—nothing. I switched on the VHF.

"Coinjock Coast Guard, Coinjock Coast Guard, this is *Serenity*. Come in, please." I gave our call numbers.

"Vessel calling Coinjock Coast Guard, this is Coinjock Bridge. The Coast Guard is out on an emergency north of their station. Give me your name and location. I will relay the call, over."

"Coinjock Bridge, this is mumble, mumble, mumble. I am hard aground in Broad Creek and require assistance, over."

"Vessel calling Coinjock Bridge, message received, but we do not read your name, over."

"Coinjock Bridge, this is mumble, mumble, mumble. I'll call the Coast Guard Station in the morning. Thank you for your help, out."

I figured if the bridge tender ever learned who we were, we would be stuck in that creek so long, we'd have to pay real estate taxes. We spent the balance of the day swimming and fishing off the tilted, immobile deck.

The next day we raised the Coast Guard, and within the hour two muscular young men on a powerful work boat arrived, passed us a two-inch braided line, and within ten minutes they had towed us off. It took another hour of struggling to free our two anchors buried in that gloop.

The days passed slowly. We read and watched the quiet river scenery drift by. I have special memories of a still, starlit anchorage on Alligator River, an outstanding meal at an old southern mansion at Belhaven, North Carolina, and a calm sail across Pamlico Sound. At anchor up the Neuse River, we watched commercial fishermen work their dragnets.

Finally, at Carolina Beach we had enough of the waterway; we had covered only three hundred miles in nine days. We topped off the fuel, reprovisioned, and sailed out past Cape

Fear, North Carolina. We were on the ocean again.

I decided to cut out across the Gulf Stream and then south to Daytona Beach. Beyond the stream the sea was heavy, and the wind strong. Es complained of being sick because she smelled diesel. When I checked the bilges, I found that they were awash with the smelly oil. We turned on the pumps, and I crawled into the engine compartment with a flashlight. There was diesel oil all over everything. After much wiping and checking, I discovered that the oil was pouring out of the top of the starboard tank. *Serenity* had formerly been powered with a gasoline engine, and when the new diesel engine was installed, the two 40-gallon tanks and fuel lines had not been reworked properly for the new system. With the boat heeled to starboard and the tanks filled, the oil was draining from the port tank into the lower one and flowing out of the top fittings. With rubber tubing and a hand pump, I transferred fuel to the almost empty port tank, blocked the flow back, and the leaking stopped. I wiped and washed everything I could reach. Then the bilge pumps stopped; first one, then the other. I spent the night with my head down in the rolly, smelly bilge, disassembling, cleaning, repairing the pumps, and scrubbing out the bilges. By morning my crew was too sick to compliment me on my night's heroic effort.

The day passed quickly. *Serenity,* my beautiful lady, sailed on effortlessly. We were averaging 6½ knots, and the self-steerer was doing all the work. The easy sail revived my mates. Even they began to enjoy the grace of our track across the green sea that stretched to each horizon.

With the rising of the moon that night came the porpoises —dancing, splashing, tumbling at the bow, their silver bodies iridescent in the moonlight. I stood leaning against the sail and watched those wonderous animals leading, beckoning *Serenity* on.

When I went aft to check the heading, several of them slid back to keep me company, just an arm's length from the rail.

They lifted their smiling heads, black eyes glistening, and talked to me in high, squeaky voices. I'm certain I talked to them as well.

The nighttime is for sailors. I'll give up the noon watch any day for a turn at the wheel at midnight. There are no words for the feeling of belonging to yourself and to the sea at night.

When the dawn turned the coast of Florida pink and white in the distance, I woke Es. She found Marineland on shore right where it belonged. I altered course to the south, and we practically sailed into Ponce de Leon Inlet. By 1400 we were tied up at the marina in New Smyrna Beach. After covering three hundred miles in 2½ days, the night in the bilges was forgotten. It had been a well-executed sail.

Jim Bruce was put on a plane to return to school, and we made ready for the completion of the trip to Fort Lauderdale. The pumps were checked again, the jury-rigged tanks were checked again, the bilges were scrubbed with strong detergent, and the boat smelled fresh and clean.

The afternoon we were leaving, a garishly painted Camaro, complete with louvers, spoilers, and roll bar, screeched to a stop in the marina driveway. A crazy man dragging a gorgeous but bewildered girl behind him ran down the dock towards us. Michael Brockmann had arrived.

Mike could be one of the country's fastest race car drivers— he is certainly one of the most exuberant. I met him for the first time when I was chairman of the Trans-Am Race held at Donnybrook in Minnesota. His home was Orlando, and during our stay I had called to say hello. Without discussing it with me, he decided I needed help sailing the boat to Lauderdale and had arrived to volunteer. While I stared at his girlfriend, he loaded his gear aboard. His gear consisted of one large cooler filled with beer, another cooler of ice, and three more cases of beer.

"What the hell are you doing? We're going to Fort Lauderdale, not Tahiti."

"Yes, sir, captain, sir. But a man can't go to sea without a little beer."

I don't know how he knew that. He'd never been on a boat before in his life. He kissed his silent centerfold goodbye, and we were on our way again.

The plan was to stay close to the coastline and ride the countercurrent and the offshore breezes for an easy thirty-six to forty hour sail south. At nightfall an enormous loom of light appeared. It was almost as if the sun had failed to set and hung just below the horizon. The closer we sailed, the brighter the loom. I've flown over Chicago and Los Angeles at night, but nothing can compare to the brilliance of Cape Kennedy the night before a moon shot. We sailed by for hours until the entire western horizon was ablaze with the energy of a million lights.

Early the following morning I sighted the radar station at Jupiter Inlet and announced that we would be in Fort Lauderdale by dark. Then I went below to catch up on my sleep. Several hours later I stuck my head out the hatch—there was the Jupiter radar dome!

"Are you two crazy? We haven't moved for hours. We're aground!"

We weren't aground. We were caught in some freak loop of the Gulf Stream in spite of being only a few hundred yards off shore.

I turned on the engine and started taking sights from the nearby landmarks. We weren't going backwards, but we sure as hell weren't going forwards very fast. It took us seven hours to cover the next fourteen miles.

Brockmann developed a new navigating technique Nathaniel Bowditch never thought of.

"See that apartment building? That's Palm Beach. I used to go with a stewey who lived there."

"That's Lake Worth. I used to make out with a widow from Des Moines there."

"We're at Del Ray Beach. I know a bird with great wheels who swings in that hotel." (That means she has nice legs, for my age group.)

And so on and on and on.

At 0900, we picked up the sea buoy off Fort Lauderdale and finally motored in. It had taken eighty hours to travel 220 miles!

We still weren't out of trouble. When Mike called his sister in Miami, she was hysterical. She was positive we were lost at sea and had called the Coast Guard to find us. I immediately called the local office and found *them* a little hysterical.

"We've got a full air and sea search out for you. Some crazy dame called, said you had been lost, and knew only the name of your boat. Where have you been?"

I explained everything as best I could, including the fact that I never gave an ETA to Mike's sister or even knew she was expecting us. I apologized for the trouble I had caused, but I stoutly maintained I didn't need rescuing.

I was able to control my emotions when Mike left, but he was right about one thing—there wasn't a can of beer left on the boat.

We planned to wait out the hurricane season at Harbor West and finish some improvements on *Serenity*. But the marina turned out to be a disaster area. The gentlemen down for the Southern Ocean Racing Conference some months before had ripped the toilet stalls from the walls, stolen the shower heads, broken the tile, and in general wrecked the place in their exuberance. In the interim Harbor West was going bankrupt. Nothing was being maintained or repaired, and the marina looked like the Holiday Inn in Beirut after a skirmish. We moved over to Pier 66, expensive even in the off-season, but a clean and friendly place.

I completely rebuilt the fuel supply lines and valves and installed a refrigeration and hold-over-plate unit. The salt-water-cooled system never really worked well, but that was mainly the fault of the old insulation in the icebox. Before venturing into the tropics, I would advise doubling or tripling the thickness of the insulation around your icebox. You can't have too much. Another necessity in the tropics is a well-designed, well-constructed sun screen that is easily put up and stowed and one that covers as much of the boat, including the cockpit, as possible.

We stripped all of the exposed varnish except the mast, boom, and wheel, and oiled the teak. We found that oiling every few months keeps the wood looking nice and is a hell of a lot easier than keeping up brightwork. In fact, if I had to do it over, I would paint the mast and boom white and throw away the varnish pot.

Based upon our previous experience in the islands, I replaced our alcohol stove with a Primus kerosene type. Alcohol is a very expensive way to cook, and on many islands you can't get it at all. Kerosene, on the other hand, is available everywhere and will boil a kettle of water faster than anything I know. Later, down island, we picked up an English "Tilly" lamp—a pressurized kerosene lamp that gives off a brilliant white light. If you like to read at night, it's the best way to save your batteries. At the time I was still worried about the Coast Guard warnings concerning bottled gas. Now I think it's bunk. At least 90 percent of all the cruising and charter boats we met used bottled gas for cooking. There are many ways to put together a safe system, and I wouldn't hesitate to use this simplest of cooking methods.

While we worked, we had a series of vacationing friends, including my father, stop by to bid us "Bon Voyage." One day we had two unexpected visitors.

Just as we left Connecticut, we had heard a shocking news story on the radio. Ginny Piper, wife of Harry S. Piper, the chairman of the board of my former investment firm, had been kidnapped. Two armed men, their faces covered with stockings, had abducted her from her home and were holding her for ransom. A few days later we were relieved to learn that this lovely, gentle lady was found, unharmed, tied to a tree in northern Minnesota. Harry Piper paid one million dollars in small bills for her release.

My two visitors were dressed in gray suits, button-down white shirts, and narrow rep ties. I didn't need to examine their credentials to know they were FBI. They removed their brightly polished brogues and came aboard. It seemed that my "friends" back home in the financial district had decided that I was plenty smart. I must have knocked off a million bucks, bought a boat, and sailed off into the blue horizon. The FBI wanted to check out the accuracy of that speculation.

"First of all, I'd like to think Ginny Piper would recognize me if I had a dozen panty hose over my head. Second, I was at sea when it happened. And finally, if I had a million dollars, do you think I'd be sweating my guts out scraping varnish in this heat?"

They weren't overly impressed with that argument. In the heat of the saloon, they took off their jackets, exposing ominous-looking pistols in holsters. They checked our log and questioned me for at least an hour before they finally decided I probably didn't arrange the kidnapping. They further admitted that the FBI didn't have a clue as to who did.

Recently, on a visit to Piper, Jaffray, some friend yelled across the boardroom, "Hey, Zane, tell the truth, what did you do with the million?" I need friends like that.

Among the many new cruising people we met during our stay at Pier 66 were the Mazzareses—Nick, Bev, and five children, aboard *Shearwater* out of Boston. We met them after their oldest son wandered over to admire *Serenity*. He recognized her as a Hinckley and considered her the prettiest yacht in the basin. I took an instant liking to that kid. We were invited over for a farewell drink—the Mazzareses were leaving on an extended cruise through the Bahamas and Virgin Islands the next day. We had to go to Miami and left our boat for a couple of days. When we returned, we saw their green ketch in her accustomed berth, and they called us aboard to tell us their sad story.

The morning they were to leave, one of the boys filled the tanks with water, and they motored over to the fuel dock to top off the diesel. The attendant told them the fuel tanks were already filled to the top. The son had put water in the diesel tanks. They had spent the last two days draining the tanks and lines and washing them out with alcohol. Now they were waiting for everything to dry out. The son was so embarrassed he had been hiding in the forepeak for two days. The luckiest part was that they discovered the error at the fuel dock, not in the middle of the Gulf Stream. Ultimately *Shearwater* had a very successful cruise, and they are back in Sudbury, Massachusetts. At least one young man aboard knows how to read the label on a deck filler cap now.

Despite repeated letters and phone calls, our documentation papers had still not arrived. It was time to leave, and we were getting desperate. Dr. William B. Woolf, living on a Cheoy Lee at the dock, knew about our troubles. Since he was heading back to his office in Washington, D.C., he volunteered to aid us. We suggested that he contact Walter Mondale, then a senator from Minnesota, and see if he could help. Two days later Fritz Mondale called. The papers were in the mail. He had accomplished in one day what we failed to do in six months. I often wonder how most of us could fight the battle of bureaucracy without a concerned representative in Washington. I spent the next day carving our new registration numbers on the main beam in the saloon.

Our last phone call was from John Ebin, my former partner. He wanted to cruise with us for a couple of weeks. It was to be a honeymoon. John and Debbie had been married that day.

And so we had another unexpected crew for the next leg of our voyage.

3 Christmas in the Bahamas

The crossing of the Gulf Stream was rough but not too bad, considering it was November and the stream is never very gentle in the winter. We picked up Great Isaac Light at sundown, had a peaceful night sail, and finally homed in on Great Stirrup Light. By dawn we were anchored in Bertram Cove. I can't speak for the others, but I was so excited I didn't know what to do first. For years we had talked and planned, and for seven months we had worked, fixed, changed our plans, and worried, and up until this day we had accomplished less than what amounted to a three-hour jet ride.

Now at least we were out of the country, on our own sailboat anchored in a deserted bay, on the clear turquoise waters of the Bahamas. Our anchor and the multi-colored fish playing around our anchor rode were clearly visible. A barracuda lounged in the shadow of our hull, teaching us to relax—the hunt was over. The sun was brighter, the air cleaner, the sky bluer. We had accomplished something at last.

John and I went diving for dinner, but we were out of practice and ended up with hamburgers charcoaled on the stern. As we sat around the cockpit that night, we congratulated ourselves on our good fortune without a thought for the less fortunate 200 million tired, harassed people we had left behind. That first night was a big night for me.

Our route through the Bahamas had been chosen with two objects in mind. The first, our draft of 7 feet. I hit bottom in the Abacos once with a centerboard bare boat drawing 3½ feet. When I jumped overboard to push us free, Es sailed off, leaving me yelling after her while the tide slowly rose toward my chest. Quite naturally, I wanted to avoid as many shallow banks as possible. We had sailed a number of the out islands in the past, so our next object was to get somewhere new.

But first we had to check in with Customs and Immigration. We decided on a midnight sail for Nassau and arrived in that busy harbor in the forenoon. I cleared customs and received a six-month cruising permit. We passed up the night-clubs, hotels, and gambling joints and anchored at Rose Island for the night. Who needs calypso bands and two-dollar drinks? We made our own rum punch and fell asleep to the soft lapping of the waves against the topsides.

My favorite anchorage in the Bahamas, at least up until that time, was Warderick Wells. The next day we sailed down the deep Exuma Sound side of the chain and eased our way into the north bay. This uninhabited island provided the seclusion and isolation we were seeking. The white beaches, varied greens and blues of the waters, the burnt green of the cay, and the stillness lent a mysticism to the small bay that is rare in the Bahamas. The island is considered haunted by the out islanders. It is said that on still nights you can hear departed souls singing hymns. A thoroughly satisfactory place to spend a few days, and we spent several of them diving, sunning, and relaxing. At night everyone but me claimed to see silent ghosts drifting among the Casuarinas and along the low hills enclosing the bay. Within twenty yards of *Serenity,* we discovered a Countess 44 ketch in about fifteen feet of water. She had apparently burned to the waterline and sunk. Her engine, compressor, stove, and burned-out settee were clearly discernible. Snorkeling over the complete bottom half of that yacht was spooky.

The conversation quite naturally turned to the "Devil's Triangle," that vague area that stretches from Bermuda to Florida's east coast and across the Bahamian Archipelago. I have always viewed the supposed supernatural dangers in the triangle as a lot of nonsense. I did envy the smart writers who could get rich dreaming up the scam and having it published. With all the inexperienced sailors and private pilots crisscrossing the area, I think it's supernatural that more people aren't reported missing. But Es firmly believes in witches and the occult. She warned me not to be a smart ass and bring down a curse on *Serenity* from Warderwick Wells's neighborhood ghosts. The hundreds of chalk lines streaking the sky—contrails from the high-flying planes—proved that at least the commercial airlines were not very worried about spirit manifestations.

We had been sailing election day 1972, and it was here at Warderwick Wells that we finally heard of Nixon's never-doubted victory (if victory is the right word). But the delayed news of the election didn't bother me. I didn't care who was elected, at least not at that time. It didn't seem to matter who was president. The mess back in the States bubbled and grew whoever stirred the pot. That's why we went sailing.

When it was time for John and Debbie to think about going home, we chose another night sail for Georgetown on Great Exuma. The next morning we were anchored in the best hurricane hole in the Bahamas, Stocking Island. We dinghied the Ebins across to Georgetown, and they left for the bitter cold of the Minnesota winter.

Alone once again, we were free to explore the island. There are four small connected bays, each almost completely land locked. When the northerns blow hard across these islands, there is hardly a ripple on the water of the anchorages. In fact it's almost too still. The one disruptive element in this paradise is bugs—sandflies, mosquitoes, and those horrible little creatures called for good reason, no-see-ems. This is a good time to discuss a recurring problem on a cruising boat—getting the bugs out.

Es is not fond of insects. A fly aboard will set her flailing the air with a flyswatter so forcefully that when she finally hits the little creature, she loosens the planking. A mosquito at night will bring forth a stream of language so blue that even the current Supreme Court would have no difficulty in defining it as obscene. She once deserted her car in the center of Interstate 494 because a bee dared to fly by her open convertible. And a cockroach—my hand shakes and cold chills envelop me just spelling the word—a cockroach aboard *Serenity* would send her off to Menninger's wrapped in wet sheets.

Serenity was so spotless that I could eat on the cabin sole, but my wife wouldn't consider letting me do such a gross, slovenly thing on her immaculate floor. She scrubbed the floor with powerful aromatic cleansers. Ammonia, pine oil, or kerosene-base detergents may make your boat smell like Leavenworth just before the governor's visit, but the odor will disappear in a few hours and the residue repels flies.

Our wooden sloop had all manner of nooks, crevices, and crannies. Es sprayed undiluted laundry bleach between the frames and ceiling, through the bilges, under the sole, at the base of all the lockers, and under the galley sink and the head fixtures. This not only prevents mildew and musty odors, but will also help kill insect eggs that you cannot see. Incidentally, spraying your docking lines with laundry bleach—or better still, the strong chlorine solutions used in swimming pools—will prevent ants and other little devils from coming aboard.

If your boat is properly ventilated, normal insect sprays are useless. You need the kind that has a residual effect, so read the labels carefully. As for ventilation, the new fiberglass boats with one hatch forward, an entry hatch aft, and five fixed portlights are great for getting bread to rise, but almost unbearable in the tropics. If you have a choice, try to pick a boat with at least four top opening hatches and at least eight opening ports, even if they all leak. It's easy to wipe up water, but gasping for breath all night is hard on the heart. You'll end up sewing wind funnels to capture any breeze you have.

Plenty of ventilation means plenty of mosquitoes, so you'll need screens. On our boat all the portholes had been screened, but the screening was torn or corroded with age. We bought the plastic kind, cut them to size, hemmed them, and sewed on Velcro tape and labeled them. We glued Velcro tape to the hatch openings with epoxy. Such screens are quickly mounted or removed, and because the plastic is flexible, they are easily rolled and stowed. Don't forget to screen the ventilator openings, even the ones for the engine compartment. In mosquito-infested anchorages we kept the boat screened all the time and carefully closed the entrance-hatch screen every time we passed through. The full set of screens does cut down on the flow of air, but it's worth it.

Bahamian no-see-ems can get through any screening made by man. We discovered the solution is to wipe down screens frequently with a sponge soaked in diesel oil or kerosene. It really works. I've seen what appeared to be dust on the deck below the ports, and it turned out to be dead no-see-ems.

Finally, there's cockroaches. Contrary to popular belief, they are not put aboard by the builder immediately before delivery. You bring them and their eggs aboard in cardboard boxes, paper bags of groceries, and newspapers. I once borrowed a book from a nearby yacht, and when I opened it, a two-inch red brown creature crawled out of the binding. This literate *Blatta orientalis* met his death between the pages of Will Durant's *The Age of Reason Begins*. I had to put the carcass in my pocket until I could dispose of it for fear of my wife seeing it and lapsing into hysteria.

Las cucarachas live, love, and lay eggs in paper surroundings in the dark, humid heat of tropical warehouses. You don't have to be an entomologist to find them. I once saw a three-inch black monster crawl out of a cardboard beer carton in a spotless supermarket. I hate to think what goes on in most native groceries we shop in.

Es had a rule: no paper containers below decks. We unloaded all liquor and beer cases on deck, all grocery bags were emptied on deck in sunlight, and all newspapers and magazines were flipped through and left on deck to sun. The boxes, bags, and wrappings were put into the dinghy tied astern until they could be disposed of ashore or at sea.

This all may seem a little paranoid until it happens to you. Once roaches are aboard, there seems to be no way of getting rid of them. Other boatmen tell me of trying sprays, powders, pills, and paints to no avail.

The only solution I know of is to hire a professional exterminator, and there are plenty of these specialists around, even on the smallest islands. They seal up the boat, spray it, and uncork a couple of fumigating bombs. After several hours one can return to what hopefully is a roach-free boat. Exterminators don't guarantee to kill the eggs, however.

Ultimately, it really gets back to cleanliness. Garbage must be kept in a sealed container, the smallest particle of food picked up before it can work itself into a crack to the bilges, and a spilled drink wiped up immediately. A piece of hard candy left on deck two hundred miles at sea will have flies or ants on it the next day. Don't ask me how or where from, but it happens.

So on those days when my wife seemed to be scrubbing down the boat in preparation for open-heart surgery, I held back my smart remarks. At least when I flicked on the light for a midnight trip to the head, I didn't have any little creatures scurrying around my bare feet.

Stocking Island has a unique facility not mentioned in any guidebook that is passed on from one cruising boat to the other. Over the hill that separates the outer bay from the eastern one, there is a path that leads through the sea grape and palmetto groves lining the shore. The path ends at an abandoned cistern filled with fresh rainwater. You have found the Stocking Island shower. The technique is to carry along a plastic bucket, soap up, and then throw buckets of cold water at each other until clean. It's primitive but a real luxury for boat dwellers.

The seaward side of the island has a two-mile white sand beach admirably suited for walking, daydreaming, and shelling. The rocks and cays off either end are filled with lobster and grouper in easy diving depth. We had seafood cooked so many ways that when Thanksgiving rolled around, Es rebelled. There was no way to make lobster taste like turkey. The village of Georgetown is less than a mile across Elizabeth Harbour from Stocking Island. In the town there are grocery stores, marine supplies, fuel, water, and ice. There are several good hotels and restaurants, but our favorite spot is the Peace and Plenty Hotel.

I dressed for dinner at the hotel by putting on a clean shirt. Es had to be fancier. She packed her clothes and shoes in a plastic bag and took the wet dinghy ride across wrapped in a beach towel. She shocked the resort guests into a second pre-dinner drink by climbing up to the dock clad in bra and bikini pants, calmly putting on her fancy long dress, fixing her hair, and regally climbing the stairs past the disbelieving diners. Thanksgiving dinner was British style—roast pork instead of turkey and no pumpkin pie.

The transient sailing community numbered eight or ten boats some days; other days we were alone. We visited on other boats, exchanging sea stories and marking each other's charts based upon our experiences. We met one group in a different way.

Mischief had been careened, pulled high on the sloping beach, when the tide went out so that her keel and bilge were exposed and her mast winched down. Then she was scraped and repainted with bottom paint. When the tide came in, the process was repeated on the other side.

I was reading on my bunk, half asleep, when I looked up through our top hatch and saw a mast where no mast should be. I leaped up the ladder to find *Mischief* nudging our life-lines. Left unattended as the tide was coming in, she was slowly drifting out the entrance when *Serenity* blocked her. I pushed her free and jumped on board. Now both of us were drifting out to sea. I couldn't figure out how to start the engine so I ran forward and got an anchor down, and we dragged to a stop. Es had been clanging our ship's bell and finally roused the crew on *Helio*. They rowed over to help secure the boat, now well out into Elizabeth Harbour.

Meanwhile, the owners of *Mischief* were approaching in a power boat. When they first saw the two masts together, they assumed a new schooner had arrived; then it became a yawl. Suddenly, it dawned on them that it was their mast drifting out. Two chagrined sailors arrived and towed their boat back to its normal spot in the bay.

We gave up our salvage rights to *Mischief* in exchange for an invitation to the rum punch party held aboard her that night.

With the perfect setting and the good company of fellow sailors, it would be easy to be seduced into staying on Stocking Island forever. But we wanted to push on. The first try for Long Island ended with a split seam in the mainsail, and we returned to a surprised group in the bay. I ended up flying to Man of War Cay in the Abacos with the sail; Uncle Norman Albury has the only sail loft in the Bahamas I would trust. The second try was more successful, and we scudded into Clarence Town harbor minutes before the black clouds and strong winds of another northern blew in.

Clarence Town is a picturesque little village dominated by two huge, twin-spired churches. They were both built by Father Jerome during an ecumenical change of heart. I don't know which came first, Saint Paul's Anglican or Saint Peter's Catholic, but few small islands can boast two such imposing structures as landmarks for approaching sailors.

The local wisdom has it that northerns will blow themselves out in three days, but this one lasted twelve long, cold, windy ones. The harbor is open only to the north, and white caps built up on the long fetch. It was rolly and uncomfortable in the bay and downright dangerous bashing up against the mail boat dock. We alternated first out, then in, then out, then in; on neither mooring did we get much sleep.

One day we had C. S. Marche, the District Commissioner, and Leland Turner, Inspector of Police of Long Island, aboard for lunch. Commissioner Marche was an amateur archeologist and diver, and his knowledge of the history of the island was encyclopedic. Inspector Turner's story was equally as interesting. At two-thirty he looked at his watch and said he had to go to the airport to make an arrest. He was expecting a U.S. plane loaded with pot.

"Your young hippies," he said, looking at me in the mistaken impression that I was an aged representative of all the youth in the U.S., "they think we're just a bunch of dumb black cops. We know when every plane leaves Jamaica, we know exactly how much dope they have on board, and we know how much gas they have. Most of them have to refuel somewhere here in these southern islands, so we just go to the airstrip and wait."

The two left in their jeep, and I later learned that just as the inspector had predicted, a rented plane landed, dropped two bales of marijuana at the end of the runway, and taxied up to the fuel pumps. The attendant stalled until the bales were picked up and the two would-be smugglers were arrested. I don't know if it was true that you could get a high from the constant aromatic burning of the confiscated pot, but I do know that almost every airstrip in the southern Bahamas has a row of confiscated airplanes rotting in the sun. Smuggling dope is a hard way to make an easy buck.

One day when the wind had died a bit, some of our number

tired of the rocking and rolling, and two of the boats left the harbor. Back within hours, they reported that the waves had built up to a dangerous height. And still it blew from the north; we registered forty-five knots on the amnometer at anchor in the supposedly protected harbor.

Many months before, a mail boat had run aground on the sandbar that extended out from the now-unused Old Clarence Light. The steel boat had caught fire, and her hulk was a marker defining the dangers of the sandbar. One day when I was at the telecommunication office, the high waves built up by the northern floated her loose, and she was drifting straight for *Serenity.* From the hill overlooking the bay, I could see everything, and I ran my lungs out down the hill, through the only street in town to the dock. Es, alone on the anchored boat, was terrified. She anxiously resigned herself to the coming collision. As I watched from the dock, the rusted hull veered in the current, missed *Serenity,* missed the dock, and beached herself on the shore, fifty feet away.

That night the crew of *Sea Queen II,* the Canadian schooner, came up with a scheme to salvage the two diesels on the burned-out mail boat, but all I wanted to do was get out of that place. We had two decent days in a row and I had had enough. We left.

We wanted to stop and explore Crooked and Acklin islands, but with the lessening wind and following sea, we decided to sail on. Within thirty-six hours we found what later turned out to be the lights of a very large Morton Salt Factory on Great Inagua and minutes later picked up the famous old light at Matthew Town. Exhausted, we anchored in the uncomfortable roadstead off the town.

Great Inagua is one of the largest islands in the Bahamian chain. It is known for its bird sanctuary, the home of enormous flocks of pink flamingos, roseate spoonbills, ducks, and countless other species. It has produced and exported salt since early Colonial days. But more importantly, it is the home of the kindest people we had met thus far.

After sleeping most of the day, we checked into the commissioner's office, and he arranged to have us move into a man-made harbor north of town that had been dredged for the mail boat. When we tied up along the concrete walls of the harbor, carloads of locals came down to welcome us. It was Christmas week, and the Inaguans celebrate with a week long *junkanoo*. (Junkanoo is Bahamian for too many rum drinks, too much to eat, and too many steel bands.)

We had hardly settled when Hugh Board and John Donkey, our friends from Georgetown, showed up on *Helio*. They had a disastrous sail down, during which they blew out all their sails and tore out two chain plates. Their boat was anchored in a cove north of the salt works, and they were living with Father Carleton, the local Anglican priest, while they attempted to repair the damage.

John Donkey was a local hero. He had gotten his name sometime earlier when he attempted to walk across the forty-mile island. The interior is a desolate barren desert, and when John collapsed from the heat and lack of water, he was rescued by local hunters. They hauled him back through the center of town lashed to a donkey. The kids followed him wherever he went, admiringly shouting his name.

We were invited to Father Carleton's for Christmas dinner, a cooperative affair. Hugh did the cooking, John baked the pies, we furnished a canned ham, canned turkey, canned cranberries, and the last two bottles of California wine on board. (It was better vintage than communion wine.)

Father Carleton was by far the most famous personage in the room. He had been the priest on Anguilla during their weird revolt. When the English Foreign Office "granted" Anguilla independence and made it part of the State of St. Kitts-Nevis-Anguilla, the people revolted. For sure, they didn't want to join with the tyrant on St. Kitts, and they really didn't want to be cast off by England. When British paratroopers landed on Anguilla, they marched resolutely through the shower of flowers and with great ceremony lowered the British Union Jack and hoisted some crazy flag of independence. Anguilla was going to be "free" whether the people wanted to be or nót! Father Carleton was banished from Anguilla for his part in this rebellion and had been assigned to Inagua.

Es was fascinated as Father Carleton presided over our festive dinner in an old T-shirt and grubby shorts. When it was time to conduct the midnight service at his church, he put on a lovely white robe over his tattered clothes and tennis shoes and bicycled off to his priestly duties. The Inaguans have a custom that should be considered everywhere. The entire population starts at the Baptist church, proceeds to the Presbyterian, the Seventh-Day Adventist, and the Catholic, and ends up at the Anglican church, participating in all of the services and singing carols as they go. What a demonstration of Peace on Earth and Good Will to Men. God bless them every one.

We turned in our Bahamian cruising permit and received our clearance for Haiti. It had been recommended that we cable the Haitian government about our expected arrival time and give a description of our boat. The cable cost five dollars a word, and no one in Haiti ever acknowledged receiving it.

Father Carleton, Hugh, and John Donkey led a group of Inaguans to the little harbor to see us off. They were waving and singing something that was a cross between calypso and a Christmas carol as we pushed out of the opening in the sea wall and turned the bow of *Serenity* southward.

4 Report from Cap Haïtian

On Christmas night 1492, Christopher Columbus was sleeping off the effects of a three-day celebration in the master's quarters of the *Santa María* as she sailed the north coast of Haiti. Unknown to him, the captain and crew were also below decks asleep, leaving the helm to a fourteen-year-old cabin boy. Instructed to follow the stern light of the *Niña,* the youth was forced to yaw the vessel back and forth in order to see around the *Santa María's* high forepeak. On one southerly swing, the seven-foot draft of the *Niña* passed over the long reef guarding the bay, while the twelve-foot draft of the *Santa María* ran hard aground and began to sink. A surprised and hung over Columbus salvaged enough supplies and materials from the sinking ship to build a fort and thus establish the first European settlement in the New World near Cap Haïtian.

On the day after Christmas 1972, we were luckier than old Chris, despite our equally heavy celebration of the Christmas season. We had a fast run down toward Tortuga until the wind died and left us in a heavy, obscuring mist. About 0930, the mist lifted, disclosing Point Picolet Light and mountains—great, green, cloud-capped mountains. After months of cruising the coast of Florida and the flat, almost featureless Bahama Cays, we felt as overwhelmed as Columbus must have felt upon first seeing the beautiful island of Haiti.

Rounding the ruins of Fort Picolet and keeping close by the shores to avoid Le Grand Mouton shoals to starboard (they are well marked with two buoys and the tall mast of a sunken freighter), we saw the long red-roofed government dock, which extends 900 feet eastward from Cap Haïtian.

As we readied the docking lines, the humor on the deck was more than a little forced. In fact, it bordered on hysteria. Throughout the Bahamas, whenever we discussed Haiti, other cruising yachtsmen reported as absolute fact:

1. American yachtsmen are not welcome, and Haitian officials will drive you crazy trying to prove it.

2. Custom officials charge outrageous fees and tear your boat apart searching for guns.

3. Release from quarantine requires medical inspection with appropriate Miami Beach fees.

4. You must leave someone aboard your boat at all times, otherwise they will steal the rigging from your deck.

5. You cannot walk the streets at night for fear of being robbed, raped, or murdered.

With all this information in mind, we were pleased to find Les and Kris of the *Karina,* unrobbed, unraped and unmurdered, smiling on the dock, ready to handle our lines.

Within minutes, a pleasant English-speaking customs official and a stern army officer invited "le capitaine" ashore to the port office at the end of the dock. After a thorough check of our yacht's papers, clearance from Inagua, and a three-dollar fee, we shook hands and were welcomed to Cap Haïtian. So much for absolute facts 1, 2, and 3.

With such a nervous beginning, we raised the black and red Haitian flag and started a most interesting month in our cruise of the Greater Antilles.

First the harbor at Le Cap: the anchorage south of the dock is well protected from almost all winds and seas by its shape, the reefs, and the long dock. Holding was good in about three fathoms in thick mud. Cleaning the gook from your anchor when you leave is another matter. The water was filthy but seemed to cleanse itself with each tide. The day we arrived, the anchorage was filled with those remarkable Haitian gaff-rigged workboats drying their sails like so many multicolored moths. Outstanding sailors casually make passages to the Caicos, to Nassau, and up and down the coast of Haiti with these boats loaded to the gunwales with fruit and sugar cane, with no engine or compass, and in complete indifference to weather or winds.

Help can be hired for a dollar a day to sand, scrape, and clean. We had a broken stanchion on our pulpit brazed for five dollars. A similar job cost me fifty dollars in Fort Lauderdale. *Karina* had a new mahogany hatch assembled and mounted in her after cabin for sixteen dollars.

There are ample grocery stores, hardware stores, and pharmacies in town, where almost all supplies can be obtained, but at fairly high prices. The best news was fresh pineapple at twelve cents, oranges and grapefruit two cents, limes five for a penny, and a huge stalk of bananas for one dollar. A loaf of fresh bread was twenty cents, and ten pounds of ice could be had for ten cents after considerable bargaining.

A word about bargaining: everything must be bargained for, and a price arrived at before purchase or employment. It is all very good natured, but expected. My wife inquired about the price of some avocados from an old lady squatting amongst her wares and smoking a pipe.

"Fifty cents American," was the smiling reply.

"No, no, too much."

"Okay, five cents." And a bargain was made.

Two cruise ships call at Cap Haïtian each week. Part of the local entertainment is to watch the swarm of tourists descend on the shops and rush back to their ship to hurry off to the next island to repeat the process. We would wait until the streets were quiet again and begin bargaining for the remaining folkcrafts. With patience and perseverance we collected a beautiful assortment of wood carvings for gifts back home at one-tenth the Miami prices. The teak boom crutch on *Serenity* was carved by one of the local young men for less than five dollars and remains the best souvenir of our travels.

We were taken only once—the day of our arrival. We gave our laundry to a man on the dock for an agreed price of two dollars and a bar of soap. When he brought it back, he wanted six dollars or no laundry. After much yelling and gesturing, we took the matter to the sergeant of the police, who had his office on the dock. More yelling and gesturing, and the sergeant closed the deal with my four dollars, but he barred the man from ever coming on the dock again.

Which brings us to facts 4 and 5. Haiti is a semipolice state, and visitors and their possessions are protected without question. Punishment is swift and violent and frequently dealt out by the police without benefit of the courts. Without discussing the social morality of this form of justice, it does provide a sense of total security for yachtsmen. Tools and belongings can be left on the deck without concern. Many nights we walked the quiet streets of the city without the slightest fear. Where in the United States can you say the same?

Once ashore, Cap Haïtian is a fascinating city. Founded by the French buccaneers in 1670, it was once the wealthiest, gayest colonial capital in the world. Just outside the city gates is the battlefield where Jean Dessalines defeated the French in 1803 in a final battle for independence and established the first black republic in the world. All around the city are the ruins of the forts with their tumbled cannons and mortars that wrote the turbulent history of this blood-tinged country.

The city streets with its overhanging balconies, grillwork, massive doors sporting wrought-iron hinges, and high walls hiding lovely flowered patios remind one of old New Orleans. At one end of the city are beautiful houses painted a rainbow of pastel colors, a seventeenth-century cathedral, the neat colonial army barracks, and scattered throughout, well-tended parks with the inevitable statue commemorating some ancient battle. On the other side of the town are the tightly packed homes of the poor, and poverty is everywhere. Yet even here you are greeted with a quizzical smile and a "bon soir." These are a proud and independent people.

But the poverty is of such soul-crushing enormity that many visitors find it too depressing to stay on. Feelings of helplessness and compassion hang like a cloud over one's tours of the island. The current government does less than nothing to change the plight of its citizens.

New Haiti North, a Swiss-financed corporation, was active while we were there. They were busy drawing plans, training local workers, and building roads as part of a multimillion dollar development program. The Haitian government has since put them out of business. Dupont Caribbean and Translinear had a concession to develop Tortuga and invested more than three million dollars in the local economy just to begin their project. Corrupt, bribe-seeking Haitian officials blackmailed both companies out of business and thus threw several hundred Haitians out of work.

In the city there are three first-rate hotels and several pensions. The Hôtel Mont Joli, sitting high above the city and the harbor, serves the best food in town. The owner, Walter Bussinius, is a good friend to visiting yachtsmen. He will hold mail addressed to the hotel for your arrival; he is available for interpreting (your high school French won't help much, since Creole is the common language); he will help with arrangements or purchases that seem undoable; and finally, you may use the freshwater pool at the hotel when the harbor gets too much for you.

The must trip at Cap Haïtian is to San Souci Palace and the Citadelle, the eighth wonder of the world. Local drivers will take you to Milot for about ten dollars. The bus ride is wilder and costs but a few cents. San Souci dominates the village of Milot and looks like a surrealist setting for an opera.

Built by King Christophe, it was substantially destroyed by an earthquake in 1842, yet the remains are still impressive. One can imagine the marble floors, the mahogany paneling, and the ornate luxury wherein Christophe held his bizarre court in pompous imitation of the French.

The trip to the Citadelle was arranged at the army post in Milot, where horses and guides were hired. The climb to the top of the 3,000-foot mountain took about two hours along a narrow, rock-strewn path and was no rougher than a beat across the Gulf Stream into a thirty-knot wind.

If you are not too busy hanging onto your horse for your life, the scenery is something special. Waterfalls cut through the rain forest. Trees of oranges, bananas, cashew, avocado, cocoa, and breadfruit line the way. Halfway up, in a shaded glen, the enterprising Haitians hauled up cold beer to refresh us while we rested our backsides. From here the trail opens up great vistas down the mountain range to the sea, and above hangs the ominous fortress. The day we made the trip, winter rain clouds shrouded the peak, and the Citadelle looked like a great ark shipwrecked on the mountain top. This useless monument to the futility of man's pride was started in 1803. Its walls rise 400 feet in some places, and are 30 feet thick at the base. More than twenty thousand slaves lost their lives hauling the rocks, cannons, and supplies to build this royal castle and fortress. Inside, there are hundreds of rooms, court-yards, and battlements strewn with engraved bronze cannons. In the center is the lime pit where Christophe's body was buried after his suicide.

Several yachts visited Cap Haïtian during our stay, but none caused so much interest as a fifty-foot Surinam canoe, fiber-glassed and fitted with four sailfish masts and sails. This strange craft glided silently to the dock one day, and her four American crewmen nonchalantly greeted the huge crowd that had gathered to stare in disbelief. The open canoe had no engine, instruments, or accommodations, but she had sailed from St. Croix. She stopped long enough to drop off two of her crew and reprovision, and then she sailed off to Jamaica.

When we had enough of the noise and hustle of Cap Haïtian, we lifted anchor and motored around the point westward up the coast five miles to Pt. St. Honore and into what is named Port Français on the chart, but is called Coco Beach and La Bar Di locally.

Here is an anchorage all yachtsmen can envy—deep water to within twenty-five yards of an almost circular beach, high mountains to the south and east, and a long spit curving from the east around the north side. Behind, across the bay to the west are more mountains. The water is clean and blue, and there are two coral reefs at either end of the bay for diving and exploring. Across the beaches to the north is the long rolling surf of the Atlantic. Along Coco Beach are the ruins of a famous seventeenth century brothel that once catered to the whims of the pirates from nearby Tortuga. High over the bay perch the ruins of still another fort. Its ancient cannons pointed at *Serenity* lying below.

Early each Friday evening, the voodoo drums begin their rhythmic pulse high in the mountains to summon their disciples. The drums continue all night, all the next day, and are stilled Sunday morning by ringing of the Catholic church bells in each village.

Deep into the bay is the village of La Bar Di. Small mud-covered houses with banana leaf thatched roofs are scattered under huge trees. Since there is no road, the houses are randomly placed, each with its own little yard. If it is true that good fences make good neighbors, these Haitians have solved an ancient problem. Their fences are made of thickly planted, neatly trimmed cactus with very large spikes. Here also is a good freshwater spring and a public bathing pond. Most of the men in the village are fishermen and weave their own fish traps of sisal when they are not at sea. They were far more interested in my little plastic dinghy and two horsepower outboard than they were in me. Es said it was like walking through the pages of *National Geographic.*

At La Bar Di we learned a lesson in Haitian officialdom which was to be confirmed again. At every city, town, and village, there were officials, police, and army officers who wanted to see our papers and fill our reports. Once at La Bar Di, a village official came out to the boat, asked a lot of questions, and carefully wrote the answers on the reverse side of a sheet of paper he had used the previous day for the same questions. The best thing to do is to grin and bear it. It is all very polite and is, as they say, "for your own protection."

The Haitians and the Dominicans, with whom they share the island, suffer from a paranoid "invasion syndrome" that, with the obvious exception of Cuba, is unique in the Caribbean. Every boat that approaches their shores they assume is intent on invading them. With the terrible overpopulation, horrendous poverty, and lack of resources, it's not clear why anyone would want the place. Yet both countries spend a crippling proportion of their annual budgets for defense. Haitians hate the Dominican Republic and vice versa. Armed guards constantly patrol their common border. What they are defending themselves against, nobody says.

One Haitian told us, "The good Lord treats the Dominicans better—they have all the highways and the airports. We just have poor people and no food."

We returned to Cap Haïtian after ten beautiful days at Coco Beach and made ready for our departure for Puerta Plata, Dominican Republic, with a stop at Fort Liberté. Clearance papers and a manifest were obtained. We were told to have the Dominican counsel co-sign our clearance papers, but he was in Port-au-Prince, so we decided to skip that formality.

Walter Bussinius and his sister asked to sail with us to visit a friend, who was the manager of Plantation Dauphine at Fort Liberté, and in company of *Karina,* we set off. The entrance to Fort Liberté is a little hard to find since it is only 100 yards wide, but from close in, there is a sharp break in the white sand beach, and still closer in you can see the ruins of Redoubt St. Louis on the eastern side of the channel. The channel has a number of sandbars extending into it along its mile-long run into the bay, but they are easily read and present no serious problem.

The landlocked bay is about five miles long east and west and one mile wide. The town of Fort Liberté is on the southern shore of the bay. It is clearly visible upon entry, and the plantation we were to visit is on the extreme western edge.

Knowing the Haitian interest in paperwork, we approached the government dock for entry procedure even though we had left another Haitian port just twenty miles away. When it became apparent that *Serenity's* seven-foot draft prevented her from docking and no one on shore seemed interested in coming out, we headed down the bay to the plantation.

The plantation maintains a private dock with electricity, water, and diesel fuel available. Unfortunately, we ran aground within fifty yards of the dock. Sisal wastes and dredging remains had formed a small hump with less than four feet of water over it. After a lot of swearing and a little kedging, we were off and floating again. Instead of trying for the dock in the fading sunlight, we dropped the hook and dinghied ashore where Herbert Vittenberg and his wife had been waiting. Before we could tie up, a jeep pulled up and out jumped two army officials, and we were at the favorite Haitian pastime again. Our clearance papers from Cap Haïtian clearly said that we had permission to stop at Fort Liberté, but no matter. Still more discussion in broken English, fluent French, and rapid Creole, more notes were written, more papers were filled out, and finally the army drove away with my clearance papers, saying they would see me in the morning.

The Vittenbergs invited us all up to their club for a much-needed drink.

Karina had left with us, but her engine had overheated, and she was proceeding much more slowly. We had kept in touch all afternoon by radio, and now in the growing darkness they entered the bay. We jumped into the dinghy and headed out to meet them. *Karina* slowed down as we approached and promptly went aground on the same mud bank. The pile was about twenty feet in diameter and in a five-square-mile bay, but both boats managed to find it. Les said the hell with it, threw an anchor overboard, and we went aboard for another drink.

The next day, when *Karina* was safely tied to the dock, we located a mechanic to work on Les's diesel and then dinghied four miles back to the village to retrieve my clearance papers. As we had grown to expect, they were no good. The local officials, with much rubber stamping and signing, gave me another set in quadruplicate, wished me "bon voyage," and we were on our way again. While time-consuming and more than a little irritating, all this paperwork cost nothing and since it seemed to provide employment for a lot of Haitians, we just learned to live with it.

We spent the next few days exploring the 50,000-acre sisal plantation. Now nearly deserted, it was once the largest privately owned sisal producer in the world. It has its own narrow gauge railroad, machine shop, power plant, school, and hospital, a beautiful-but-empty owner's residence, and a private club with a swimming pool and bowling alley. The plantation waits quietly for the day when nylon and dacron rope will fall into disfavor with the sailors of the world.

After the heat exchangers on *Karina's* diesel had been disassembled, cleaned, and re-attached, the engine still overheated, thus putting an end to our plan to sail to Puerto Plata in tandem with *Karina*. We left one sunny afternoon for what was to be *Serenity's* most difficult passage.

5 Our Cruise Almost Ends in Puerto Plata

The night became a long black tunnel. Heavy dark waves broke over the port bow and exploded into a white obscuring spray. *Serenity's* starboard rail had been buried in water since nightfall, and what I really needed was another reef in the mainsail. It was a useless idea. Es had been sick for hours and was asleep on the bridge deck. Wrapped up in her foul weather gear and sleeping bag, she remained motionless, even when a wave dumped over her. The only advantage of her huddled body was that she obscured the wind speed indicator and knotmeter. We were going at least nine knots, which had to be *Serenity's* hull speed, and I didn't need to be reminded of *that* all night.

Earlier, I had struggled forward and cranked in a reef. With the wind and water blowing, that's a murderous job. Hanging from your safety harness, you slack off the main halyard and simultaneously crank the boom to wrap the mainsail around the boom. Single-handed, with no one to bring you up into the wind, it's almost impossible. Besides, with the mountainous coast of the Dominican Republic less than a half mile off to leeward, I was as interested in being able to steer as I was in keeping the mast in one piece.

Serenity took it like a tough old lady. Her rigging hummed and vibrated, and her timbers creaked; water poured down her decks. Her long overhangings lifting us out of the waves left a white, boiling wake in the darkness. Crouched over the wheel, in the red glow of the compass light, I could almost enjoy it if I weren't so damned cold. The sea water, now a good six inches in the cockpit, was warm, but the wind and the rain squalls that tore through the night were cold, bitter cold. I was soaked and shivering.

This passage had begun innocently enough. I had planned to leave Fort Liberté in the late afternoon, work my way through the Seven Brothers in fading light, pick up the light off Montechristi in darkness, and then have an easy sail down the coast to arrive at Puerto Plata in daylight the next morning. The northeast trade wind that I had counted on shifted as a full-blown northern swept out of the Bahamas. And here I was at midnight, peering through salt-burned eyes for the light off Point Patilla.

Normally, Es does the spotting of lights and buoys. She can see a navigation mark minutes before I do. But this night she was useless. Every thirty minutes or so, she would untangle herself, lean over the bulwark, head down, and throw up into the water rushing by. Then without a word, she would tumble backward, cover her head with the drenched sleeping bag, and collapse in a heap.

Finally, it was there, flashing in the night. Blink, blink— pause, slow count to ten—blink, blink. I sailed past as close as I dared, freed the sails, and ran for Puerto Plata.

In another hour and a half, I saw more lights—too many lights—white, red, green, flashing bright—the lights of Puerto Plata. There is supposed to be a set of red range lights leading into the harbor and a tall searchlight flashing every five seconds near the entrance. Through the rain I couldn't pick them out or anything else that made sense. I drew close enough to determine the moving headlights of automobiles and wondered who was crazy enough to be driving around on a night like this. I'm not brave enough to try a nighttime entrance into a strange harbor, so I came about.

We headed out into a wind that had built up enormous seas. As the waves rolled onto the sounding of the bay, great combers were formed; the gale blew spume off the tops to mix with the rain. We would sail diagonally up the face of a wall of water to plunge over the crest into the black trough. Over and over *Serenity* would slide down, bury her bow, lift out, shake off the heavy water, and climb the next comber. When the lights of the city were no longer visible, I came about. Leaning with my back against the wheel, I readied the jib sheet on the leeward winch, spun the wheel to windward, and cast off the windward sheet. Then tailing hand over hand, I cleated off the sheet and returned to the wheel for a wild broad reach across the bay. When the shore lights appeared too close, I repeated the drill and pounded back out to sea.

Each tack took about thirty minutes, and I soon lost track of the trips. As the storm wore on, I began to get a little goofy. The compass swung around like an insane merry-go-round in the red light. Despite the noise and the wet, I would fall asleep at the wheel only to snap awake in seconds, looking around frantically as I tried to remember where I was. Each time we tacked, Es would slide on her bench—first head down, then feet. Still she would lift up, making a horrible retching sound and then slump back and bury herself without looking at me. The night seemed endless, and yet without my being aware of when it happened, the eastern mountains were lit in a pale gray dawn under the clouds.

I yelled to awaken Es.

"Take the wheel, we're going in," I ordered.

I crawled forward, dropped the main, and tied it into a lumpy mess on the boom. Back at the wheel, I pointed *Serenity* toward shore.

"You've got to find the entrance buoys. I can't see a thing." In silence, she turned to search as the city grew larger on the bow.

With the jib flying, the wind and the sea on our stern, we flew in. Sometimes we surfed on the crest of a breaker like those maniacs on TV who surf the curlers in Hawaii; sometimes we dove into the trough until we were lifted to the peak of the next wave. I wasn't steering so much as hanging on. Es found the red and black buoys and they flashed by, but we weren't in the center of the channel. We were much too far to the west. From the top of a twenty-foot comber, I looked down on the dirty green bottom cleared out by the trough. Later, Es told me I said calmly, "Hang on, this is going to be rough."

Serenity hit the bottom with a shuddering thud and swung over on her side with her mast almost parallel to the bottom. In a second the next sea lifted her upright, and we shot into the relative calm of the harbor. I rounded up, put down the anchor, dropped the jib, and staggered back to the cockpit. Es sat huddled in her corner, hair and clothes dripping water, staring at me. I curled up on the seat and fell asleep.

Sometime during the morning, Customs and the port commandante came out to inspect the boat and clear us in, but I have only a vague memory of the boarding. I slept until late afternoon. The seas were still pouring into the harbor opening, and the anchorage was rolly, but the storm was breaking up and the sun warmed through ragged tears in the clouds. While I slept, Es had refurled the sails and hung up all the wet furnishings. I stripped off my still damp clothing, and Es brought a bowl of hot soup up to the cockpit.

"I have to talk to you. I'm leaving," she said tonelessly.

"Leaving? What do you mean, leaving?"

"Leaving, getting off this boat. If there is a plane in this God-forsaken place, I'm going to get on it and go home."

"Home—this boat is your home. There is no place to go."

"Look, we've—I've made a terrible mistake, and when you make a mistake, you try to correct it."

"But we've just started. I can't turn around now."

"You do what you have to do. Let me do what I have to do."

"What the hell kind of arrangement is that! Look, Es, you'll forget about last night. After all, you had a good time up until last night."

Tears were beginning to form now. "No, I haven't, I hate the boat. I'm always sick—I'm terrified every time we go out into the ocean. This is one time you're not going to talk me into anything. I'm leaving."

With that she went below. Es has never wanted anyone to see her cry.

I sat alone in the cockpit and tried to think. The soup had grown cold in my hands. The thin sliver of a moon did nothing to light up this dark and angry place.

I now found myself tired, cold, and miserable, facing a decision I didn't want to make. The dilemma was overwhelming my ability to think. I couldn't face the possibility of turning back. But going on alone while Es returned to the States would destroy the entire purpose of our new life. I didn't view cruising as a means of traveling but a new way of living, of thinking—of being. It was something to be shared. To be enjoyed together. I fell asleep without even beginning to resolve the problem.

Over breakfast coffee, neither of us mentioned a word of what was occupying our every thought. I suggested we get off the boat and go for a walk around the city. At the comandante's office, we picked up our papers and were directed toward the center of Puerto Plata. In less than a block, a teenager approached us.

"Buenos días, Captain, cómo está? My name is José, and I would like to practice my English. May I walk with you?" His English was ten times better than our guidebook Spanish, so we welcomed him along.

José led us to a restaurant called Corral, decorated with symbols of the Old West. They served, of all things—pizza! They also served the standard drink in Dominican Republic,

El Presidente beer, ice cold in a quart bottle. Fantastic! We visited with the two young American owners and were invited back for dinner, a shower, and the use of their phone for some long-distance calls.

We walked up to the public market housed in a new free form concrete structure. Wandering among the stalls, we picked up fresh fruits and vegetables, eggs, meat, and some more El Presidente. José did the pricing, and when he felt we were being overcharged, he took us to another vendor to strike a better bargain. Loaded down with goodies, we headed back to the still rolling *Serenity* and a silent meal.

Both of us had a troubled, sleepless night.

José met us the next morning and took us to meet Mike Roan, an ex-Peace Corps worker who had settled in Puerto Plata after his assignment in Dominican Republic was completed. Mike helped run the travel bureau, and Es checked the flights back to the States via Santa Domingo. I was pretty discouraged.

I asked José to leave us alone for a little while, and we walked to the main square and seated ourselves in front of the brightly colored Victorian bandstand. I began hesitatingly.

"Hear me out and then think about it awhile. Don't give me an answer now. We can't leave *Serenity* here—this is a foreign country. We can't sell it—there are no facilities to store it. We have to go to Puerto Rico. At least that's part of the U.S., and we might have a chance of doing something there."

"I won't go across the Mona Passage," Es interrupted. "The Mona Passage is supposed to be the worst place in the whole world."

"You don't have to. I'll hire a crew to help me over. You fly to San Juan and meet me at Club Nautico. Once we get settled there, you can fly home, visit your mother, get some rest, and then when you come back, we can talk it over again. We both need time to think this out."

Es was a long way from being sure.

"I'll let you know tomorrow."

The first step in winning Es over was to get out of that miserable, rolly harbor. I cleared out at the port authority for nearby Sosua. I asked the comandante to try and find a crew member, and we left. It was an easy ten-mile sail down the mountainous coastline to what is considered the most beautiful beach in the Dominican Republic. The palm-fringed crescent of pink sand outlined a small bay of clearest water. In the center, a long wondrous coral garden—orange slabs of stag coral—came within inches of the still surface. We moved in slowly and anchored in between the reef and the shore. On the beach an ominous squad of armed uniformed men beckoned me in. I rowed ashore and found a bilingual nun to explain to the army officer that I had just left Puerto Plata ten miles away. I said that I had cleared with the port comandante, and he had assured me that he would call ahead to announce my arrival.

"Of course," the answer was translated back, "we are here to welcome you. It's just for your own protection."

"From whom!" but I asked the nun not to translate that remark.

A foreign yacht anchored in the bay was an unusual enough occurrence to bring many of the nearby residents down to meet us and invite us to their homes.

From our new friends we learned the story of Sosua. The area had been settled in the 1930s by Jewish refugees from Hitler's Germany. While our country ignored their plight, Rafael Trujillo offered (some said sold) visas to thousands of fleeing Jews. Land was made available to them along the north coast, and they established dairy farms among the rolling hills. These immaculate, well-tended farms still thrive in the area. When their products grew in demand, they built meat and dairy processing plants at Sosua and today supply most of the milk, ice cream, meat, and sausages consumed in the Dominican. The modern pastel-colored homes, the flower-lined streets and walkways, and the famous beach have made Sosua a showplace for tourists.

We were invited for dinner by the president of the corporation and spent the evening meeting many of the charming multilingual residents. But they were all the elders of the village, well past middle age. There are no young people in Sosua. Like so many parents before them, they sent their children off to fine schools in Mexico and the States and when they returned, failed to permit the young people to move into positions of importance in the farms and plants. The young ones have all left for the major cities of the Americas. Now the older generation sits alone with no one to take over the fruits of their long labor. It is sad to see this beautiful place begin to decline for want of some vigorous young minds.

The wife of a U.S. engineer working on the construction of a nearby jet airport drove us back to Puerto Plata where Mike Roan had found us an ideal crew member. Ramón Arturo Torres, a handsome young employee of the Bank for Agriculture, had sailed to San Juan before and enjoyed the trip so much, he wanted to try again.

Back at Sosua, I dove in the clear water to check out *Serenity's* hull after her near disaster. Except for a couple of scars, she seemed sound. The weather cleared. It was sunny and warm as we snorkeled over the coral reef and relished the seclusion of having this tourist attraction all to ourselves. Es was cheerful and relaxed, and without ever saying anything directly to me about it, she seemed willing to try at least one more sail, even if it meant the Mona Passage.

Arturo arrived with his visa and mariner's papers and duffle, excited and eager to be leaving. His enthusiasm was infectious, the weather perfect. As we rounded the headlands, we were a happy crew.

6 Puerto Rico and the Not-so Virgin-Islands

The seas were light and the breeze on the beam, and we were really honking. By 1400 we passed Cape Viejo Francés and gave up any idea of a stop on the north coast. We altered course directly for Puerto Rico. The next morning was cloudy, the wind picked up, and the passage looked ominous to the south, but *Serenity* was flying along with an easy motion. The self-steering was doing most of the work. All we had to do was keep a lookout for the several freighters and ocean liners that steamed past us. That is one active route. At 2030 we spotted the fifteen-second light at Borinquen Point. We had crossed the Mona Passage, more than two hundred miles, in thirty-six hours!

The bash up the Puerto Rican coast into the strong current was long and hard. But I was the only one on board who was feeling miserable. The months of work in the bilges and the engine had chewed up my hands, and the constant immersion in salt water left them looking like two lumps of spoiled hamburger. Whether it was an infection or some form of tropical flu, I never knew, but I had a first-class fever and was alternately shivering and shaking or sweating in my foul weather gear. I didn't say anything then because we still had to negotiate the entrance at San Juan, and it was getting dark.

San Juan is the best-marked harbor in the Caribbean. Two

tall lights guard the entrance, there are range lights, and the channel buoys are all lit. Hundreds of vessels of all sizes enter the harbor night and day.

It looks easy on the harbor charts, but the most nerve-wracking task on a voyage for me is the entry into a strange harbor at night. I hate the job and try my best to avoid the necessity. There are always too many lights, they are in the wrong place, or they don't flash in the proper sequence, or they don't line up according to the chart, or they are the wrong color. Everything seems wrong. The entrance is like an impenetrable black wall decorated with too many flashing lights, that lure you in to make a mistake.

We made it safely, but by the time we rounded El Moro, I was shaking from more than my fever. We located the San Antonio canal and tied up in the only open slip at Club Nautico. We were dirty and tired but more than anything we were *hungry*. Arturo remembered a McDonalds nearby, so we closed up the boat and walked over.

I didn't have to tell Es I was sick. My normal suntan had faded to a gray green, and my teeth were chattering. Sweat poured down my face. In addition I couldn't eat my Big Mac. McDonalds was next to a hotel, and Es didn't get any argument when she left to make a room reservation. When she returned, she ordered me up to the room to take a hot shower and go to bed. She and Arturo would go back to the boat to get dry clothes and some medication.

I have neglected to mention that Es is an R.N. Before we left, her doctor friends had given us a complete first aid kit, surgical instruments, and enough sample drugs to equip a fair-sized pharmacy. In medical matters I defer to her.

I weaved into the hotel lobby and asked the desk clerk for my key.

"Do you have credit cards or cash?" he wanted to know.

"I have both, but at the moment they are in my wife's purse. She was just here, but now she's back at the boat."

"No credit card, no room."

"Look, I'm sick. I can't walk all the way back to the boat. I need to lie down."

"I don't make the rules, I just work here. No credit card, no room."

Screw the rules, I thought. I'll get even with him—I'll die in his lobby. I picked out a big couch in front of the elevators, so my body would be sure to be found, covered up with my day-glow orange jacket, and passed out.

I was awakened by the sound of Es's voice ripping the head off the room clerk. She slammed the money on the desk, grabbed the key, lifted me bodily from the couch, and led me to the room.

I was soaking in a hot tub of water when Es came into the bathroom. She had just called her friend the room clerk and asked him to turn off the air conditioning and send up three blankets. Now he really thought we were crazy.

I took some antibiotics and fell asleep under the scarcest commodity in ninety-degree San Juan—three wool blankets.

I was feeling much better when I got to the boat at noon the next day. Es had called Customs and Immigration. They were a little testy when they found me gone and even more concerned when they learned that Arturo was from the Dominican Republic, but everything was smoothed out and Arturo had gone shopping before flying back.

The only problem I had to face was Club Nautico. The dockmaster was an angry little man who wanted a week's dockage in advance and warned us that we wouldn't get a refund when he kicked us out of the slip. My two stateside yacht club cards didn't impress him a bit. I called my only friend in San Juan, Emilio Casailles. Emilio had been an officer of the Puerto Rico Bank for Development during a time when I was underwriting a lot of their bonds. He had recently been appointed commissioner of something by the new governor. He came aboard *Serenity* for a drink, and it turned out that the slip belonged to his uncle and would not be needed for the balance of the month. He convinced the club management to quit hassling us. Club Nautico is a very exclusive yacht club that caters to the wealthy owners of large sports fishing boats, and they weren't too interested in having a U.S. sailboat tied at their dock. Despite our renewed friendship with Ralph Christiansen, one of the owners of *Wishbone* and vice-commodore of the club, our stay there was short and uncomfortable. If a Puerto Rican yacht at a U.S. yacht club were treated as we were, the Puerto Rican Anti-Defamation League would close the club with a storm of lawsuits. Leaving was the easiest thing to do.

As we motored down the river to the main harbor, a large gray ship pulled away from the seawall lining the channel. Others joined her until there were five in all. We were being escorted by a squadron of Brazilian destroyers. To the captain of an aircraft carrier these destroyers may be small, but to us, on our forty-five foot sailboat, they seemed enormous. I pulled as far to starboard as I dared and held a steady five knots. The fleet skippers displayed amazing seamanship and courtesy by maintaining their position at that slow speed and did not attempt to overtake us until we were out into the wide bay. As each destroyer slipped gently by, the crew lined the rails and saluted a greeting. By the time we left the sea buoy, the squadron had maneuvered into formation and were steaming off toward Roosevelt Roads, where they were to engage in joint war games with the U.S. Caribbean Fleet. Quite an experience for us.

The thirty-five-mile sail to Fajardo on the east coast was another dead beat into the coastal current, and again our arrival was at night. We rounded the bright light at Cape San Juan and then went from one lighted buoy to the next until we anchored off Isletta Marina.

We were awakened the next morning by a hail from a nearby yacht. We had anchored immediately over the electric cable crossing from the mainland! We gingerly pulled the hook and moved deeper into the anchorage. I went over to thank the skipper who had warned us away from the potential danger. We met Dudley and Kay Pope and their eight-year-old daughter, Jane, aboard *Ramage*. Dudley Pope is a noted British naval historian who has published a number of volumes describing famous English naval battles and heroes, but only recently has he become famous himself with his Ramage series. Lieutenant Ramage is a Hornblower-like hero whose adventures take place invariably in the same place that Dudley is anchored at the time of his writing. The family has been cruising for years, first in the Mediterranean and now the Caribbean. They were to become good friends and advisors.

Isletta was our home port for almost three months. During our stay, Es flew back to the States for a visit, and I had *Serenity* hauled. The garboard strakes had been making water during hard beating, and we had them recaulked and the bottom painted. I had read for years about the dangers of worms in the tropical waters. In the three years *Serenity* sailed these waters, we never had the slightest sign of worms. The answer in our case seemed to be using the best, highest-copper content paint we could buy and hauling out at least every eight months. I replaced all three bilge pumps: a manual gusher type, an electric Jabsco, and an automatic submersible type. All three were troublesome and spent more time apart than working.

We were the source of considerable amusement for the workers in the yard. Before leaving the U.S., we had acquired two home study courses in French and Spanish taught by means of a tape cassette. While the workers walked around with their transistor radios blaring Spanish rock, we walked around with our cassette player, mumbling

"*¿Buenas tardes. ¡Cómo está?*"
Good afternoon. How are you?
"*Necessito un intérprete, por favor.*"

I need an interpreter, if you please.
"¿ Qué profunda es la agua?"
How deep is the water?
"¿Dónde está el baño?"
Where is the bathroom?

They collectively decided to help us in our quest for fluency in Spanish. No one, thereafter, spoke a word of English to me, even when I filled in for a couple of weeks at the marine store in the yard. A worker would order four 2½-inch bronze screws, and I would get four rolls of toilet paper. It was a hard way to learn Spanish. By this time I was burned a dark brown and had raised a huge black mustache. I looked *too* Puerto Rican. When I went to town shopping, I could never convince anyone I couldn't speak Spanish.

Isletta Marina was an ideal place to stay in those days. During the week it was quiet. The workers took the ferry back to Fajardo every afternoon, leaving the island to the five or six cruising families anchored in the bay. We visited back and forth, sharing experiences and advice. We had frequent communal cookouts on the beach side and afterwards sat around the dying coals of a palm frond bonfire, talking late into the night. Many of the sailors had cruised to the southern islands, and they were our source of information on future anchorages, mail drops, places to explore, and places to avoid.

On the weekends the marina was crowded with busy, happy people. On Friday, the ferryboat loads of families burdened with food, fishing gear, and children would swarm into the many power boats docked at the marina and then roar off to the abundant fishing grounds that extend to the Virgin Islands. The sailors would arrive Saturday morning, carrying their sailbags and the latest racing gear. The island was the home of a racing yacht club, and almost every weekend there was a race program. The races were sometimes casual, but more often they were serious, hard-fought contests, including one of the toughest—the annual round Puerto Rico race. All of these people were unfailingly kind to us as strangers and soon became close and lasting friends.

This is all changed now. The island is slowly sinking into the ocean burdened with two skyscraper condominiums, and there is no room for ordinary sailors. The sailing fleet is moored at various marinas that have been built up along the east coast, and the feeling of friendship and good will is similarly diffused. I guess it's called progress.

Bill and Monica Peters flew down to spend their vacation with us. We had chartered in the Virgins and bareboated in the Bahamas with them and had looked forward to their first cruise on *Serenity*. You could not find better guests. Bill was president of a large meat-packing business but much preferred tinkering with machinery to sitting behind a desk. It is said that when a sausage machine broke down, he was the first one down to the production line to fix it. He had maintained his own race cars, built his own airplane, and restored several classic cars. That's the kind of talent that always gets invited on cruises. During the three weeks he fixed, cleaned, and tuned every mechanical device on the boat and claimed it was the best vacation he ever had.

Monica made Es a deal she couldn't refuse. Monica would do all the cooking if Es made the drinks and hors d'oeuvres. Years ago the four of us had invented a drink called "Elizabeth O," in honor of a Soverel ketch we had rented at the time. It consisted of several kinds of fruit juices, canned and fresh, mixed together with one shot of rum and one of vodka. Since there was an obvious limit of two to a customer each sundown, drink mixing wasn't that hard. Bill had smuggled in a duffle bag full of his fanciest sausages so hors d'oeuvres were also taken care of.

Vieques Sound, where we spent most of our cruise, is so perfect in every way that I hesitate to write about it. Its main attraction is that almost no one goes there. In the next few years we found other areas with beautiful, protected bays, clean sandy beaches, and reefs full of fish and lobster, but these were found after long, hard sails to remote places. Vieques and Culebra, the two major islands of the sound, are clearly visible from the mainland of Puerto Rico, and St. Thomas can be seen from Culebra. Even so, most of the anchorages were empty, and we went days without seeing another person. Each island has a deep land-locked bay, each named Ensenada Honda, that would serve as a very safe hurricane hole. In addition, each island is ringed by little bays and inlets that make tranquil overnight anchorages. There are also several smaller islands, again each with its own charm, its own special spot. Obviously, care must be taken moving in and out of these reef-bound anchorages, but since there are several charts and an excellent guide to the area, there is no reason to get into any trouble.

Our favorite, number-one spot on the cruise was the north bay on Culabrita. It could prove untenable in a northern, but in the normal prevailing easterlies it should be high on the list of perfect harbors. The beach is a multihued pink made up of sugar-fine crushed shells. The extensive reef that curves around the opening is shallow, filled with fish, and perfect for snorkeling. The water is absolutely clear and deep enough to anchor just a few yards off the beach. A cut in the hills surrounding the bay allows the trades to air-condition the boat constantly and keep it bug free. A path leads from the beach up the hills to the highest part, where there is a nineteenth-century Spanish lighthouse, now fully automatic, that points out the sparkling constellations every night as it sweeps the endless sky. From the hilltop, the broad Virgin Passage is clearly visible. In the mornings we could watch the vivid white tourist ships move majestically across the shiny blue water on their way to St. Thomas or San Juan. Although the whole island is barely a mile in each direction, we spent several happy days swimming, sunning, and hiking there. I'm ashamed to say that despite seeing hundreds of lobsters, they were so experienced I was able to snare only two. They weren't enough for dinner, but boiled and served with one of Monica's special sauces and our daily ration of "Elizabeth Os," they were a delicacy unavailable in the finest New York restaurant.

The main reason the archipelagos off eastern Puerto Rico are so little used is that for years the rocks and cays northwest of Culebra have been used as a bombing and gunnery range by the U.S. Navy. We were there during a night exercise. The star-burst shells and parachute flares lit the night in a giant Fourth of July display. But it is no problem now. After years of protest, including a sit-in on the scored rocks by locals, the navy no longer uses the area for target practice. About one quarter of Vieques is a U.S. Marine installation, but none of their activities should interfere with cruising yachtsmen.

On weekends you will share many of these anchorages with Puerto Rican boaters, but during the week you can have most of Vieques Sound to yourself. If you plan a charter out of St. Thomas, you might want to get permission from the charterers and sail west to these seldom-cruised islands before everyone finds out about them.

After our tranquil stay in Culabrita we decided to revisit the Virgin Islands for old times' sake. It turned out to be a mistake. St. Thomas is only thirty miles away from Culabrita but dead downwind, so we motor-sailed, purposely bypassing the customs people at Charlotte Amalie, who at that time had a reputation as the snottiest, most arrogant, time-consuming officials anywhere. We cleared in at Cruz Bay on St. John, where you'd think you were in another country. The customs officer has been there for years and welcomes you rather than resents your arrival. In minutes we were sailing up the coast to Francis Bay.

That night I could have walked ashore on the boats banging together in the bay. Houseboats, bare boats, power boats, charter boats—there must have been fifty boats in the anchorage. Radios and hi-fi sets blared, the laughter of partygoers shrieked through the night, and curses rang out as boats dragging at anchor swung into one another. Sleep was impossible, and getting out in the morning was no better. Anchors were fouled; some with long scopes, some with short. Anchor lines knitted themselves together in a tangled macrame. We were too spoiled to find another spot, so we headed for St. Thomas and some shopping.

Since the four of us had visited the U.S. Virgin Islands for the last twelve years, we knew our way around. It had become our favorite vacation area, but in the winter of 1972-1973 St. Thomas was a war zone. Blacks pushed whites off the sidewalks; salespersons in stores either ignored you or slammed the merchandise on the counter and dared you to buy it. Cabdrivers charged outrageous prices for rides, and if you complained, a surly policeman would side with the local in any rip-off. Cruise ships had warnings on their bulletin boards that directed passengers to return to the boat by 5 P.M. to insure their safety.

Thievery was a way of life not only unpunished but also admired. Dinghies and outboards disappeared from yachts every day. Jeff Lane, a young ship surveyor, had his arm broken in broad daylight two blocks from Yacht Haven. If you were white, it was useless to go to the police. A friend of mine had his whaler and outboard stolen, chased the two young thieves in another power boat, and finally caught them on Water Island. When he brought one of them back to the police he was arrested for "assault on a juvenile."

I am aware of those sociologists and economists who claim that tourism as an industry is personally demeaning and unreliable as a stable base for the islands' economy. Maybe it is. But if they didn't want "honkies" crowding their stores, why did they advertise in honky magazines, extolling the virtues of the islands and inviting the tourist and his dollars down there? What they should have asked for is that Whitey stay home and ship the money down.

And incidentally, we do that as well. Rightly so. The U.S. Virgins are as entitled to U.S. tax dollars as any other part of the nation. We have spent millions building roads, schools, water systems, and low cost housing projects. We have provided technical training and education and helped to finance local industry. The citizens of the U.S. Virgins have the highest standard of living of any islands in the Caribbean. After the local citizens drove most of the tourists away, we provided unemployment checks and welfare payments.

The day we tied up at Yacht Haven, I wasn't interested in social reform or the world's problems. All I wanted was a new lens for my camera, a good meal in a favorite restaurant, and to be left alone. It didn't work out. After a few minutes in that oppressive atmosphere, after being harassed and insulted, I gathered up the crew and we headed back to the boat. The best part about cruising with your own boat is that if you are not wanted anywhere you can pull the anchor and leave. And leave we did—the warm, friendly people at Fajardo would never look so good.

I must make a few things absolutely clear. First, I have written only about the U.S. Virgins—St. Thomas and St. Croix—not the British Virgins nearby. This chain of at least fifty islands, rocks, and cays has been the scene of more pleasant cruises than probably any place in the world and the subject of hundreds of articles and cruising stories. The population is only a small fraction of that of the U.S. Virgins—in fact, most of the small islands are uninhabited—but wherever you meet a local, you will be cheerfully welcomed. Even in Road Town, now a rapidly growing commercial and tourist center, you can stroll down the streets without the slightest concern. In fact, it's hard to get any strolling done; several times people have stopped their cars and offered us rides. These islanders have a long heritage of seamanship, and there are many skilled mechanics to help you with repairs. Tortola is a startling contrast to nearby St. Thomas.

The Virgins have been written about and photographed so many times that there is little to add. The bare boat business has multiplied so rapidly in recent years that Sir Francis Drake Channel is a mighty busy place. If you are thinking about a cruise or charter in the area, my strong advice is to plan on the off-season. The weather is better, the crowds smaller, and the islands are just as beautiful. By a careful study of the charts and cruising guides, you can still find plenty of anchorages that don't look like the Block Island Regatta.

Now a final word about St. Thomas. Last year, entering from Anguilla, we spent three wonderful weeks poking in and out of our favorite bays and renewing acquaintanceships with old friends. We ended up in Red Hook in southeastern St. Thomas. Dyke and Inga Wilmerding, who chartered *Zulu Warrior* and are two of the nicest people in the charter business, offered to take us to town, but my memory is long and my prejudices firm. I stayed on the boat while Es did the shopping. Loaded with groceries, she returned raving about how things had changed.

The lure of a new marine store proved to be the clincher, and Dyke drove us to Charlotte Amalie. His old jalopy had a leaking water hose, which necessitated several stops to refill the radiator. At one stop a taxi coming from the other direction pulled off the road, and the driver came over. I instantly assumed he was going to steal the tires off the car, but I was wrong. He cheerfully volunteered to aid us. Maybe things had changed. Despite two shiploads of tourists crowding the streets and shops, the atmosphere was different. Everyone, tourist or local, seemed to be enjoying himself.

Even the hippies were gone. Hordes of these aromatic nonconformists used to hang out at Yacht Haven, their semiconscious bodies blocking the docks. One of the great ironies of the year caused the counterculturists to abandon Yacht Haven. A British TV company was shooting a film series in the Virgin Islands. Since the script involved early English naval exploits in the West Indies, the casting director needed dirty, bedraggled, bearded, long-haired types to act as crews on eighteenth-century warships. St. Thomas had a corner on the world's supply of such characters, and most of the hippie population was put to work at $120 a day as extras in the picture.

The old Yacht Haven has been torn down. It has been replaced by a multimillion-dollar marina and hotel complex, including a new marine store, that is almost complete.

I am delighted to report that all is well in St. Thomas—at least from a tourist's point of view. There must be a way to achieve black power and black rights without pushing people off the streets.

Back at Isletta we said our sad goodbyes to Bill and Monica and began thinking about our next voyage.

During our stay in Puerto Rico, we met a couple who were to become our closest cruising friends, Jeanne and Curt Harding on *Posh* out of Boothbay. They had been living aboard for over five years. They had sailed to Grenada and back and were anchored at Isletta while their teenage sons went to school. Jeanne was the enthusiastic organizer of most of our interboat parties, and Curt was a willing participant in any boat repair project. We have sailed and raced on each other's boats, shared a hundred meals, and visited over countless drinks. Jeanne drinks "Doowahs and soder." Those downeasters are great sailors, but they shoowah do talk funny.

The Hardings had participated in Antigua Race Week for the past two years and were trying to sell us on joining them this year. It was a gathering of most of the famous yachts in the south. The races were low key, fun races, and the parties were great.

We were easily sold and prepared *Serenity* to sail down with *Posh*. I'm such a clumsy idiot. The morning of our departure, I fouled a docking line, caught our running backstay on the edge of the dock, and ripped the fitting from the deck. Reluctantly, we told Jeanne and Curt to sail on without us, and we would try to join them before entries were closed.

That day I was struggling with the badly bent bronze fitting when Kris and Les of *Karina* climbed off the ferry and greeted us. After a whole series of engine troubles and misadventures in the Dominican Republic, they had just arrived in San Juan and driven out to find us. When they learned that it was only because of the accident that we weren't on our way to Antigua, they insisted that we needed their help and wanted to go along. While they rushed back to close up *Karina* and get their gear, I continued busting my knuckles refastening the back stay. Finally, everything was together, the gear stowed, and we left—thirty hours late.

Even in the protected harbor of Culebra that night we were aware of a good blow going on outside, but we didn't learn until later that *Posh* had been caught in a fierce gale and had lain ahull, being blown off course for many hours. The next morning we picked up a good northeast wind and set a course direct for St. Barts.

7 Antigua Me Come From

Our crossing of the fabled Anegada Passage was one of those sun-filled, then moonlit, sails we had waited for. The only incident of the night occurred when the dumb navigator of *Serenity* mistook the lights of Saba for a giant oil tanker. We arrived early the next morning, having made the 140-mile passage in twenty-four hours.

St. Barts is a miniature jewel of an island. The harbor is a tiny, snug little basin with small, red-roofed houses arranged around the hills. You almost expect Lilliputians to stroll down the quay to greet you. I located the gendarme, gave him my crew list, and he looked bored. That was it. And I guess that's as it should be.

Since St. Barts has been supplying smugglers since 1784, you might as well take advantage of it. The island is famed among cruising yachtsmen as a booze stop. Rum is eighty cents a quart, the best scotch, two dollars. Beer, cigarettes, and boat supplies from one of the most complete chandleries in the Caribbean are sold at similarly low prices. We loaded aboard a good supply in anticipation of the coming stresses of the competition and slipped out of the harbor at 1900. The breeze had freshened, and after another silver-tinted night, we arrived at English Harbour by 0700 the next morning. In fact we did the eighty-five miles almost too fast, since finding the opening for the harbor in early dawn is not that easy. When they say English Harbour is the best land-locked hurricane hole in the Antilles, they are right.

As we rounded Barclay Point into the multiple small bays that form the harbor, we found more than one hundred sailboats of every size and shape, from little fiberglass rule beaters to huge schooners, some anchored out, others tied stern-to at Nelson's Dockyard. As we dinghied ashore, we were greeted by old friends and strangers alike, all up and busy themselves in preparation for the big race. *Posh* had arrived only minutes before us. Clearing customs at the police station within the dockyard was quick and painless and polite.

The form used is my all-time favorite. To quote in part from it:

> These are to certify all whom it doth concern that *Zane B. Mann* Master or Commander of the *sailing vessel Serenity* burthen *22* tons, mounted with *naught* guns, navigated with *4* men, *USA* built and bound for . . . hath here entered and cleared his vessel according to law.

I would like to think that young Captain Horatio Nelson of H.M.S. *Boreas* used the same form when he cleared into this same harbor.

Later we moved over to Antigua Slipway to meet David Simmons, the official measurer. File away for future reference that David runs one of the best yards in this part of the ocean. He has a railway that can haul up to 150 tons and a good engine and outboard shop. Diesel, gas, and water are available at the dock, and there is a reasonably complete chandlery. David can be a mighty good man to know if your boat is in trouble down this way.

After he did some mysterious things with a tape measure and a plumb line, we really shook him up when we told him we were racing with only a working jib, a light drifter, and a main. My only jenny was at the sailmaker being repaired. As long as we were at the dock, we topped off the fuel and water tanks, and David just stared as we lashed down several jerry jugs, our diving gear, self-steerer, and awning. With enough canned food and supplies aboard to try a circumnavigation and enough whiskey to last at least a week, we were riding two inches below the waterline. When we pulled away from his dock, David observed, in a clipped British accent,

"That's the trouble with you bloody Americans, you're just too damned competitive."

The first race started the next morning at the entrance to English Harbour. *Serenity* had a smashing start. Once in free air we flew out our big drifter and ran down the coast. As we approached the first mark, we were lying in a close fourth, and Es was rehearsing her speech for the victory banquet. We closed on *Treena's* stern as she rounded the mark, then— disaster. *Treena* overtacked, went into irons, and was dead in the water. With inches to spare I pulled an all-standing jibe and sailed off for Montserrat. By the time we got everything sorted out, nine-tenths of the fleet had passed us by. For the balance of the race Es said terrible things about *Treena* and threatened her skipper with bodily harm. She was still mumbling when we took the gun well down in the standings.

That night just as the first party was getting started, a tall, handsome movie-star-type strode across the room, swept Es into his arms, kissed her and said,

"That was a bloody awful thing I did. It was all my fault. I'm dreadfully sorry."

The skipper of *Treena* was Graham Kerr, the Galloping Gourmet.

Es just stared up at him and stuttered, "It's all right, it's all right. They're just fun races."

If they are low pressure fun races, you must have to mount three inchers and a torpedo rack in preparation for the Bermuda Race. Entering a cruising yacht, loaded with all your worldly possessions, in Antigua Sailing Week is a little like entering a mobile home in the Indy 500. But they were right about one thing, the parties were something else.

The races started each day from one of Antigua's many harbors, churned out to sea, and went up and down the coast for twenty to twenty-eight miles with one traditional round-the-buoys race. Then it was time for a different harbor with a different hotel hosting a dinner. If you didn't have a good time, you just weren't trying. Several mornings, crew members, male and female, would rouse themselves on the beach and swim back to their boats barely in time for the warning gun. If we did not star in the races, we were outstanding at the parties.

When the week was over, I felt as if I had played middle linebacker for the Vikings in the Super Bowl. I vaguely remember saying goodbye to Les and Kris, who flew back to San Juan to recuperate. For two days, I would climb up the hatch, stare at the brilliant sunlight through slitted eyes, and return in pain to my bunk. All the effects of some poisoned ice I had forced on me, no doubt.

When I finally recovered, we were able to explore the anchorage which was to be our home off and on for the next three years. Antigua, pronounced An-tee-gah, is a small, oval island about fifteen miles east to west and ten miles north to south. Its highest point in the southwest corner is only 1,300 feet. The rest of the island is dry, rolling hills. The temperature is always in the eighties, and a constant trade wind cools the evenings. With the exception of morning showers and a few rainy days in the fall, there is an endless procession of billowy, cumulous clouds in a bright blue sky.

After Antigua was discovered by Columbus on his second voyage, the Spanish, English, Irish, and French all attempted to settle here, and all were discouraged by the lack of water and the nearby Carib Indians, who had a bad habit of eating them. In the early 1700s the English, determined to create a keystone for their conquest of the great crescent formed by the islands of the Caribbean, fortified the point that guards the entrance, and thus began the fame of English Harbour. More forts were built on the hills that surround the harbor and command the passage to Guadeloupe. Inside the harbor, facilities were constructed to service and outfit the navy. British naval heroes Rodney, Hood, and Horatio Nelson all served in command here. The Duke of Clarence, later King William IV, built an imposing home overlooking the harbor when he captained a man-of-war in these waters. The dockyard remained the center of British naval activities throughout the eighteenth century, and with peace and stability finally established, it was abandoned in 1889.

In 1949, when Commander V. E. B. Nicholson, R.N. (Ret.), his wife, and two sons arrived on their schooner *Mollihawk,* the yard had fallen into a crumbled, weed-grown ruin. In 1951, the Society of Friends of English Harbour was formed to restore and maintain the old Royal Navy Dockyard, and slowly, with contributions from interested visitors the world over, the work of restoration has progressed. Armed with original drawings, workmen have duplicated the eighteenth-century building method. As you walk the narrow streets today, it must look as it did when Captain Nelson returned from Nevis with his new bride. Clarence House is also restored and furnished in its original condition.

The yard is not, however, a sterile historical site. In part, thanks to the Nicholsons, father and sons, it is the most interesting and convenient stop in the Leewards. The Nicholsons abandoned their plans for a world cruise and stayed in Antigua to establish their very successful charter business. At the dockyard, housed in restored old buildings, are a grocery store, marine supply store, a travel agency, gift shop, snack bar, sailmaker, and a hotel and pub. Showers, fresh water, and ice are available most of the time. The Nelson House has been converted into a naval museum, and the old officers' quarters into apartments for the charter captains. The Nicholson office maintains a radio watch and broadcasts weather every morning at 0900 on 2527 Khz. Mail and messages are held for visiting yachtsmen.

Every Sunday, Commander Nicholson and his wife have a cocktail party at their home, a converted powder magazine. Here the sea tales really flow, told in a babble of languages and accents. One Sunday, Mrs. Nicholson confided in me that the entire harbor is haunted, but with congenial ghosts, not the ghoulish kind. Her favorite ghost rows ashore on bright moonlit nights, his oarlocks creaking, and leaves a silvery wake across the quiet waters. Heading for a ghostly pint at the pub, I presume.

The great fascination of the harbor is the boats. Almost every evening a new one slides in through the entrance, sails still set, silently picking her spot in the bay or at the quay. The sails drop with an audible sigh, and another new friend has arrived to tell stories of adventure. Tied stern-to at the quay is the charter boat fleet. They are magnificent old yachts, 70 to 120 feet long, built by royalty, either economic or heredi-tary, that have no use in today's world but to provide the temporary pleasures of chartering. They are immaculately cared for. Brightwork and topsides gleam, heavy rigging is served and painted, huge sails are formally furled, and multi-colored awnings vie with the flowers of the dockyard. Husky young men and bikinied young girls scramble around the deck, scrubbing, sanding, and polishing in anticipation of the next charter. If you prefer girl watching to boat watching, every morning the ladies gather to swap last night's gossip and to shop for fruits, vegetables, and bread brought to the yard by the locals.

For years the Nicholsons have maintained scrapbooks of their visitors. On each page, many with pictures and maps, written in the skippers' own hand are the stories of trans-

Atlantic and Pacific crossings, circumnavigations, passages from New England and Miami, and harrowing descriptions of hurricanes and dismastings. The most famous sailors and boats are represented in this pile of scrapbooks. The modern history of cruising is all here.

The strangest story in the books is the passage of the *Stella Maris,* a twenty-six-foot gaff cutter. She cleared Bermuda June 10, 1966, with her owner John J. Pflieger alone on board. On July 19, her storm stays'l set with eased sheets, storm trys'l bent on, and her tiller lashed amidships, she crossed the dangerous, almost solid reef that surrounds northern Antigua and came to rest at Prickly Pear Island, unharmed but empty. The chart of her daily positions and the last noon sight work-sheet are in the scrapbook, along with this last entry in the log:

> July 10th. I estimate my noon position at long.
> 61° 18′ and lat. 20° 20′ N* but the arrival of
> a ship somewhat interfered with my noon lat.
> It was a large tanker overtaking me also going
> S.W. She sailed within half a mile of me. I
> waved my American Flag. Seeing ships at sea
> after this immensity gives me a tremendous
> boost, and at least I knew I was heading in the
> right direction.

Sitting in this picturesque anchorage with its constant good weather and good companionship can be addictive. It requires some effort to break out and explore the rest of the island. Nearby are the ruins of several forts and the remains of sugar plantations with their unique conical-shaped windmills. There are two archeological digs being conducted by Yale University. Desmond Nicholson met us at the Nelson House Museum where many of the Arawak Indian artifacts are displayed, briefed us on these early inhabitants of Antigua, and drove us out to the digs. Here the ancient history of this tribe, dating

*This is approximately 240 miles north of Antigua.

from 2000 B.C., can be read in the trenches filled with flint stones, pottery, and seashells.

St. Johns is the major city on the island. Its newly dredged harbor is well lit and buoyed and is the only harbor to be attempted at night. Other than that, it has little to offer. It is a typically busy, dirty commercial harbor.

The best way to see St. Johns and Antigua is by bus. All of the islands of the Caribbean have a unique public transportation system that takes some getting used to. Here on Antigua, the buses range from new school buses to some ancient types that I think Hemingway drove through the mud of Italy while under artillery fire from the dastardly Hun. The drivers are all cheerful, grand prix aspirants, who have an encouraging word for all the pretty girls that they pass as they careen around the island. The drivers seem to know everyone and where they live and where they are going, which is just as well, since conversation is impossible. The radio is going full blast on the local rock station at a decibel level that will eventually loosen the rivets on the bus. They pick you up wherever you are and drop you wherever you are going. If you are a tired old lady with a large bundle, they will drive you to your doorstep blocks from the main route. Route may be the wrong word—if there is a system or schedule to the whole madness, we never figured it out. But it all works and it's cheap. About thirty cents U.S. from the dockyard to St. Johns.

In St. Johns you can find almost anything you need. There are good hardware stores, lumber yards, several banks, two big supermarkets, and numerous small shops. The people are generally pleasant and helpful, although there are a few sullen types who lean against the buildings and stare at you as if you were an avocado ripe for picking.

The post office is down near the waterfront, and you can have an all-day hassle running between there and customs to clear a package. Have all your U.S. supplies marked "Ship's Stores" before they are mailed, and they will be duty free. And be sure to have them sent airmail: surface mail takes forever. A wedding gift for Captain and Mrs. Horatio Nelson only recently arrived.

Antigua was the first in the chain of islands known as the Associated States of the British Commonwealth. The list includes Antigua, St. Kitts-Nevis-Anguilla, Dominica, St. Lucia, and St. Vincent. These governments are fully independent for internal affairs with a democratically elected legislature and premier. The queen appoints, with the approval of the premier, a governor as her representative. Britain is responsible for foreign affairs and defense and still provides economic aid for her former colonies. The totally independent island nations, or at least they were by the time we finished our cruise, are Grenada, Barbados, and Trinidad-Tobago.

The standard currency in all of these islands is East Caribbean currency, or E.C., as it is called. The official rate of exchange with U.S. dollars varies from day to day, but for easy computation it is thought of as 2 to 1. That is, $2.00 E.C. = $1.00 U.S. Since the actual exchange rate will be different on the same day at various banks, it is wise to shop around if you are going to change any substantial sum. You always get a better rate at a bank than you can from a local store or the hotels, so it's worth a trip to town.

The currency is also called BeeWee, stemming from the day when there was a British West Indies Federation. The federation fell apart, but the term BeeWee stuck and is applied to anything indigenous to the former British Islands. Thus, a BeeWee is someone born in the islands; a BeeWee boat, one built in the islands.

There is also a BeeWee language, and if the locals don't want you to, you can't understand a word of it. It's spoken very rapidly. Sentences are inverted and words slurred together, all with the hidden remains of a few French words and a broad English accent. After I had been around the islanders for a couple of years, I could understand about a quarter of what was being said, and when I started laughing at the right time everyone around me was a little more careful of what he said.

The phrase, "Antigua me come from" is worn on T-shirts by locals and tourists alike.

Some of the other phrases I particularly like:

"Doan make me vex, Mon." (Don't make me angry.)

Less strong is,

"Doan fatigue me." (Don't give me a hard time.)

And to "suck salt" is to argue.

A "punch up" or "mash up" is a fight, and a "fete" or "bram" is a party.

"Wash yo foot and come" is an invitation to a fete.

"Oui, papa, me charged!" means, "Boy, am I drunk!"

Someone strange is said to be "bent," and if she is thought to be a witch, she has a "goat's mouth."

Grenada is "quite down" from Antigua.

"Study yo head, Mon, yo brutalize me boat!" is "Watch out what you're doing, you're damaging my boat."

And I love, "What is to is must is"—What will be will be.

If you choose, you may enter and clear customs at St. Johns. If the busy, noisy harbor gets too much for you, just to the north is Dickenson Bay, a lovely sweeping curve of white sand beach and the Anchorage Hotel. Another well-protected anchorage with a beautiful beach and a great feeling of solitude is Deep Bay, which is immediately around the corner from Fort Barrington at the southwest entrance to St. Johns. Continuing south along the lee shore, you round Pelican Islands and enter Five Islands Harbour. This is a broad, shallow bay with numerous anchorages and lovely beaches where you can usually pick a spot to be alone. When you round Johnson's Point at the extreme southwest corner of Antigua, you may stay inside Cade's Reef, but since it is normally dead into the wind with a strong current, it is safer to pass outside the reef and enter Morris Bay in the lee of Curtain Bluff.

Then by all means dinghy out to the reef for the most colorful snorkeling and diving spot on the island.

Less than five miles west is Falmouth Harbour, another broad, quiet bay which unfortunately has a shoal right in the middle of it. So be careful. On the southwest shore is the Antigua Yacht Club, where every Sunday all the sailors at English Harbour gather for Sunfish racing, cook-it-yourself hamburgers, and lots of Heineken beer, or "Greenies," as they are called.

Immediately around the next point is English Harbour. Look for the red wall of Shirley Heights and the eroded cliff, locally called the "Pillars of Hercules," and you are at the entrance.

Green Island is a side trip. We spent six great days there. It is about ten miles from English Harbour. Once past Willoughby Bay, swing northward, and the island sticks out to the east. Enter slowly and carefully, and pick one of the three little anchorages, depending on wind and weather. We chose an un-named one around the westernmost point of the island. Nonsuch Bay is reef enclosed and filled with coral heads and little islands. The white sand bottom tints the water from palest green to bright blue. The anchorage is dead still, and yet the trades blow in uninterrupted. The island itself is high, rocky, and desert dry, covered with cactus, prickly plants, and manchineel trees. The windward side has deep caves and grotesque sculpture carved by the crashing waves, while the lee side is indented with little white beaches and coral gardens filled with bright-colored fish. We climbed all over the island and, while it is hard to explain to someone who hasn't tried it, we spent hours sitting atop Man of War Point watching the endless ranks of white combers march in and break with a roar against the long reef at the foot of our perch. For days we swam and sunned and visited with each other. Minnesota was a long way away.

We returned to English Harbour to catch up on our boat-keeping chores. We quickly slipped into the routine of the harbor: painting, fixing, trips to town for supplies, and the inevitable parties. At least twice a week, rum bottles and fruit juice or a cooler full of "greenies" would appear to celebrate one thing or another, and the conversation would turn to the great passages we had made, each trying to outdo the other with our skill and derring-do. After the storms grew too violent to be believed, and the seas ultimate in the extreme, we would switch to a deep philosophical discussion of the relative beauty of the girls in the Mediterreanean vs, Martinique vs. Tahiti. I always held out for the girls on Nicollet Avenue in Minneapolis, but no one would listen to me. The women would gather whatever was available from the various galleys, and a huge dinner of spaghetti or bouillabaisse or goat water, a local stew, would be prepared. Then more rum and more beer. Finally the guitars would be uncased, and folk music from around the world was performed. U.S. country and western followed the Beatles, followed by South African sea chanties, followed by "Waltzing Matilda." I never knew there were so many dirty versions of calypso. These impromptu parties lasted well into the night, and very little got done the next day.

You should also be warned about the Sound and Light Show. Every Friday night, if there are cruise ships in port or the hotels are filled, a lecture is given on the hillside overlooking Nelson's Dockyard. A tape made by distinguished British actors to the accompaniment of the London Philharmonic Orchestra describes the glorious history of the yard. At appropriate points in the drama, colored spotlights are thrown on the buildings and the bay. Since we have a propensity for sleeping on deck and since one thing leads to another, we were caught one Friday night in the glare of the spotlight, *in flagrante delicto,* as it were. We sent some disbelieving tourists away that night after the only X-rated version of the lecture ever held.

We were in and out of English Harbour a number of times.

One memorable entrance was the time we sailed *Serenity* over from Curtain Bluff for a haul out. I had failed to close the thru-hull valve on the head, and on the tack into the harbor, the boat steeply heeled. Water syphoned in through the fitting and flooded the bilges. We made it to the railway, but just barely.

By far our most dramatic entrance was our last. We were returning from an extended cruise of many months. By this time I was confident of our experience and sailing skills. Since this was the week after the Antigua races, the bay would be filled with old friends, and I was determined to enter under sail and show off a little. We flew in past Barclay Fort, into the crowded harbor and came about smartly. I was smiling and waving inanely like some beauty queen on the back of a convertible. Denny Warner on *Lord Jim* blew his horn in greeting as we tacked back and forth through the closely anchored boats. As we approached our favorite spot, I turned on the engine, brought it up into the wind, and turned the wheel over to Es. Still beaming from the success of our demonstration, I went forward and dropped the jib, threw a couple of gaskets around it, and did the same to the main as Es steered us between two little race boats whose skippers stood on deck, wondering what the hell was going on. I readied the anchor on the bow. When it was apparent that we had much too much way on, I yelled to Es,

"Reverse!"

Nothing.

Now we were headed straight for David Simmons, who was waving frantically on the fuel dock.

"Reverse! God damn it, reverse!"

Nothing.

I threw the anchor over and snubbed the line. *Serenity* hauled to a stop with her anchor dug in the wrong way, but at least she stopped. David relaxed on the dock. I charged back to the cockpit steaming.

"Are you trying to wreck us? When I say reverse, God damn it, put it in reverse!"

Es was standing, white-faced, tight-lipped, at the wheel, the rear-shift lever in her hand. It had snapped off at the base. She pointed the bronze lever at me.

"Take your reverse and shove it in your ear!"

It will be a long time before English Harbour forgets that entrance.

When it came time to leave, we experienced again one of the most pleasant rituals of the harbor. In the pale yellow light of dawn we dug out the anchor and lashed it to its chocks. Horns began to blow, and across the still water a sleepy voice called out, "Fair winds, *Serenity.*"

8 The Bypassed Islands— Nevis, St. Kitts, Barbuda

From the heights surrounding English Harbour you can almost always see Montserrat, forty miles southwest, and on clear days, Guadeloupe, fifty miles to the south. Clear is a relative term in these islands. There is, of course, no fog or smog, just water vapor that can appear as a distant haze. The local fishermen say that if you can see Montserrat clearly for three days, a blow is coming. The idea that a dry, stable high will be followed shortly by a windy low works out pretty well. The one thing you can count on is that the wind will blow. In the summer the trades blow from E to ESE at ten to twenty knots. In the winter, they shift to ENE to E and blow constantly at fifteen to twenty-five knots. I've spent ten days holed up when so-called Christmas winds blew twenty-five to thirty knots day and night. At least when you start for someplace, you don't have to wonder where the wind is coming from, or if it will last long enough to reach your destination.

We were booming along before the wind on our way to Nevis, our attention fixed on the cloud-covered volcano just ahead of us, when a white squall hit. It gave us no warning. There were no black heavy clouds; there was no rain beforehand—just a sudden blast of wind. *Serenity* leaped forward, her sails full out, and rotated toward the wind. With a terrible ripping sound, two seams in her main let go. Before I could get the flogging sail in, two batten pockets ripped and the battens were lost. In minutes the squall passed. The torn main was furled on the boom on its crutch, and we proceeded evenly with just the jenny.

When I finally took the mainsail ashore at English Harbour to have the seams resewn, I cut off the 2½-foot roach, leaving a straight leech and no battens. Roaches and battens may be fine for racing boats, but I've decided they have no place on a cruising sail.

The island of Nevis is only thirty-five miles in circumference. Its conical peak, which rises to 3,200 feet, could have been the inspiration for Zumi, the triangular-shaped Arawak island god. The island has no harbor, but the roadstead at Charlestown was surprisingly calm when we anchored late in the afternoon. As we finished our chores, we watched two island sloops ghost in to the pier.

These boats are about fifty feet long. They sail back and forth between Nevis and St. Kitts so loaded with people and goods that there is less than three feet of freeboard. The boom of an island sloop is at least fifty feet long and extends half its length beyond the stern; the main is peaked up with a short gaff. This design has been used to sail the lee of these islands for hundreds of years. And I thought I had an overpowering mainsail! I wondered what happened to a sloop when a squall blew through the narrows.

Here in Nevis, where young Captain Nelson wooed the Widow Nesbit, our visit followed by a few days a visit from another famous young British Naval Officer, Prince Charles. Everywhere we went that week, whenever we signed guest books, just above our signatures was the bold inscription *"Charles—June 5."*

Our first stop was the Bath Hotel built in 1778 over some hot sulphurous springs. Elegant ladies and gouty gentlemen from as far away as England traveled to this once imposing structure to seek relief in the thermal mineral waters. Surviving hurricanes and earthquakes, the stately building is now falling into decay. Weeds clog the grounds, and goats graze where wealthy plantation owners once gathered.

Further on, Fig Tree Church stands amid aged tombstones and tall flamboyant trees, their scarlet flowers filtering the light in the picturesque old church. In the marriage registry we read:

> 1787
> March 11 Horatio Nelson, Esquire His Majes-
> ty's Ship the Boreas, to Frances Herbert Nesbit,
> Widow.

Less than a mile from the church is the steep, curving road that leads to Morningstar. Here there is a bougainvillea-trimmed manor house, the base of a stone sugar mill, a large, rolling lawn interrupted by banks of multicolored flowers, and a view beyond belief. Behind us towered the cloud-covered mountain, and shafts of sunlight painted the hillside a brilliant, changing green. Before us, the cultivated lowlands sloped to the blue, blue ocean. The 300-year-old sugar plantation has been tastefully restored by Mr. and Mrs. Robert D. Abrahams of Philadelphia. It's a vacation home for them and a museum housing their large collection of Nelson memorabilia. They had flown to Nevis to welcome Prince Charles, who had expressed an interest in visiting the museum. We, too, had a personally guided tour conducted by this charming couple.

Whenever we pulled off the road to photograph a particularly stunning scene, someone would always approach us and visit with us. I have never met a group of islanders so proud of their history and the beauty of their island. Maybe living amid all the flowers on that bountiful island made them so kind and thoughtful.

We drove along white beaches where the ocean tumbled in, through thick groves of breadfruit trees and forests of coconut palms, and past the ruins of stately old plantations, homes, and sugar mills that could not survive the abuse of time and the changing sugar economy. The question people ask us most frequently is, of all the islands you have visited which is your favorite? Es always answers, Nevis.

The cruising guidebooks say that when the roadstead in Nevis is calm, it is rolly at Basseterre and vice versa. I don't know about the vice versa, but it was miserable the day we anchored at St. Kitts. We were so uncomfortable, in fact, that it was one of the few times we couldn't sleep on the boat and checked into a hotel.

Basseterre is the capital of the Associated States of Nevis-St. Kitts-Anguilla, having been granted independence from England in 1967. It probably has the most corrupt, autocratic government of any of the islands in the Caribbean. Unlike their neighbors in Nevis, where a proud, industrious people work their own carefully tended land, St. Kittians work for the government or the absentee owners of large land holdings. Their livelihood is dependent upon a widely fluctuating sugar market. All of this is exploited by a demagogic premier who foments strikes and disturbances. The premier reinforces his turbulent rule with a gang of bullies once called the Bread-fruit Tree Boys. Nevis accepts the government of the Associated States reluctantly and passively, but the Anguillans rebelled and became the "mouse that roared," seeking realignment with England or anyone except St. Kitts.

The Anguillans have many sound reasons for wanting to be free of St. Kitts. One of the minor incidents was the "Great Dock Caper." For years Anguilla needed a dock from which to off-load their supplies, and the Canadian government donated the money for its construction. When the money arrived in Basseterre, the premier had the dock built—on the east coast of St. Kitts. It is rusting away, unneeded and unused, but it *is* called the Anguillan Dock.

St. Kitts is spectacularly beautiful. The mountainous spine

of the island is dominated by a 4,000-foot cratered peak whose lower slopes are swept by broad green waves of sugarcane fields. To the south there is a narrow panhandle lined with white beaches that extends to the Narrows, a two-mile cut that separates St. Kitts from Nevis.

Our main purpose for visiting St. Kitts was Brimstone Hill. This fortification, rising 750 feet above the western coastline, was constructed by the British in the early 1700s and was known as the "Gibraltar of the West Indies." Ironically, the British lost the only battle fought here, but they defended the fort so valiantly that the French permitted the defeated troops to march from the fort with their guns and their colors flying. The citadel has been partially reconstructed, and there are fine old cannons remounted in the gun ports. From the ramparts atop thick masonry walls, a magnificent panorama of blue sea swept from Nevis in the south to Statia, reaching up into the clouds in the north.

We didn't continue on to Statia and Saba as we had planned because of the torn sail. Instead, we motored all night back to English Harbour. We had made some pretty strange entrances in the harbor as I have related, but this one was peaceful enough. We were more than a little self-conscious, however, because it was obvious that we were being watched through binoculars from a lovely maroon ketch. The anchor was barely down and set when we got a hail.

"Ahoy, *Serenity,* may we come over and see you?"

Es wanted a few minutes to clean up the boat, so I went in and cleared customs and then invited the party on *Holger Danske* to come over. The reason for the visit was immediately apparent. John Wilson, the owner, had as his guest Aage Nielsen, the designer of *Serenity*. The famous designer remembered each detail of her construction twenty-seven years before and was still angry with Hinckley for changing small items without his approval. But it was clear that he was as proud of *Serenity* as we were.

As we listened to this distinguished architect reminisce, another strange scene was unfolding in the harbor. When I was ashore, I had noticed a luxurious power yacht, *Romantica,* taking on fuel at the quay. While we visited in the cockpit, a jet plane buzzed the harbor. A few minutes later several cabs arrived and the drivers unloaded stacks of luggage. Robert Vesco, the renegade financier, and his family hurried aboard *Romantica.* The yacht immediately cast off her stern lines, moved forward on her chain, and as the anchor rose, turned on power. Unfortunately, she snagged the anchor chain of *Ariels,* a large steel schooner moored alongside. As *Romantica* gathered speed, she snapped the schooner's chain and towed it toward the outer bay. *Ariels* swung toward the quay, threatening to crush a small sailboat tied next to her. We watched in disbelief, yelling and waving, as David Simmons, across the way at the boat yard, jumped in his power boat and rushed out to the bay where *Romantica's* crew was still struggling to disengage the schooner's anchor.

Alongside, David yelled up, "Where the hell are you going? Who's going to pay for the bloody damages?"

Vesco called down, "You know my address. Send me a bill."

With the anchor freed, he powered out of English Harbour. We never found out which address he meant: Costa Rica, where he lives in exile, or Nassau, where he was headed to help the Bahamians celebrate their independence (an independence that included no extradition procedures with the U.S.).

Certainly among the reasons one adopts cruising as a way of life is the rebellion against clock-watching, timetables, and schedules. The freedom to go where and when one pleases is as good a reason as any to buy a boat. Unfortunately, it doesn't always work out that way. After talking to other cruising yachtsmen, I found that most of us had drifted into another form of the rat race. All too often, we had to get to the next island to pick up friends, or because we were due for a haul out, or because the shopping was better than where we were and on and on.

Our excuse for bypassing Barbuda the first time seemed valid enough at the time. We were hurrying down to English Harbour to participate in Race Week. Later we learned that there was more to cruising than rushing from one anchorage to another on some self-imposed schedule. There is too much to see, too many places to explore, and too many people to meet to hurry on.

It was with all of this in mind that we backtracked to one of the rarely visited islands—Barbuda.

Our cruising companions were ideal. Colin Beazer, a native Barbudan, would be returning home on *Serenity,* and Graham Knight, the sailmaker at the dockyard in English Harbour and a professional diver, wanted to come along, too. Even Es, a reluctant sailor at best, was ready for the trip.

Low, flat, and scrub covered, Barbuda is the last of the true coral islands in the Leeward chain. From here southward, the islands are volcanic in origin, and they become higher and greener. Barbuda is about fifteen miles long and ten miles wide. The highest point on the island reaches only 200 feet. Its north, east, and south shores are almost totally reef enclosed; its western approaches are pockmarked with reefs, shoals, and coral heads. There are more than one hundred wrecks on the reefs surrounding the island, so it is hardly necessary to advise caution.

We had all the charts but more important, we had Colin high in the ratlines, conning us in to his home. The major danger in approaching the island is that you don't see it until you are almost on it. The first thing you see is either a cliff, which is actually on the east side, or, sailing in from the south as we did, the Martello Tower, thoughtfully painted white by the locals. Keeping the tower bearing no less than twelve degrees in accordance with the sailing direction, we glided in until the hotel on Cocoa Point was due east and then slowly powered our way in among the heads. The water here is clear and beautiful. In sunlight the coral can be seen thirty to forty feet, and it can be assumed that if you have gone this far in your sailing, you have developed the skills to pick your way toward the bright sand beach.

The next morning *Serenity* motored northward along one of the most magnificent beaches to be seen anywhere. It stretches unbroken for twelve miles, sloping some fifty yards toward the underbrush of the interior. The beach itself is bright pink, and the water is an indescribable pale turquoise, so clear that we could see fish, turtles, and rays swimming below as we moved along. Around Palmetto Point, opposite a group of palm trees called Oyster Pond Landing, we re-anchored within fifty feet of the beach. The trade winds whistled high in the rigging, but there was hardly a ripple in the water as we dinghied ashore. A short walk across a narrow spit of land brought us to the Great Lagoon of Barbuda. This shallow saltwater body, about five miles long and one mile wide, opens to the sea through a narrow creek to the north. The only village on the island is on the east coast of the inland lagoon. Two local fishing boats were waiting for us, and in typical West Indies fashion, we roared full throttle toward the north end of the lagoon. As we approached the mangrove swamp, thousands of magnificent frigate birds wheeled high in the sky.

These graceful birds are familiar to all southern sailors. With a wing span that can exceed seven feet and long, deeply forked tails, they glide high in the air and never seem to move their wings. The rookery on Barbuda is said to be one of the only two known in the Caribbean. The bird lays a single egg, which is balanced on a platform of droppings built on the shrubs. Parents feed their white-headed young beak to beak for more than a year until the fledglings learn to fly.

When we climbed ashore through the mangroves, we sometimes sunk up to our knees in the slough. But it was worth it to watch these strangely awkward offspring sun themselves as they waited for their next meal. There are no natural predators on the breeding grounds, and our presence did not seem to disturb either the young or the parents.

Back in the boats, we headed through the creek to the northeast coast. Codrington Village is supplied by interisland boats from St. Johns, Antigua, but the lagoon is too shallow for the boats to sail in fully loaded. Small sailing lighters meet them at the entrance of the lagoon, and part of their cargo is off-loaded. We saw several lighters loaded to the gunwales, hard on the wind, bringing their cargo to the village.

The balance of the day was spent beachcombing and scavenging amongst the clutter of a windward beach. Unlike the immaculate leeward shore, this area is covered with bottles, light bulbs, and the plastic junk of civilization tossed up by an angry sea. I have no idea how long it will take to fill in the trenches of the ocean and choke off all life beneath a huge pile of debris, but when some extraterrestrial archeologist lands on the dead Earth someday, he will probably call us the "Bottle People."

Farther up the road is the village of Codrington, the home of the thousand inhabitants of the island. The village is neat, clean, and spacious. The houses are well built, and all are fenced against the constant grazing of goats and sheep that wander freely around the island. While we were there, we walked out on the larger dock that extends into the lagoon to watch the arrival of the supply boat. All the villagers expecting deliveries gathered on the dock, and the captain, armed with little slips of paper, called out their names and passed out the merchandise. We didn't see any money change hands, so I'm not quite sure how that part works. All the Barbudans we met were pleasant, handsome people who shared a communal life on the government-owned land and the bountiful sea.

Barbuda's major export is lobster. One day we went diving with the lobstermen to watch the process. They ranged up and down the island in small outboard motorboats until they found a likely coral head. Free diving down as far as forty feet, they snared the lobsters with a wire noose attached to a stick. Graham and I made up two snares and found we learned to use them very quickly. The lobsters were brought to chicken wire pens on shore and collected there until there were enough of them to warrant air freight delivery. They sold for $1.50 E.C. (about $.75) a pound. By the way, these bugs are spiny lobsters, clawless relatives of the Maine lobster, that sometimes grow to more than three feet in length.

When we left Codrington, we headed for the highlands on a road impassable to anything but a Land Rover. Here, high in the limestone and coral cliffs, are a series of caves first used by the Carib Indians and now by native fishermen, who work the waters of Two Foot Bay. As we ate our lunch, we watched the brilliant blue Atlantic come crashing in against the reef that encloses the eastern shore. Large black pigeons darted in and out of their nests in the coral walls.

The next several days were spent lazily enjoying the beauty of the long, quiet beaches and diving on the extraordinary reefs. We supplied Colin and his neighbors with big groupers and parrot fish shot with ease among the coral gardens. One day we discovered two huge cannon lying in eight feet of water that had been untouched since colonial days.

I recommend our next trip ashore only for the hardy. We were met by some local hunters, who set off walking inland at a pace slightly slower than the Boston Marathon. The trail across sharp coral led through head-high underbrush and cacti. As we trotted breathlessly behind the hunters, they told us of the deer they had shot at this spot and the wild boar at that. I just nodded and swore again to give up smoking. Five miles later we were on a plateau a hundred feet above the flat surrounding land. A great section of the tableland had collapsed, and at the bottom of the sinkhole, the trees that had sprung up were so huge that their tops were even with where we stood. Scrambling down into the hole, we were led to a series of great caves. After all too short a rest, we climbed down into the darkness and by torchlight found ourselves in a huge room the size of a football field. Passages led off at all angles into the blackness. The irregular floor was filled with ponds of water so still and transparent that you stepped into it before discovering that it was water. Graham stripped and swam into one of the passages, and when his waterproof flashlight turned out not to be so waterproof, swam back in the eerie black stillness. It was an unusual trip, but on the long hike back, I decided I would rather sail and leave spelunking to others.

Having concluded that we had enough of the land for a while, we moved the boat around to Spanish Point. Within a few yards of the beach we anchored in eight feet of crystalline water; even at that depth the ripples in the sandy bottom were clearly visible. We had barely enough swinging room since there were coral heads on all sides. Across the narrow beach in front of us, the ocean broke in towering fountains. To the south, Palaster Reef blocked the swells, and our new anchorage was like sitting on pale blue glass.

Each day sparkled in the bright sun; each night was luminous, calm, and so clear that the Southern Cross and Scorpius were undiminished by the full moon. We dove on the endless reefs, bringing back fish, lobster, and shells. We napped through lunch so that we could dive all afternoon.

The coral was fantastic. Stag corral rose twenty feet from the bottom. We found brain coral ten feet in diameter, and fan coral eight feet across waved gently in the current. The fish were beyond belief. Every species, every color, and every size seemed to be there. They were so tame we could swim among them and even touch them without disturbing them. Barracuda hovered nearby, watching, threatening, and then slowly swimming away. Some of these big bluffers of the sea were more than five feet long.

The scattered remains of many boats that had sailed up on the island in the darkness or had been tossed up by tropical storms surrounded the point. Their salvage was a profitable pastime for the locals. Colin's family still eats and cooks on dishes and kettles removed from a wreck by his grandfather. I found two freestanding cubes, ten feet on a side, that were coral encrusted, but presumably made of metal. I'm not certain of their former use, but one was the recent home of a giant lobster. He made a fine dinner for all of us with enough left over for salad the next day.

We finally sent Es to her cookbooks for new ways to cook fish. She prepared our first sting ray by skinning the wings, cutting the meat into strips, and deep frying them—delicious. The number-one meal of the cruise was pure invention. We had brought in whelks gathered in the tidal pools of the rugged windward shore. Es diced and sauteed them in garlic, onion, lime, and butter. She served them over pasta with our last bottle of Martinican vin ordinaire. There are oil sheiks who do not live as well. We were able to take two burlap bags full of lobster back to English Harbour for our less fortunate friends.

By far the most important pleasure of our stay was the reinforcement of our decision for our new way of life. The peace, the cleanliness, and the beauty of our surroundings were all rediscovered in Barbuda.

9 *Guadeloupe and a Real Emerald Isle, Dominica*

For weeks Guadeloupe had beckoned us across the channel, and we were on our way to visit our first real French island. Our short stay in St. Barts didn't really count. Guadeloupe is part of the submerged volcanic mountain chain that separates the Atlantic from the Caribbean, and it rises to a lofty 4,800-foot height above the sea. We watched it slowly grow tall, green, and lush on the horizon as we made the fifty-mile passage. When we rounded the twin mornes that mark the entrance to Deshaies, we were greeted with a warm fifteen-minute rain shower that washed the accumulated salt from *Serenity's* sails and deck. It was to be an almost daily occurrence on the lee of the high, rain-making mountains.

The deep bay at Deshaies is enveloped by the heavy green of the foothills that rise steeply from the quiet waters. The mass of the tropical forest is slashed by the flame of scarlet flamboyant, or royal poincia, trees. These striking trees, named for a former governor of the French West Indies, M. de Poinci, were in spectacular bloom. I reminded Es that after the beauty of the flowers fade, they are followed by the growth of long dangling pods. The natives call these pods "women's tongues" because of the breeze-borne clatter they make.

We dinghied ashore and hiked up the hill to the south of town to locate the gendarmerie and check in. We had been told by many cruising yachtsmen to be certain to arrange for a meal at Madame Racine's, and that was our next stop. Her brasserie was in back of a grocery store on the waterfront, and while it didn't look like much of a place, we asked Madame to prepare dinner for us. The tiny woman, her face wrinkled in smiles, spoke a few words of English and assured us that she could find something from which to cook us a meal.

At 6:30 P.M. we were seated at a rough wooden table covered with a plastic cloth. The ambience left something to be desired. The dining area was a courtyard formed by sheets of corrugated metal roofing that was painted a horrid green and draped with tinseled Christmas decorations. We were the only guests, and we were suspicious. Then Madame's teenage granddaughter, immaculate in a starched lace apron, began the first of her many trips from the scent-filled kitchen. Big bowls of onion soup, with a long, hot loaf of French bread, and a bottle of white wine. Coquilles served in large shells topped with thick, gooey melted cheese. A table-filling antique tureen of fish stew. Es delicately picked out the squid but managed to finish her share. Then escargots, not in those phony hand-stuffed shells, but served in a little ceramic bowl, hot from the oven, in a garlic sauce so thick you could smell it coming. More hot bread and another bottle of wine. Next a whole snapper baked with a delicate white sauce and a steaming bowl of yams. Es turned the platter so the fish wouldn't stare at her as she ate. When Madame came out of her steaming kitchen to see if the food was all right, my mouth was so full, I just nodded. Next a tray of baked lobster tails with a spicy creole sauce and a cut glass bowl of salad tossed with crisp vegetables, half of which I couldn't identify. I kept shoving the food down, just pausing for the cool white wine. At last we stopped—exhausted and embarrassed at our gluttony.

When I pantomimed that I wanted our check, the granddaughter, obviously unhappy, fled to the kitchen, and Madame hurried out to explain. Her helper had picked wild cherries from a tree in the yard and had prepared our dessert herself. We couldn't disappoint the lovely young cook, so out it came —a lighted chafing dish of ripe mahogany-colored cherries in a syrup spiced with nutmeg and cinnamon. Madame proudly opened an ancient bottle of cognac and poured a few drops to set it ablaze. Cerises Flambées à la Racine. Magnifique!

We had been eating for three hours when I received the bill—forty-three francs (less than ten dollars) for the two of us. I was more than a little embarrassed to tell Madame Racine that all the currency we had was either U.S. or E.C., and we didn't have any francs to pay her, but it didn't seem to bother her. She went in to the dining room and returned carrying a fat light chocolate baby with a gurgling face and curly blond ringlets—her great-granddaughter. The four of us sipped a bonne nuit cognac.

The next day Madame Racine gave us enough francs to pay for the bus ride to Pointe-à-Pitre so we could change our money. Is it any wonder that we love the French islands?

And French they are and proud of it. Guadeloupe and Martinique are departments of France, not colonies. They are as much a part of France as Hawaii is a part of the United States. The islanders enjoy a higher standard of living than most. The housing is modern and neatly kept; the educational system is outstanding, and literacy approaches 100 percent. The bus we took was modern, and the highways broad and paved. At each bus stop the persons boarding would kiss all their friends on both cheeks as they worked their way up the aisle. There were an awful lot of pretty girls getting on, but I got kissed only twice.

Guadeloupe is shaped like a butterfly. Basse-Terre, the western wing, is mountainous. A highway cuts through the dense forests to the river that divides it from the eastern wing, Grande Terre, which is broad, flat, and heavily cultivated. At the union of the two is Pointe-à-Pitre, a city of fifty thousand ringed with concrete high-rise apartments, which is the busy commercial center for the island. The shops and boutiques that line the narrow, twisted street of the old section are filled with the best Paris has to offer. Interisland schooners can dock in the center of town, and the waterfront is crowded with fish and produce markets.

It took more than a week to explore the island. After arid Antigua and Barbuda, we were especially impressed with Basse-Terre. We climbed up to the Carbet double waterfalls and bathed in the 377-foot torrent that poured down the cliff face in a white shower, a perpetual rainbow at its base. These falls are the first thing Columbus saw on his second voyage. "A bridal veil from the sky," he called it. I remembered that just a few days ago in Antigua, I had paid ten cents a gallon for the water we put aboard *Serenity*. Here in Guadeloupe there were rivers, springs, lakes, and waterfalls of pure fresh water. The center of the island has wisely been set aside as a national park. Hiking paths led through the dense rich forest on the rain-soaked summits and the natural hothouse valleys. Ferns, philodendrons, and weird epiphytes clung to the steepest slopes. We picnicked on wine, cheese, and crisp bread amid the fragile scent of frangipani and wild orchids.

Sailing down the lee coast of Guadeloupe, we discovered a technique that we would use as we passed all the high islands. During the heat of the day, the land warms and the clouds lift, the trade winds are blocked, and you are left in a calm. Then a sea breeze blows in from the west to take the place of the heated air rising above the island. The effect is tacking in a straight line. First there is a starboard tack as you ride the light sea breeze. Then as you pass a deep valley or a saddle in the ridge, the easterlies pour down the slope, and you are snapped on a port tack. When the mountains blanket the trades, you are back on a starboard tack. And all the time you are making good progress on a rhumbline course. You can usually read the coming changes on the rippling water ahead of the boat. The only danger is being lulled by the beauty of the scenery or the sail and failing to see a hard puff coming off the shore. There have been a number of ripped sails when helmsmen underestimated the power of the cold rush of air blowing momentarily across a calm sea.

Sailing in this manner, just a few hundred feet offshore, we watched the landmarks slide by—Basse-Terre, the capital city; the lighthouse at Vieux-Fort; and then a group of islands called Îles des Saintes in the channel. Let me tell you about that ten-mile pass. The wind really howls through there—all the time. It has been uninterrupted since Africa, and when it is channeled by the venturi of the high land masses, it blows. Since the wind reinforces the normal westerly current, you can be set miles off course in minutes. Once, coming from the other direction, our knot meter read over ten knots for forty-five minutes. Don't show me any mathematics to prove *Serenity* can't go over ten knots. She did, and the elapsed time proved it. Anyway, after that peaceful sail down the coast, the ten-mile pound to the Saints is one helluva ride. We were going so fast when we got in the lee of Terre d'Haut that we coasted all the way to the town dock.

Students of the French language may wonder how Terre de Bas, the highest island, and Terre d'Haut, which isn't so haut, got their seemingly mixed-up names. They were named by sailors, naturally. *Bas* in this case means down or downwind, not low, and *haut* means up or upwind, not high. Clear? Wait until I try to explain the meaning of the Leeward and Windward Islands.

We anchored between the dock at Bourg des Saintes and the strangest-looking house I've ever seen. Built in the shape of a bow of a ship, it projects into the harbor and is complete with an anchor chain. My line, "that son of a gun must have really been going fast when it hit the other side of the island," turned out not to be very original. Everyone who sees it says the same thing.

When I went ashore to find the gendarme to show him my crew list, I had to track him all over the town. I finally found him astride a bicyle, flirting with a large, round lady hanging out her clothes. He indicated his displeasure at my interruption for such a trivial matter. A very civilized nation—France.

As you walk through the hilly streets of Bourg, the main occupation of the islanders is readily apparent. Each yard has bright yellow foul weather jackets drying in the sun, and every beach has the distinctive Saints boats pulled up above the tide line. The long boats are painted a rainbow of primary colors and have a high, flared bow that sweeps back to a low, heart-shaped transom. Once sailed with a detachable mast, they all now carry a large outboard motor. Each morning the dawn's stillness is broken with a roar as the fishermen power out, their prows lifted out of the water, the outboard almost awash. They are back by noon and spend the balance of the day sitting under the trees in the square at the foot of the dock discussing the day's catch.

Our anchorage in L'Anse du Bourg was the exact apex marked by the ferryboats crisscrossing to the mainland and the traffic pattern for the light planes landing on the field carved out of the hills. We moved to a tiny, palm-fringed beach around the corner from Pain de Sucre (Sugar Loaf. See how much French I learned?). From there we could hike around the pretty little island without all the disturbance.

Fort Napoléon, a traditional tourist stop, is in good condition, having been used as a prison in World War II. From the heights of Point Mire, you can see Dominica, a green lump in the white-flecked blue sea.

When leaving the Saints for Dominica, I recommend looking backward at the channel between La Cloche and Grand Ilet and getting a good picture of what is called Passe des Dames. Coming from the other direction you will be going like a bat out of hell, and there is no time to start checking charts to find the right passage in. We've done it a couple of times, and both times there was a lot of tense screaming and yelling until we picked up the right two islands to pass through.

It is said that when a certain king was planning a military campaign in the West Indies, he asked an aide to describe Dominica. The aide crumpled a ball of paper and tossed it into his majesty's wine goblet. The king wisely chose to do battle on another island. This convoluted mass, rising peak upon jagged peak from its wave-pounded coastline and covered with inpenetrable forest, was no place for a military campaign. If the terrain was inhospitable, so were the fierce Carib Indians, who made Dominica their last stronghold. The last few hundred of these Indians, whose name is the source of the words cannibal and Caribbean, still live on Dominica. The island is as ruggedly beautiful as the day Columbus first saw it, but he, too, was unwilling to tangle with the Caribs and sailed on by.

We saw it first from Prince Rupert Bay, the only protected anchorage on Dominica. After an easy twenty-mile sail from Les Saintes, we were greeted by a flotilla of small boats manned by small boys all yelling at the same time.

"Hey, Mon, you gotta job? Me a plenty fine sailor."

"Hey, Mon, you want limes—figs?"

"Hey, Mon, you got laundry? My mama's the best on the island."

"Hey, Mon, gimme a dolla."

They were banging into my freshly painted topside, and the only way to get rid of them was to dinghy ashore myself and clear customs. They were out every day that we were in the harbor. Even after buying a load of limes and figs (green tasteless bananas) and having our laundry done, we still couldn't stop them from scarring up our white topsides. In self-defense we moved *Serenity* to the north side of the bay opposite a small white beach, where we could enjoy some privacy.

While we were in Portsmouth getting our clearance and cruising permit, we met Bruno, who, with his wife, a Carib princess, runs an open air restaurant tucked in the palm grove behind the beach. In exchange for fixing his ancient phonograph we got our evening meal at a discount. Although the dinner was excellent creole cooking, it turned out not to be much of a bargain. We ended up baby sitting for the five children while the parents went to a late night tribal meeting.

The next day, *Spartan,* a converted twelve-meter, arrived after a tough sail, her foresails blown out. Mike, her skipper, and an old friend from Fajardo, came over and asked for help. He had ten young men aboard as a boys' camp charter, and since he couldn't sail without some kind of foresail, I lent him my furling jib. When he sailed out, my jib looked like a handkerchief on his big yacht.

Mike urged us to make the trip up the Indian River, which enters Prince Rupert Bay near the town. We clamped our little 2-h.p. outboard on the dinghy, packed a lunch, and worked our way through the lighters moored at the opening of the river.

We entered another world. The river wound inland through a green tunnel of enormous bloodwood trees, their strange twisted roots framing either bank. The canopy of leaves was so thick that only an occasional sunray filtered down to dapple the clear, fresh water. Schools of mullet swirled to the surface and then sank down to feed among the roots. Fluted vines and creepers wove an impenetrable wall around us as the river narrowed and twisted its way toward the highlands. Then the current increased, and our way was blocked by short tumbling rapids. I tilted up the motor, and we pulled the dinghy over the water-smoothed rocks into the next quiet pool. Then more rapids and we repeated the process. We alternately hauled and paddled our way up until we were blocked by a waterfall. Here we pulled the boat up on a sandbank, stripped off our clothes, and swam in our own private Eden. On the far side of the pool, flowing from some volcanic cleft far above us, the water was hot enough to make staying in it uncomfortable. We warmed our bodies and then drifted back to the center of the cool, clear pool.

We lunched on the remains of our French cheese and bread and shared a bottle of wine. Then we sat silently, absorbing the serenity of our leafy cathedral. The sound of the falling water was interrupted occasionally by the raucous call of a parrot hidden in the greenness that surrounded us. There is no time in such a place, and yet the thought that we had worked our way at least two miles upriver forced us to turn our little boat around and start back.

We drifted down on the slightest current. Without the noise of the outboard to frighten them, the inhabitants of the river bank came out. Huge pale frogs watched us with unblinking eyes, and little orange crabs clattered sideways along the banks. Birds broke through the green roof and wheeled and sang their way down the tunnel. Schools of fish hung in the water undisturbed as we drifted over. Too soon, we rounded the last bend in the river and saw the bridge filled with jabbering kids. Their fishing lines parted as we passed under and out into the bay.

My fascination with boats is such that I never refuse an invitation to inspect another man's boat. If the invitation is not forthcoming, I sometimes invite myself. The strangest-looking catamaran anchored near us and unasked, I rowed over and hailed the crew. Reluctantly I was allowed aboard.

It wasn't a normal cat, but two 40-foot deep-keeled sailboats without masts, fastened together with a complex bridge of steel girders and winches. After some small talk the three Californians who comprised the crew took me below. One half was a normal cruising boat, but with a more elaborate navigation section than most and a much larger auxiliary generator than the average sailboat carries. The other boat had been stripped out, and in the center section was a complete dive shop. Tanks and gear lined the sides, and in the center there was a full bottle bank and large compressor. Forward, where the V berths would normally be, there was a machine shop and racks of tools. What would be called the aft cabin had been converted into a walk-in cooler that had its own compressor. Empty now, it was large enough to hang several sides of beef. The bridge that joined the two boats had two big electric winches, and hooks dangled down to the water.

"For the mini-sub," one husky young crewman said cryptically.

That's it. I never heard any more. Every day they would motor off somewhere, and the next day they would be back. Sometimes they left at twilight and returned the next morning. They never again spoke to us or even acknowledged our presence. What brought that strange craft all the way from California? What were they looking for? What was the purpose of the walk-in cooler? I've thought about it many times. I'll never know for sure.

The main reason that many yachtsmen pass up Dominica and miss the opportunity to explore this pristine wilderness is that the roadstead at Rouseau, the capital, is so horrible. It's rolly and filthy with oil and garbage. The bottom is so deep and rocky that it is impossible to get an anchor to hold. Carl and Janis Armour are trying to change all this. They built the Anchorage Hotel about a mile south of Rouseau. They put out four moorings in the deep water in front of the hotel, but time after time thoughtless skippers sailed off with the moorings, and maintenance became impossible. Now you are invited to edge up to their seawall, take the heavy line that is offered to you, and fasten it to the wall, then back off, drop a stern anchor in the very deep water, and snug up. You should be very secure.

The Armours welcome yachtsmen. You are free to use the freshwater pool. Water for your tanks is available. They'll have your laundry done. Dinners are good Creole cooking and inexpensive. When Es and I ate at the hotel, they invited us to change and shower in an unoccupied room. A thoroughly delightful place and wonderful, warm people. The Armours rent cars at the hotel, but they also have a safari service. If you don't want to drive the narrow, mountainous roads to see the wonder of the tropical jungles, they will supply a driver, Land Rover and lunch. We've stopped there four times, and as you may have gathered, enjoyed each trip.

There is so much to see on Dominica that it's hard to begin. The sadness is the poverty on this lonely isle. The rugged mountains and primeval forest that we viewed with awe have overwhelmed the natives. There is little of the steep land that can be cultivated. Bananas can be harvested only by the toughest workman hacking his way through with a cutlass and carrying out the fifty-pound bunches. Some of the copra can be harvested, but limes, the major export, barely survive the encroachment of the ever-enlarging jungle. When the English discovered the value of limes to combat scurvy, L. Rose and Company developed a secret technique to process lime juice so that it could be shipped from Dominica. Now that vitamin C is artificially produced, only gimlet drinkers are thankful that Rose's lime juice is still made here. There are tall virgin stands of timber, untouched since Columbus saw them. There have been several attempts to begin a lumber industry here, but so far they have been the schemes of con men and promoters. What is needed is a skilled lumberman who can convert this enormous natural resource to benefit the depressed economy of the island. Someone, somewhere, with a heart and a brain could do it.

We rented a car at the hotel, and armed with cameras and lunch, we set off each day to explore. The roads on the mountainous island are paved but very narrow, seldom more than a single lane. When you meet a loaded banana truck swinging around an S curve, you must back up until there is a place wide enough to pass. The roads have been carved out of volcanic rock. On one side there is a sheer wall covered with ferns and thick hanging vines that brush the car; the other is a straight drop to the valley floor with only tangled underbrush to break a fall. Despite the fact that Es was riding with one of the world's greatest drivers, she spent the day clutching the dashboard and staring straight ahead. You are instructed to sound your "klaxon" at every blind turn, and since the curves and cutbacks come with great rapidity, you drive with one hand on the wheel and the other on the horn. Fortunately, there are few cars on the island, so your main worry is not the traffic, but staying on the road as you wind up through the clouds.

Dominica has the highest rainfall of any of the islands. Up to 250 inches a year fall along the 4,500-foot ridge. Every cliff has a waterfall, and every valley a rushing white river. The islanders say there are 365 rivers on the thirty-mile island, one for every day of the year. Rain forest is no idle description here; each vista layered green upon green as the opulent slopes stretched before us.

The Emerald Pool is about a one-mile walk off the road in the direction of Dominica's highest peak. The general location can be found on a map, but there are no road signs to help the tourist find the way in. We picked a likely spot because there was a cab pulled off the road nearby. The narrow muddy path that had been hacked through the jungle of foliage wound around rock outcroppings and giant trees 100 feet tall and 8 feet in diameter. We found the cabdriver lounging on a rock, and he pointed us on. Clambering down a slippery ledge, we saw a silvery curtain of water cascading into a cool basin— and a young couple swimming nude. They grabbed for their clothes and crouched behind the rocks to dress. When I uncased my camera, they looked as though they would like to claw a cave into the moss-covered walls. After I apologized for interrupting them and promised not to take their pictures,

I explained that I had to wait around in hopes that the sun might burn through the overhanging mist to give me proper lighting for my shot. They were polite, but it was clear that we had ruined their afternoon and they left in a few minutes. The light never got much better, so in addition to interrupting a rendezvous, I took pictures that mostly turned out to be nothing but a spectrum of green tones.

We were eager to visit the Carib Reserve and watch the construction of the famous Carib canoes. The design and method of construction has been unchanged for centuries, and the canoes are widely used throughout the Windward Islands. We have been out in the center of a windy passage hanging on for dear life, when we passed one of the canoes tossing in the waves, its occupants calmly fishing with drop lines miles from shore.

Canoe construction begins with the selection of a tall, stately gommier tree, which is felled and trimmed. The canoe is rough shaped by the side of the trail and then hauled down to the shore where it is further shaped and hollowed out with an adze. More than half of the circumference of the dense golden log is used so that the upper edges of the partially formed canoe curve inward. These edges are bent out with sticks, and the hull is filled with water and heated stones. When a fire is built under the canoe, the heat warps the edges to a straight sheer. After a twelve-inch plank is added to each side to increase the freeboard, the dugout is ready for finishing. Today a small transom is added for the ubiquitous outboard, but many times I have seen canoes slipping through the seas under tattered burlap sails.

The Caribs that we met were small muscular people, with straight black hair and slanted almond eyes. They looked much more oriental than the Plains Indians we had known at home. The women still weave a straw basket so tightly formed that it will carry water.

There was still more to see. Fathomless Freshwater Lake,

which occupies a deep crater in an ancient volcano, is a tranquil geologic contrast to Boiling Lake, where columns of steaming geysers jet into the air from the turbulent surface. The latter is a reminder that all the volcanic forces that created these islands are not yet extinct. The twin Trafalgar waterfalls, just six miles from the hotel, not only provide a spectacular view but also energy for the hydroelectric power station downstream. If Dominica could package and ship its scenery, it could be the richest island in the Antilles and still have enough left over to delight the tourist.

One more thing, be sure to have Janis Armour prepare a platter of fried mountain chicken for your dinner. I don't want to ruin it for you, but the Colonel never saw chickens like these! They are *crapaud,* the enormous frogs we saw along the banks of the rivers.

The morning we left Dominica, we passed a British frigate anchored offshore. We came within yards of the man-of-war, and on impulse I went to the stern and dipped our yacht ensign. Whistles blew, gongs clanged, and pipes piped. A hundren white-clad sailors formed ranks along the rail. On shouted orders they snapped to attention, and the quartermaster smartly dipped the Royal Navy White Ensign in return. *Serenity* sailed the length of the frigate, our crew standing in a semblance of awestruck attention.

10 Martinique and Hurricane Christine

Although I've never been to France, I'm convinced that Martinique must have broken off from the mother country somehow and floated off to this tropical place in the sun. I've never met a yachtsman who didn't consider his stay in Martinique memorable. The one thing France can't surpass is the beauty of the women of Martinique. Gaugin, no mean authority on the subject, wrote enthusiastically of the island's "sweet, soft-eyed, sentimental country girls." Some country girls! Tall, supple, and graceful, they walk with an easy elegance that invites admiration. After all, these beauties, whose colors range frome café-au-lait to café noir, are direct descendents of Josephine and six other European queens. There can't be a bra on the island, and in arrogant disregard for the couturiers of Paris they wear *les minimum mini-jupes*—the miniest skirt in the world. I've overheard Es say that she wouldn't fear leaving me in Fort-de-France because nothing could happen.

"I want that one—no, I want that one. Look at that one! I can't believe it. Look at that one."

By the time I'd make up my mind, the indifferent lady would have disappeared long ago with her amoureux.

The first time I went ashore, I walked into the side of a moving taxi—girl watching.

One of the most pleasant features of our arrival in Fort-de-France was our reception by M. Le Breton, the most helpful officer we met anywhere. The government must have known how eager we were to visit this delightful city, for a customs and immigration office had been set up at Martinique Yacht Charters on the inner bay. M. Le Breton guided us through the bilingual paperwork and directed us to marine and hardware stores for much-needed spare parts.

Spartan, the charter boat we had helped in Dominica, was in the bay. We learned that her troubles were not yet over when her crew came over to borrow my diving gear. While they were stowing the provisions they had bought in town, one of the teenagers dropped a case of vintage wine overboard. After spending hours in the sludge of the bottom, they brought up lots of empty bottles but none of their valuable case. If you want to get a case of good French wine the hard way, I can show you where they were anchored.

Robert Vilo, a wealthy Martinican importer, took us to Plantation de Leyritz nestled in the foothills of Montagne Pelée on the far northeast side of the island. This plantation, built around 1700, has been restored with loving care and respect for authenticity. The manor house has been remodeled with all the conveniences, but the two-feet thick masonry walls and elegant tile floor remain intact. Each room is furnished with antiques of the period, and the formal gardens that surround the house show the care that has been lavished on them for more than two hundred years. The manor house is open for guests, and the rows of slave quarters have been remodeled into guest cottages. The former sugar mill is a bar and dance hall; the former chapel and storehouse have been combined into a large restaurant. Both Es and I considered Plantation de Leyritz to be the most beautiful hotel complex we had ever seen.

It was here that Robert Vilo introduced me to two Martinican traditions—sea eggs and rum punch. Sea eggs are the orange roe, or eggs, found in the black spiny sea urchins that everyone has been taught not to step on. Some people eat them raw, slurping them down like raw oysters. At Plantation de Leyritz, they are browned in a garlic-onion-butter sauce, by far my preference. The French attribute remarkable aphro-disiac powers to the eggs, probably because there are so many black sea urchins around. But then, the French are pre-occupied with aphrodisiac powers.

I can personally testify to the powers of Martinican rum punch. It is in no way related to the benevolent, health-giving, fruity punch served elsewhere in the tropics. This demon rum is mixed at the table by the host. The mixture consists of one large part dark rum, one equally large part clear rum, and a slight dash of sugarcane syrup. Add lime, stir, and watch out! It tastes like sweetened kerosene. One makes you think you will live forever; two will knock you to your knees. I don't remember much about the trip back except Vilo laughing at me as he set a new land speed record over the mountainous roads.

As the guests of Maria and Bernard Walker, we explored all of Fort-de-France bay and most of the inlets on the west coast of Martinique. Their yacht *Santa Maria* is a luxurious fifty-eight-foot Matthews, and she could cover in one day what *Serenity* could do in a week or more, so it was a comfortable way to see the island.

We were picnicking on the beach at Les Anses-d'Arlets when we heard a large commotion on the beach on the oppo-site end of the bay. Hundreds of shouting people were launch-ing six boats for the start of a race. The boats were twenty-five-foot versions of the Carib canoe; the sprit sails were mounted on a mast of at least thirty feet, and a bent bamboo sprit held the peak taut. Some had jibs, some not. They had to be carrying five hundred square feet of sails on those slim, keelless canoes. The crew of ten to twelve hung over the sides on poles locked to the gunwales, alternately spilling air from the giant sails and pulling the mast upright by climbing out onto the poles until they touched the water. The course was marked by anchored rowboats. The rest of the spectator fleet must have occupied every outboard-powered boat on the west coast. They wove in and out of the racers, cheering their favorites on and occasionally passing a bottle of rum to the hiking-pole men. The boats flew around the course, and it was a wild, happy scene. Serious thought should be given to making it an Olympic event. Those Martinicans could teach the stuffy one-class sailors how to have fun.

We went out to photograph Rocher du Diamant (Diamond Rock), and as we circled it close up, its often-told history became even more impressive. This volcanic piton rises a sheer 573 feet out of the water with hardly a toehold on its rocky sides. In January 1804, the British somehow winched up five cannon to the summit, and a lieutenant with 110 men held this bleak position for seventeen months, effectively preventing the French fleet from using the channel. In honor of their courage the British commissioned the forbidding pinnacle, H.M.S. *Diamond Rock,* and it still draws a salute from passing Royal Navy vessels.

Not as well known is the recent saga of another British sailor and the rock. Ships of the French Navy were scheduled to attend a celebration in Fort-de-France. In anticipation of their arrival, Joel Byerly, a British charter captain, led an expedition up the rock at night to festoon its seaward side with a British ensign. Somehow the men managed to get down without killing themselves. When the French Navy sailed by the next day the admiral went into shock, and it took the crew of a helicopter to remove the offending flag. All is peaceful now, but I bet Joel has trouble every time he checks into Martinique.

Because of my way of living, I would be the last man on earth to criticize another man's lifestyle. As far as I am concerned, you can do anything you please so long as you don't hurt anyone else. I do admit to being very uncomfortable, however, around the hippie sailors and boat freaks that have invaded the West Indies. It certainly isn't for reasons of hair-style—mine is longer than most. Or even manner of dress. After all, I lived for three years in the same four pair of shorts. I do find their artificially old clothes a little irritating, though, like the jeans that are carefully but unnecessarily patched, aged, and bleached. I consider it an affront to the natives of the island with whom they purport to relate. The locals wear old patched clothing because they are desperately poor, not because it's the "in-thing." The hippies' affectation in clothing is a lot like talking with an imitation harelip to a person afflicted with a cleft palate. I also freely admit an unreasonable jealousy. I worked for many years to be able to afford my boat; it gets to me that they can earn theirs on just a couple of trips with smuggled dope. I am frankly resentful that the major U.S. export down here has been our drug culture. The youth of these islands need decent food a lot more than they need pot. And it bothers me that most yachts flying the U.S. ensign are assumed to be dealing dope.

"You got 'erbs to sell, Mon?" is not an unusual greeting on arrival.

I admit to my prejudice, but it is not based on rumor or hearsay.

One midnight I was awakened by a rapping on the side and climbed topside to find two long-haired, ghostly figures in a dinghy alongside.

"Greetings, brother, may the Lord be with thee."

"At midnight?"

"Ah, look, man,—ah—like our boat is ah—like sinking, you know."

I thought it was some kind of put-on.

"What do you mean, sinking? What exactly is happening?"

"It is the Lord's will, brother."

"Christ, Luke, will you shut up!" said the second with some

wisdom. "It's sinking, you know—ah, like the water is above the floor, you know. Sinking. Could you, like, come over and see?"

I got into the boat. The Jesus freak was out of it, but the young blonde rowing seemed to know what was going on. Their yacht appeared in the moonlight to be a pretty wooden ketch about fifty feet long. We climbed aboard and down into the saloon. It was lit by candles, and the air was thick with the sweet smell of marijuana. Another youth was spaced out on the bunk less than two feet from the water which was, indeed, over the floorboards.

"That's Brother Paul," said Brother Luke.

"I'm Sandy," said the big blonde, giving me a reverse "soul" hand grip.

"Sandy? What happened to John, Matthew, Peter, and Paul?"

"I'm not one of these nuts, you know. I just met them like a week ago."

"Well, it is my judgment that it is the Lord's will that you get some buckets and bail this damned boat out, and like, fast."

Sandy got his dazed companions mobile and organized a bucket brigade, and the water level began to lower. He explained that the yacht had been purchased for cash, without a survey, two weeks ago in St. Thomas. Since neither of the disciples had ever sailed before, Sandy, who had done some sailing in California, had been recruited to handle the boat while the brothers spread the word. The boat had made water for days, but the pumps kept up with the flow until the pumps went out the day before. Since then they had been sitting there, slowly sinking.

With the bailing, the water level dropped enough to open the Henderson hand pump, where I found the discharge valve flap torn. I carry a truck inner tube for just such an emergency, and since there didn't seem to be a tool on the boat, I had

Sandy row me back for supplies. I dug out the piece of rubber, a caulking iron and mallets, oakum, epoxy, screwdrivers, and wrenches and headed back. After I got the hand pump operational, we got the water down low enough to find the electric bilge pump. Head down in the bilge, I unfastened it and found that it was clogged with an accumulation of sludge and that one wire had corroded off at the plastic case. While I cleaned and repaired the pump, I had the crew scoop out the muck in the bilge. I finally got the pump working and re-mounted. We pulled up the sole and located the leak where it usually is, in the garboard seams in the way of the mast step. The caulking had worked out of the seam and was laying inside the hull. I pushed some oakum into the seam with the caulking iron and sealed it with my two-part underwater epoxy. Truly remarkable stuff. The flow slowed to a trickle, at least temporarily. I recommended that they dive over the side in the daylight to work some more oakum in the seams and explained how to use the caulking tools and epoxy. Sandy rowed me back to *Serenity* at 4 A.M.

"Go in peace, Brother," called Brother Luke.

I slept until noon, and when I got up on deck, the ketch was gone. So were my caulking irons, oakum, epoxy, and tools. I never saw them again.

Go in peace, Brother.

There is no place to begin and no place to end when discussing the food on Martinique. You measure the success of your stay by the number of pounds you gain. We never had a bad meal. Even the smallest cafe in the smallest fishing village served a creole dinner that was a gourmet's delight. Gaston Athanase, the owner of the ferry service at Fort-de-France, took us to a restored eighteenth-century manor house at Ste.-Anne, where he, too, recommended sea eggs and rum punch. In between, we had an extraordinary seven-course, three-wine meal. Those who know claim that the yacht club on the inner basin, of all places, serves the finest meal in town. It surely has the fanciest dining room and the best service of any yacht club I've ever seen. There is even a French pizzeria. The Bakoua Hotel may not rank four stars among the galaxies of other four stars, but it features the Groupe Folklorique Martiniquais, a ballet troupe so colorful in costume, so sensuous in dance, and so rhythmic in music that they intoxicate the senses. The beguine, a dance popularized by Cole Porter, originated in Martinique. But the merengue! Even I tried that although I haven't been on a dance floor since I stumbled through my obligations with Es at our high school prom. You clutch your partner in a bear hug, shuffle your feet to a heady African beat, freeze—do what comes naturally during the hesitation—and then resume the rhythmic motion. Es said I had a natural talent for the merengue, and I decided to eat more sea eggs.

The most highly recommended restaurant in Fort-de-France is Chez Gerard. M. Gerard is no longer around, but Philippe Mays is the current owner. He personally selects in the local markets every item of food served and jealously guards his wine cellar. Our enthusiasm for his stupefying meals and his overwhelming service led to our friendship. Philippe and his wife Annak, who deserves to be on the cover of *Vogue,* ended each of our meals by sharing a cognac with us. Their repeated interest in our life aboard led us to invite them for a day trip to St.-Pierre.

St.-Pierre was once the "Paris of the Indies" and outdid even Fort-de-France in beauty, culture, industry, and gaiety. At the turn of the century, St.-Pierre was the principal city on the island although Fort-de-France was the civil capital. Its population of thirty-five thousand was double that of Fort-de-France. St.-Pierre could boast of one hundred rum distilleries, twenty sugar factories, and the largest cathedral on the island.

The volcanoes deep within the bowels of Montagne Pelée had on several occasions given warning to the people of St.-

Pierre, who lived and worked on its verdant slopes. But the skies were too blue, the air too perfumed with the scent of flowers, and the hillsides too green to brood about the dangers that had hovered over the city for centuries.

At 7:50 A.M., May 8, 1902, the mountain's side split open, belching a blast of incandescent gases and an explosive rain of molten lava. Buildings fell under a barrage of huge boulders that shot like projectiles from the force of eruption. People on the streets of St.-Pierre dropped in their tracks, dead of suffocation, and were burned beyond recognition. Then more craters burst open, and white hot lava flowed down the valleys to engulf the city. Within three minutes every person, save one, was dead. Raoul Sarteret, a prisoner, was found alive, protected by the walls of his dungeon.

At least twenty ships lay at anchor in the roadstead; all but one caught fire and sunk. The steamer *Roddam* escaped destruction by fleeing the harbor aflame. During the month that followed, continuous eruptions buried the northern end of the island beneath a layer of ashes. The destruction of St.-Pierre and the surrounding countryside left over forty thousand dead and thus became the worst disaster in the western hemisphere.

When we sailed into the bay, Pelée was wreathed in fleecy white clouds. Her steep slopes were reforested, and now only the flames of flamboyant blossoms interrupt the green, peaceful hillsides. The people of Martinique, however, no longer trust their sleeping giant. A new town of St.-Pierre has been built south of the old city, but today it has a population of only three thousand. There is a museum housing melted twisted artifacts, stark remains of the disaster. During a walk through the ruins, you can reconstruct the former beauty of St.-Pierre from what is left: the broad sweeping steps of the opera house, broken statues and a rusting cross amid the tumbled walls of the cathedral, and the carved stone columns that once fronted the crumbled building. In contrast, hibiscus and bougainvillea grow out of the cracks in the rubble, and vines of bright yellow allamanda cover the blackened walls. Even the birds still sing in this fallen city.

When we moved over to the little bay at L'Anse Mitan across from Fort-de-France, we joined a community of about six cruising boats, three of which were Brittany fishing yawls. Ever since we had been sailing in French waters, I had admired these boats, which have a gaff-rigged main and jigger with long overhangs and a bowsprit. They make very handsome traditional yachts of forty to fifty feet in length. I was delighted to be invited aboard one of *Serenity's* Brittany neighbors to inspect it. Philippe, a young Swiss, had purchased *Marjana* in France and then sailed her around to the Mediterranean, where he rebuilt the interior and outfitted her as a proper yacht. He and his wife sailed across to Martinique and were doing some charter business during the tourist season. The other two Brittany yawls in the bay had been acquired and maintained in much the same way.

One morning Philippe came over and with some alarm in his voice told us that Martinique radio was announcing a hurricane alert. I switched on English Harbour, and while I couldn't transmit that far, I could receive the 0900 weather broadcast. Sure enough, a tropical storm was swirling southeast of Barbados and was formed up enough to be named Christine. It was the last day of August and certainly in the hurricane season. The possibility of a storm had been on our minds all month.

Statistically, the danger of hurricanes hitting Martinique is pretty remote. Only a dozen have attacked the Windward Islands in the last three hundred years. The breeding area lies well to the east, and the pinwheel-shaped storm normally tracks northwest. The few that have crossed the Antilles do so at about the latitude of Guadeloupe and Antigua, hit Puerto Rico or Hispaniola a good whack, and continue curving northwest until they reach the continental east coast. The sailors in New England have a lot more to fear than those in

There, rising slim and graceful among her ugly covered neighbors, was the most beautiful boat I had ever seen.

Below, all was teak.

The skipper and mate on their first sail. The sound was like glass, and Serenity sailed like a dream.

In Haiti, Serenity *acquired a stempiece hand carved from solid teak.* Comme elle est belle!

San Souci, built by Haiti's manic king, Henri Christophe, looks like a surrealistic setting for an opera.

*Puerto Plata's graceful bandstand, where Es and I de-
clared the truce that made the rest of our voyage possible.*

A visitor appears in the dreaded Mona Passage.

Curt Harding, Posh's *skipper, during Antigua Race Week. It was Curt who had talked us into joining the races.*

The racers churned out to sea and sailed up
and down the coast each day.

English Harbour, Antigua, which was our home, on and off, for three years.

Don't start the party without us! When Antigua Race Week was over, I felt as if I had played middle linebacker for the Vikings in the Super Bowl.

The skipper with Colin Beazer, the Barbudan who conned us in to his low-lying home.

Hunting for whelks on the windward coast of Barbuda. Sauteed in butter and laced with lime, they make a memorable meal.

What might be called a "houseboat" in Bourg des Saintes.

Dominica, an emerald isle. Each vista layered green upon green as the opulent slopes stretched before us.

Indian River on Dominica. There is no time in such a place.

Emerald Pool, a lovely spot hidden away in Dominica's rain forest.

An unfinished Carib canoe. The craft is carved from a single log and shaped by heat and the simplest of tools.

the southern islands. It is also true that the newly formed storms have a smaller circumference and less powerful winds than the wide, destructive hurricanes that have matured on the sweep across the open oceans toward the United States.

Knowing this doesn't mean that during the months of July through October a wise sailor won't keep an eye on the barometer and have a hurricane hole picked out in advance as he moves. The hurricane reporting services are so refined today that there is no excuse for being caught unaware.

The commercial AM radio stations had picked up the news, and they were broadcasting hourly position reports on Christine. We began tracking her approach and talking about where we should move. I had located two or three likely spots in the mangrove swamps on the far eastern edge of the deep Fort-de-France bay. Philippe came up with what seemed like a better idea. Just a few blocks from us was the steel skeleton of the Meridian Hotel still under construction. On the far side of the hotel site, a basin had been dredged for a marina, concrete walls had been poured, and a few pilings were in place, but otherwise it was incomplete and unused. We received permission to occupy the marina, and Philippe led a parade of six boats into the little basin. We shared the job of lashing everyone's boat to the seawall with our heaviest lines and anchor rodes. I stripped everything on deck, including the sails, and secured everything below. Except for the possibility of flying debris from the construction site, we were in pretty good shape. We set up the hurricane watch headquarters in *Serenity's* cockpit. I mounted a large chart of the area on a piece of plywood, set up the radio on deck, and began plotting the coordinates of the storm as we received them. Over the next two days, it turned into one big party. Rum, wine, and food were contributed, and by nightfall most of us forgot what we were worrying about. On the third day it became apparent that Christine was going to miss us; she was heading well off-shore to the east and her track led directly to Antigua. It was with a deep sense of guilt that I remembered I was responsible for *Santa Maria* moving to English Harbour while I sat safe and unharmed in Martinique. The Walkers had sailed for Antigua a few days earlier.

Ultimately the storm veered out to sea and Antigua caught only the tail. The island survived two rainy, windy days easily and sustained little damage. All over the islands radios were turned off, and the hurricane scare ended for the time.

We moved back to L'Anse Mitan. The days passed quickly as we prepared to continue our trip south. In a week, yachts began arriving from Antigua with messages for us that we were wanted back there. The relayed messages were a little garbled, but it finally became clear that we were being asked to return to go to work at the Curtain Bluff Hotel.

Some months before, we had learned that the young charter captain of the Curtain Bluff's boat was being offered a chance to go to the hotel school at Cornell University and an opportunity to become assistant manager. Since the job of running the hotel's boat for the next season was open, Es and I had gone over to be interviewed. The results of the interview had seemed vague to us, and when we left English Harbour we had forgotten all about it. The hotel had been trying to reach us to tell us that we were hired and wanted us back to prepare for the season's opening.

With some reluctance we sailed north. St. Lucia and the Grenadines would have to wait for another time.

11 Day Chartering for Fun or Profit

I suppose everyone cruising in the Caribbean runs out of money sooner or later. The cost of food and services has multiplied at an alarming rate. When faced with personal inflation problems, many yachtsmen begin to think about day chartering. Those back home who are preparing to fulfill their dreams of cruising may actually plan on augmenting their resources this way. A closer look at the day charter scene may be helpful.

Typically, the guests are picked up at nine or ten in the morning for a sail to a nearby cove. There they sun, swim, snorkel with your equipment, and drink. Lunch is served either on the beach or the boat. Tired, sunburned, and more than a little smacked, they are returned to the dock about five o'clock. The charge for all of this varies according to the competition and the location and quality of your services, but fifteen to twenty-five dollars per person is the normal range.

The first consideration is your boat. Since criticizing another man's boat is in the same bad taste as criticizing his mistress, I'll discuss mine. Boat, that is. *Serenity* is just not a good charter boat. With a medium jenny up, her rail in the blue water, a lovely cooling spray over her bow, and the twenty-knot trades blowing, she is my private personal high. But she would have the average guest crushing the grab rails, his toes dug deep into the deck, and screaming in terror. Ninety-nine percent of the tourists have never been on a sailboat before; they're not looking for thrills. They want a quiet, peaceful day in the sun.

The ideal boat is a multi-hull. Its broad deck space, large cockpit, stability, and shallow draft are perfect for day chartering. A keelboat with some of the same qualities will do as well. Remember, none of your guests wants to go below. You must have room for at least eight or ten plus crew on deck if you expect any chance of economic success.

Next you need customers. There are three systems with variations and overlaps between them. The first is pure private enterprise. You put up your posters in local bars, restaurants, and shopping districts and hang around the docks at the yachting center. You buy your own food and booze and hope for the best. The main drawback is that there are probably several skippers who have been around your harbor for a long time. They have already established a relationship with the bartenders and tour guides, and about all you can hope for in the beginning is the overflow.

The next system is to develop an arrangement with one or two hotels. They will allow you to advertise on their bulletin board, and their recreation director will extoll the pleasures of your cruise. The hotel will frequently sell you liquor and mix at wholesale prices, and it is profitable for them to sell you box lunches. The obvious difficulty is to find such a place. English hotels tend to expect their stalwart, crinkly-eyed skippers to speak with a clipped British accent and wear dress whites. Naturally, on the French or Spanish islands you must speak the language fluently. United States islands require Coast Guard licenses, though few skippers have them. If your lifestyle includes long hair, a beard, scruffy clothes, and more than one bikinied beauty on board, you can forget about the whole idea.

The variation on this method is an arrangement with a

cruise ship line. While most of the passengers flee ashore to buy up all the souvenirs in sight, you take the remaining few on a seaward tour of the island or harbor complete with a calypso band and rum punches. This can get to be a bit much in a very short time.

Finally, there is the in-house charter. In this system you are an employee of the hotel or lease the concession; many times the hotel's own boat is included in the deal. The hotel takes care of the billing, and in some cases the day cruise is included in a packaged charge for the week's stay. They furnish the food, liquor, and crew if necessary. Your main job is to mix with the guests, show them a good time, and get them back safely in time for the cocktail hour. You frequently live, eat, and drink at the hotel, and except for getting damned tired of steel bands and limbo dancers, it is not a bad way to go.

Like any other business enterprise your profits depend upon your volume, cost accounting, and dedication to your job. Figure four to five dollars per person for food. Remember, these are vacationers. If you don't serve an attractive lunch, you won't get much word-of-mouth advertising. Your average cost factor will be the same for drinks. Beer, mix, and ice cost as much as rum on these islands. Day-to-day maintenance is surprisingly high; the abuse your boat will take from this hard usage will shock you. Sometimes there is a fee charged by the hotel or recommending guide. Insurance, fuel, and the extra cost of being in the right place at the right time add up very quickly. After discussions with many charter skippers up and down the Caribbean, I've concluded it's almost impossible to show a decent profit at the end of the season. At the very least, it requires a large, well-tended boat, an extraordinary arrangement with a large, well-filled hotel, and a willingness to work very hard.

There is, however, another sound reason for day chartering. If you really enjoy sailing and being with people, it can be a most pleasant way to spend the winter months at a tropical resort and with luck, break even on your expenses.

We had, for us, the ideal setup. We worked with Curtain Bluff Hotel, the most exclusive resort on Antigua. It is located on the protected southwest coast and has two beautiful beaches, fifty rooms, a gourmet dining room, and a season's occupancy of affluent, communicative, enjoyable guests.

Part of our interest in working at the hotel was to give Es a chance to get off *Serenity* for a while and be able to dress up and be a lady again. My lack of interest in dressing up was the only running quarrel I had with management. When we were first interviewed by Eddie Sheerin, the resident manager and a tough little Irishman, he explained that I would be required to dress for dinner. That meant tie and jacket. Since I didn't own a tie and never intended to own one again, we reached an impasse. We sailed down island. When we were asked to return at the beginning of the season, we met owner Howard Hulford, who introduced a compromise: because the "captain" was such a character, I didn't have to wear a tie, but I did have to wear a jacket, so I sent back to the States for some jackets and slacks. I still liked Wednesday nights best because that was beach barbecue night, and dress was informal. That meant I could wear the same shorts and T-shirt I wore anyway.

Howard and I became instant compatriots. I thoroughly enjoyed his company, and he at least tolerated mine. He was an ex-marine pilot who had fallen in love with Antigua during his travels as a commercial pilot. He arranged for the purchase of the land at Curtain Bluff and raised enough money in the States to form a corporation to build the hotel. He supervised the planting of every shrub and the placement of every stone during construction and was justly proud of his accomplishment. Howard was built like a tackle. The only hair on his bald head was a sweeping cossack mustache, and he wore a scowl that was far more theatrical than actual. For good reason we called him the Godfather. Howard and I yelled at each other a lot, but we got along fine. He used to introduce me to his guests as "the world's oldest goddamned beach boy."

We sailed the hotel's ketch *Salaamat:* she is forty-three feet long with a fifteen-foot beam and a five-foot draft. Heavy, roomy, and well laid out for day chartering, she has an easy motion downwind for the morning trip and a powerful diesel to bring us home in the afternoon. The hotel furnished everything that we could need, including our prized first mate, Luther, pronounced "Lootah." He was a tall, gangly Antiguan, a little shy and more than a little bemused with most of our guests, but an ideal companion for the young people we had on board. He was a good sailor and knowledgeable in the folklore and geography of the island.

Since I am not at all that charming, Es handled the conversation, served drinks, and set out lunch. My main job was to sail us as comfortably as possible to one of the many deserted white sand beaches for which Antigua is justly famed. I would usually lead the snorkelers over offshore coral gardens filled with multicolored fish and, at one of our favorite anchorages, into spectacular caves carved at the water's edge from a red limestone cliff.

Luther would dinghy the nonswimmers ashore for walks on the quiet beaches, and Es led shellers to a likely spot. We would gather whelks, boil them, and serve them with hot sauce as hors d'oeuvres. Lunches were always something outstanding—fried chicken, barbecued ribs, cold beef wellington, salads, and fresh local pineapple, all served on a table bright with hibiscus, oleander and frangipani.

The guests came from England, South America, Italy, and all parts of the United States and Canada. We had one cruise where none of the guests spoke English. With only a few exceptions they were great company. We averaged four and one-half trips a week during the season and cannot recall an unpleasant sail.

A memorable if not typical group was the Beverly Bridge

Club. It consisted of eight Chicagoans approaching middle age who had gone to school together and maintained their friendship through the years. Although they hadn't played bridge since 1956, they still vacationed together every year. After putting a pretty good dent in our liquor supply, they spent much of the day singing college fight songs and World War II ballads. "Don't Sit under the Apple Tree with Anyone Else but Me" really broke Luther up. A couple of the men were boat owners and had raced the Mackinac and other inland races, so I let them sail the boat home while I went below to make still more drinks. When I came up to the wheel, I found I had a mini-mutiny on my hands. Mitch, the helmsman, was on a course for Guadeloupe instead of the hotel. They were all a little peeved when I insisted we come about.

I usually wear a sheath knife and marlin spike on my belt when sailing and that, together with my red crew cap, had become my badge of office around the hotel. In a loud stage whisper I heard my former helmsman tell Luther,

"You get the knife, then you'll be the captain."

It was getting so late by then that management sent the speedboat out to see if the guests needed rescuing. My loyal crew chased the poor driver away by pelting him with our last remaining ice cubes.

We finally sailed into the harbor in near darkness, and many of the guests had gathered on the hotel dock to watch as the Beverly Bridge Club, standing at attention on the foredeck sang in loud, if slurred voices, "Just a Closer Walk with Thee." It had been a long day.

Being a captain at a resort hotel is an ego-building experience. You are looked upon as a walking encyclopedia and are the final word on geography, astronomy, oceanography and most important, weather prediction. Sometimes answering the same questions every day can drive you crazy. Even Es and Luther would get a little bent some days. From my post at the wheel I have overheard,

"What's the name of that black bird with the white head?"

"She's a white-headed black bird, Ma'am."

"What do you call those red cliffs?"

"That's Red Cliff."

Pointing to Montserrat—"What island is that?"

"Guadeloupe," from Luther.

"Grenada," from Es.

But for the most part we understood that our guests had traveled a long distance and had spent a lot of money to make what was in many cases a first trip to the tropics, and we tried to guide them toward a pleasant vacation.

The single-most-recurring danger was sunburn. However many times guests were warned, at least once a week someone would be confined to his room with a severe case of sun poisoning. And his expensive vacation was ruined. The powers of the sun's rays near the equator can easily be underestimated because you never really get hot. Antigua in the summertime is far more comfortable than Fort Lauderdale or San Diego, because the trade winds always blow and the temperature rarely gets above ninety degrees. Almost none of the hotels in the Antilles are air conditioned. The trade winds are our air conditioning.

Snorkeling, in particular, can give you a really painful burn. The sun's rays are magnified by the water, and as you float, peering down at the wonder of undersea life, they focus on your shoulders and the tender backs of your legs. Because you are cooled by the sea, your problem goes unnoticed until your evening shower when you find that you can't bend your legs or put on a shirt. Getting a proper suntan is a time-consuming, careful process. Take it easy. It's far safer to go home pale than broiled purple.

The next most common vacation ruiners are black sea urchins. These spiny balls are about a foot across and look like curled-up porcupines. They are found along the coastline everywhere—among the coral heads, in the crevices of rocks, and even on open sandy beaches. They don't stab you; you stab them. You have to step on one, stick your elbow in it, or push your hand down on the spikes to be hurt. But despite the warnings, someone does it every day. Once the quill is stuck in the flesh, it breaks off and leaves its barbed head buried in your skin. Do not attempt to dig it out with a needle—you can't do it. The only thing to try is to dissolve it with repeated applications of lime juice, vinegar, or urine. The easiest way to avoid the problem is simply to avoid the urchin. Look where you're going. Don't jump out of a boat without determining what is beneath you.

The last real danger is the manchineel tree. These shiny green-leafed trees with grey white bark grow on all the islands from the Bahamas to South America, usually in the center of the beach you want to picnic on. The Carib Indians used the sap of the manchineel tree to make poison arrows, and the little green apples are highly poisonous, too. The apples can be found washed up on a beach even where there are no trees. Do not eat any little green apples—ever!

A mature motherly type, who must have told her children a thousand times not to pick up anything off the street and put it into their mouths, bit into a manchineel apple lying on the beach and in seconds had terrible burns on her lips and tongue. A cruising friend of mine was hiking in Bequia, slipped, grabbed the branch of a manchineel tree, and stripped the leaves from the branch as she fell. She was hospitalized for three weeks. I have been told of people being burned by sitting under one of the trees in a rain shower. If you don't know what one looks like, have someone who does know point one out to you.

Incidentally, the reason you don't eat land crabs down here is because land crabs eat manchineel apples. In Dominica, the crabs are gathered in a pen and fed until they are purged of the poison and then eaten. I can get along without them.

The other supposed perils of these tropic waters are myths.

It is a shame to meet so many people—cruising yachtsmen as well—so obsessed with imaginary dangers that they are fearful of venturing out and thus fail to extend themselves and their senses in an exploration of things they've never seen before. High on the list of things to explore is a wondrous world of underwater beauty—the coral reef.

With just a few minutes of training in the use of flippers, snorkel, and mask, you can float over this ever-changing theater built of towers, archways, domes, and hardened flames of coral. Antlers of staghorn reach up to you, and convoluted boulders of brain coral strew the sea floor. Graceful purple sea fans wave in the current. Delicate sea anemones beckon with rose and lavender tentacles. Drifting and darting through the intricate structures are the reef fish. Their reds, greens, yellows, and blues make for a dazzling array in the filtered sunlight. The delicate, disclike angelfish trails gossamer wings. The parrot fish nibbling away at the coral is a tapestry of color. A boldly striped butterfly fish tries to deceive you with a false eye on its tail. An ugly grouper peers out of a crevice with its extended eyes. A crazy little spotted trunkfish sticks its long, pointed nose into everyone's business. And the truly schizophrenic trumpet fish hangs motionless on its nose—it thinks that you think it's a strand of seaweed.

All this and more is there for those who will only roll over the side of the boat and look. But far too many people deny themselves the beauty of these sea creatures because of some irrational fear that they will be injured.

You can't go diving without seeing a barracuda. Force yourself to remember that this highly selective feeder is so skilled a predator that it alone among the inhabitants of the reefs does not have to feed constantly. Admittedly, it is a savage-looking creature. Its baleful yellow eyes watch your every move; it gives the appearance of gnashing its fearsome teeth nonstop as its jaws open and close. Seeing it for the first time, hanging sleek and motionless a few yards away, can

155

stop your heart. But the barracuda is just making use of its leisure time. It is curious about you—that strange creature poking about awkwardly, disturbing its fish in its domain. If you should be lucky enough to spear a fish, get it out of the water as fast as possible, or the barracuda may want to share it with you. A lot of divers shoot barracuda (and they must be relieved when their first shot finds its mark!), but it is a practice I don't recommend. Like the 'cuda, I can find plenty of easier prey on the reef. But always remember that barracuda eat fish, not people.

The danger lies not in being eaten, but in eating barracuda —as well as grouper and snapper. Ciguatera is a tropical fish nerve poisoning that is endemic to large predators on the reef. The larger the fish, the more prevalent the poison. There are a number of myths, but scientists still can't tell you how to detect ciguatera until you get sick.

We used to catch barracuda on a trailing line on *Salaamat,* and I always gave any fish we caught to Luther.

"Hey, Mon, you sure 'cuda good to eat?" I asked him once.

"Sure they good."

"I heard you could get sick from them. Did you ever get sick?"

"Sure I got sick, but they good fish."

Luther thought Americans were crazy when they cleaned a fish and threw the head away. His mother made the best stew on the island with fish heads.

There are a lot of sharks in the Caribbean, but only a fraction of the number that there are in Long Island Sound. Despite anything you have read, any movies you've seen, or any rumors you've heard, there has never been a documented case of a shark attack on a human being in the history of the Caribbean islands.

Most of the sharks on the shallow reefs are small—four to five feet long. The larger ones, found by deep divers, have so much food on the reef that they don't need you. Some, like the nurse sharks, are bottom feeders, and about the only way they can hurt you is to scare you to death. To deny yourself the overwhelming pleasures of diving because of some sensational movies or TV shows is nonsense. I don't say that sharks are not frightening. I am saying they are not necessarily dangerous, which is quite a different thing. I am scared enough to get out of the water and move to a different place when I see one, but fear of sharks doesn't prevent me from enjoying the undersea world. The average snorkeler who confines himself to floating over coral gardens may never see a shark.

Another much maligned creature of the reef is the moray eel. This night-feeding "half-fish" lives in small caves in the reef. The only way you can get bitten is to put your hand in its mouth. The same can be said for my sister's twelve-year-old miniature sheep dog.

I love to watch rays or skates. Flat, with batlike wings that sometimes stretch six feet across, they glide through the water like giant prehistoric birds, slowly flapping their graceful wings and trailing a long whip of a tail. When they are at rest, they lie on the bottom partially covered with sand, but their widely spaced eyes are alert for any threatening movement. As you swim nearer, this timid creature will take off with a powerful thrust, trailing a cloud of sand. Some species of rays have a sharp barb on their tail that is usually located where the tail joins the body. It is said that if you step on a stingray, you will receive a poisonous wound. No one has ever explained how you go about stepping on a stingray.

The only injury involving a ray that I ever heard of occurred in Antigua. A professional diver shot one, and as he was swinging the heavy ray over his head into his boat, it slid down the spear and the barb dug into the fleshy part of his forearm, resulting in a nasty, painful gash that required hospital treatment. But you can't claim the ray attacked the man.

There is one other minor danger from the ray's tail that I

must tell you about, no chauvinist slur intended.

Once, when a Bahamian and I were cleaning two rays we had just shot, he pointed out the beaklike barb and then cut off the tail and handed it to me.

"Here, Mon, hang it in your boat. You'll have a long, happy marriage."

I had seen dried rays' tails hanging in many Bahamian homes and assumed they were supposed to have some sort of mystical power.

"Are they supposed to bring good luck?"

"No, Mon." He looked at me as if I was some new kind of idiot. "You keep it. If your woman argues too much, you beat her with it."

Es wouldn't let me bring it on board.

On almost every trip, I would bring up starfish, queen conch, or helmet shells as gifts for our guests. And while I would never break off or tear out a piece of living coral, there were always enough small pieces snapped off by the motion of the waves to keep everyone supplied with souvenirs. Despite my repeated warnings to have them cleaned and treated, invariably the guests would wrap them in newspapers and pack them among their clothes for the trip home. There had to be a lot of 747s arriving in New York with baggage compartments smelling like a garbage pit. Most people, yachtsmen included, forget that these are living creatures and when they die, they smell awful.

Contrary to popular belief, islanders are not particularly good divers nor are they fond of swimming. Mainly they dislike being cold. This is translated into their belief in and fear of the "jumbies." These demons that travel on the cool night breezes are claimed to be the source of all the troubles and disease on Antigua. At night, all the houses in the islanders' village are boarded shut in all kinds of weather against the jumbies' intrusions. It must work, because the Antiguans are extraordinarily healthy and never get colds or flu without the help of a planeload of North Americans.

Whenever Luther and I dove together, it would be only a few minutes before his teeth would start to chatter and his hard-muscled body would shiver. This is in eighty-five degree water, mind you. Then he would swim for the beach and roll over and over in the hot, dry sand until he looked like a six-foot breaded veal cutlet. Once his body had been warmed by the sand, he would rinse off quickly in the tepid shallow water, dress, and cheerfully be ready for any task—except more diving.

In season Luther would locate some mangos, which I insisted were to be eaten on the beach. There is no way to eat a mango without taking a swim afterwards! When guests came back from their walks on the beach hauling dried coconut husks, we would have to explain that they were beyond the eating stage. An edible nut has a golden brown husk that must be cut away, exposing the hard kernel you are used to seeing in the supermarket. We carried them on *Salaamat* for those who like the coconut meat fresh. But the real treat is "jelly nuts," the newly formed green coconuts. After we had found a small boy to climb up a tree to get some for us, Luther would whack off the ends with a mighty swipe of his cutlass (machete, to most people). The milk is a clear, refreshing liquid that is even more refreshing if you add rum or gin. We've had guests so refreshed they couldn't walk.

The local ladies made their own brand of suntan oil from the freshly pressed coconut oil (the white meat is pressed for oil). It doesn't smell very good, but tourists assume it must be better than the expensive stuff they brought with them. Antiguan women don't use it—they stay brown all year round.

One of the spectacles of Antigua is the blooming of the century, or dagger, plant. A lady from California once told me that they are called century plants because they bloom only once every hundred years. She was thrilled to be on the island the very day that every one was in bloom! The mature succulent grows six feet high, its base made up of tough, dag-gerlike spikes. Every spring a pole shoots up from the base and grows almost a foot a day until it thrusts itself twenty to thirty feet in the sky and bursts into golden blossoms at the top. Hummingbirds find its yellow flowers particularly attrac-tive, and each stock wears a haze of fluttering violet green birds. In a month it is over: the pole turns brown and topples to the ground. The fierce, spiky plant waits for next Easter to show off its beauty again.

The dead poles are as light and buoyant as balsa, and small boys bind them together into a raft or "dagger boat." Every day we passed the village boys fishing from these proudly constructed craft.

After the sail we would gather with all our new friends on the veranda for one last drink to await the gorgeous tropical sunset. Here the sun sinks below the horizon in a sudden blaze of coral and vermillion abruptly followed by darkness. One reason is that in this part of the world the angle of the sun's path is almost ninety degrees to the horizon, and it dis-appears rapidly. In the latitudes in the United States, the sun's path slopes toward the horizon, and so its light can be seen for a much longer time. The other reason is that the atmo-sphere in the States is so polluted with gases, smog, and chemicals that the sun's rays are reflected, refracted, and changed in color as the rays pass through the murkiness. Here we have only water vapor to bend and reflect the light, and so we have almost no twilight.

The same is true, of course, of sunrise. But that view is usually restricted to sleepy helmsmen on early morning watch. The sun leaps from the distant sea rapidly, seemingly elon-gated by its velocity and eager to flood the chilly sailor with its warmth.

To make up for our short twilights we have the "green flash." (The French call it *le rayon vert.*) I'm not putting you on. It's not the nickname for the Celtics new forward, it's not the product of a rum-drugged mind—it's real. We always alerted our skeptical guests when the conditions were right: a cloudless horizon with just enough vapor to tint the sky. A fraction of a second before the last thin segment of the sun's red arc drops below the horizon, you will see a green flash. It is caused by the difference in the degree of bending of light rays as they filter through the denser atmosphere. Since the green rays are bent more, they appear to break away from the red and—green flash! If you don't believe any of this, check Life's Nature Library, *The Earth,* pages 68 and 69, for photographs of the green flash taken by the Vatican Observatory. You're not going to argue with the Vatican, are you?

Some afternoons we would have fifteen or twenty people staring at the setting sun. One half would see the flash; the other half would not. The latter half would claim the flash see-ers were either drunk or crazy. We have simple pleasures at a resort hotel.

The hotel was twelve years old and enjoyed an extraordinarily good relationship with the natives of Antigua—something that cannot be said of many resort hotels. All of the help at the hotel had been recruited from the nearby villages and personally trained by Eddie Sheerin and Howard and 'Chelle Hulford. The training was so respected that those who were not hired were eagerly employed at other hotels. (Most of the employees had been at the hotel since the day it opened.)

One other indication of the kindness of the Hulfords was the junior tennis program. 'Chelle organized all the kids in Old Road, the village near the hotel. She furnished the equipment, and the hotel's tennis pro began group lessons. Remember, these were ragged, barefoot kids who had never seen a tennis racquet before and had to wait their turn to put on a pair of tennis shoes. Two years later, we watched the Antigua Junior Tennis Championship, and 'Chelle's boys were in tennis whites, shouting "Good shot, Mon" and formally shaking hands with their opponents after each match. More important, these teenagers had developed a tennis game that could beat most of the adults around the hotel.

Both Eddie and Howard were good sailors, who were constantly sought after as crew members during Race Week. (I won't tell you about the time Eddie, with his vast local knowledge, ran a PJ racing machine aground at Johnson's Point.) Once, when the three of us were bored with the activities at the hotel, we took *Serenity* for a sail to Redonda. That big rock is just north of Montserrat, and it was midnight before we returned. There was an empty fifth of Irish whiskey in the cockpit, and my two navigators were sound asleep as I tried to pick my way around Cades Reef and into Morris Bay. They are a hell of a lot better hoteliers than they are crew members.

Our last charter was one of the best of the year. A group of twenty-two divers from Baltimore stayed at the hotel, and every day for a week we took them out to the reefs that we had grown to know so well. With all of the diving gear *Salaamat* looked like a miniature *Calypso* except that we had many more pretty girls than Cousteau.

By far the best part of our stay at Curtain Bluff was the good friends we made. When it was time to leave, to say good-bye to management and Luther, Es cried and carried on as if she were leaving our family. And we were—Howard, 'Chelle, and Eddie had made it that way.

And then we went back to *Serenity*. We thoroughly enjoyed the season and were glad we had tried day chartering. If we didn't make much money, we had filled a whole address book with new friends. And we had lived an enviable life for months at one of the Caribbean's most beautiful resorts without its costing a cent.

12 *A Year Late but We Get to St. Lucia*

We moved *Serenity* around to English Harbour and caught up with accident-prone *Spartan*. We heard the bad news that her young crew had improperly lashed our jib on the foredeck, and it was washed overboard. That was the end of our spare jib.

Curt and Jeanne Harding brought *Posh* down again for Antigua Race Week, and we raced with them. One of the great joys of my life was racing against "Big Ti" that week. *Ticonderoga* is the ultimate expression of L. Francis Herreshoff's designing genius. Seventy-two feet long and built as a cruising yacht, she accomplished the incredible feat of holding thirty major ocean race records at one time. One of her more dramatic victories took place during the Trinidad-Grenada Race, which is set up to finish at St. George's Harbour, Grenada, in the morning. *Ti* sailed the ninety miles so fast that she reached St. George's at 0200 and had to drift around for hours until the committee boat finally arrived and checked her in.

While waiting for a race to start, Ken MacKenzie can wheel that great beauty around with a delicate skill that few skippers of thirty-feet racing machines can match. Before one race at Antigua, we were side by side at the gun. *Ti*'s sails filled with a great thud, and she heeled on the wind. She was so close that I could touch the golden dolphin on her bulwark as she whooshed by. What a sound, what a sight! The fleet navigated on *Ticonderoga's* tall spars. If given my choice, I would swap all the plastic boats in the world for *Big Ti*.

When the tiring week was over, English Harbour slowly emptied again. We had *Serenity* hauled, bottom painted, and pulled stern-to to the quay as we reprovisioned for our return to the south.

To put all this in a time perspective, this was the winter and spring of Watergate. During the past year we had been traveling so much that our knowledge of what was going on was restricted to old *Time* magazines we found along the way and the BBC's version of U.S. affairs sandwiched in between the cricket test matches and soccer scores. The "Saturday Night Massacre" occurred soon after we arrived at Curtain Bluff Hotel, but it still evoked only a passing interest from us until people at the hotel really involved us in the sordid mess. There were two, in particular—Jerry Dickler, a learned and articulate lawyer from New York, and Morgan Beatty, a news commentator who lived and taped his broadcasts in Antigua. Jerry invited Morgan to spend the day at the hotel and allowed me to join them. These two informed men discussed the implications of Watergate all afternoon, through dinner, and late into the night. The conversation concluded with the prediction by both men that Nixon would resign or be impeached before the year was out. (Beatty died of cancer a year later, but he lived to see the prediction come true.)

From that point on I became addicted to the news, as most of my friends back home had been for months. Every arriving guest was asked for fresh newspapers or *Time* or *Newsweek*. We set aside time every night for news broadcasts from the States. The two most powerful signals received on shortwave were Voice of America and the Armed Forces Radio Service. It soon became obvious that VOA news was so biased in favor of the administration that it frequently seemed as if they were talking about different events than those being reported a few minutes later on AFRS. All that spring and summer our travels were interrupted while we sat, ears to the Zenith shortwave, and listened to the impeachment proceedings and Nixon's resignation. As two of the few Americans wandering these islands, Es and I were questioned constantly about Watergate and its aftermath. Because nearly every island government is so corrupt and because bribery and payoffs are accepted as a way of life for bureaucrats, it was sometimes difficult to explain to the islanders what we in the United States were so concerned about.

Unless one shares our inherent faith in a republic under laws to which its citizens democratically agree, the betrayal of trust, the flawed concept of presidential power, and the shoddy disrespect for laws and decency does not seem to be so obvious. In general, the exorcism that followed Watergate was viewed with awe and envy by the varied islanders with whom it was discussed. These months were a strange, ambivalent period for us. At the same time that we were involved citizens, undeniably fascinated with the ugly events, we were also wanderers, who preferred to have left it all behind.

The sailing community at English Harbour is made up of two groups: the cruising types who drift in and out, and the more-or-less permanently based charter crews who use Commander Nicholson's office as headquarters. The charter captains view newcomers suspiciously, at least until it is determined that the cruising people are not going to compete by going into charter work. One of the cruising boats was a steel Dutch-built ketch named, of all things, *Zorro,* which had arrived from England that season. On her crew was Rosemary Elizabeth Barrett Browning, a Scottish lass nicknamed "George." Not the average boat bum, she was the talented product of a famous British family and a fancy finishing school. If you met her, you would agree that calling her George made as much sense as calling Raquel Welch "Irving."

George had taken a job as cook on *Zorro,* one of the larger charter boats. As the boat was coming into English Harbour after a charter, the topping lift parted and the heavy boom fell on George's head and shoulder. She was rushed to San Juan where she was treated for a severe concussion, broken ribs, and all kinds of contusions and cuts. When she returned, she still hadn't recovered the hearing in one ear and she was sore and bruised. George and Es decided that a quiet cruise on *Serenity* would be beneficial for both of them, and so we had a new crew member, a pretty one this time.

The trip to Guadeloupe was uneventful; we were old sailors now.

As the sun was setting in the opening at Deshaies, I saw a yawl sail in and anchor behind us, but it was in line with the setting sun and I couldn't tell who it might be. I heard the hail *Serenity!* and waved them over. As their rowboat drew near, I recognized Philippe, our old friend from Martinique, and a new girlfriend. I knew right away she was a girl—her pareu was knotted around her waist. A pareu, originally from Tahiti, is a rectangular piece of cloth that normally, on a woman at least, is knotted around the chest to form a baggy dress. Men usually wear them as a long, slitted skirt.

Philippe introduced me to Denise. As I helped them aboard, I called below to Es to bring up some drinks. Denise undid the pareu, smoothed it out on the hot cockpit seat, and then lounged back wearing nothing but a smile. She evidentally didn't consider bikini bottoms de rigueur with her outfit—or the lack of it.

I played it as cool as Hugh Heffner would have under the circumstances. As Philippe and I calmly exchanged stories about what had happened to us since we had last met, I learned that he had been working the past season at the Club Méditerranée at Fort Royal, just around the point from us. He had been doing day chartering for the club and was planning to sell his boat and return to Switzerland. Denise was a guest who enjoyed the club so much that she stayed on as Philippe's crew.

Es was not so calm. When she came up with the drinks, she stumbled and almost spilled the glasses. George, stunned, followed with appetizers. The funniest sight was watching two women talking to a naked lady. Their conversation and eyes were directed at Venus, just coming up over the hills. The only time Es looked at me, she glared as if I had ripped the clothes off the darling little creature.

The next day, Es and George went in to Pointe-à-Pitre for supplies—that presumably included pareus. I went on *Marajana* for a day sail with Philippe, crew, and guests. Denise's lack of inhibition was contagious. All the Club Med members followed her lead, and I ended up conspicuously overdressed in my little nylon trunks. By the time we returned, the guests had some parts sunburned that had never been burned before. I said I didn't think I could handle a whole season of it, and Philippe confided that he couldn't, either. Denise didn't keep the boat as neat as his wife.

The next day we left for Îles des Saintes off Guadeloupe. On our way there we ran afoul of a fish trap, a hazard I neglected to include in my previous list of dangers in the Caribbean. There are thousands of fish traps wherever you sail here. They are rectangular boxes, about seven by five by two feet, framed with bamboo, and enclosed with chicken wire or woven palm fronds. They have a single entrance maze that is baited with fish entrails. Once in, a fish cannot swim out. The traps are weighted with stones and are tied with a polyethylene cord to a Clorox bottle or similar float.

Fish traps are diabolically placed exactly in line with your course. Other than to catch fish, their main purpose is to catch your prop or rudder. Once wrapped around the prop, the friction of the revolving blades melts the polyethylene into a glasslike blob of plastic that is almost impossible to cut free.

We were approaching the channel to the Saints, booming

along in beautiful weather, when we slowed suddenly. The sails were still set and drawing, and we were still heeled over, but the knotmeter said we weren't going anywhere. I gave Es the wheel and checked over the stern. Sure enough, we were trailing a bobbing plastic bottle with a line that drifted off into the deep from beneath the boat. I was able to catch the line with the boat hook, but our motion through the water, little as it was, and the weight of the trap created so much drag, I couldn't lift the line high enough to cut it. In fact, I damned near lost the boat hook. I went forward, dropped and secured the sails, and we began drifting off toward Mexico. The trap line no longer trailed behind, and I could not hook it with the pole, so after much discussion I tied a line around my waist and went overboard. I cut the trapline hanging straight down and then the float line, but this didn't seem to be the place to free the mess woven around the prop. I climbed back on board, and we continued under sail into the lee of the Saints. Once anchored, it was no trick to unwind and cut the remaining cord wrapped around the prop. That was the only time I ever caught a trap, but I have helped several yachtsmen who didn't get off so easily. The traps are an omnipresent danger.

After spending some time in Îles des Saintes and showing George some of our favorite spots in Dominica, we moved on to Martinique, where I had problems with French currency once more. Seasoned travelers by now, we carried extra amounts of the various currencies so that our shopping would not be dependent on banking hours. We had francs left over from our stay in the French West Indies a year ago.

Our first stop in Fort-de-France was the hardware store since I needed some parts for our Primus stove. I picked out the parts, gave the cashier a 100-franc note, and waited for my change. She started yelling and gesturing in French and called over the manager. He looked at my bill, then at me, and then back at my bill. More rapid French and gesturing.

He took a 100-franc note from his cash box and compared it with mine. They were obviously different. I opened my wallet and showed him that all I had were the same style notes and some U.S. currency. He took a ten-dollar U.S. bill, something the French never do, gave me change, and waved me out of the store.

Curiouser and curiouser! Es decided that we should go to the American Express office at Roger Albert, a department store where she was well known and where somebody spoke English. There she collected our mail and introduced me to the girl behind the American Express desk. I explained that the previous store wouldn't take my perfectly good Martinican francs. She grabbed my franc bills, took a long look at me, and fled to the rear of the office.

Now, I admit I look a little like a benign Mafioso, but nobody has made me feel paranoid about it before. The girl returned in a heated discussion with a man, presumably the head of the department. He looked at me, looked at my francs, and with obvious reluctance took all of my bills and gave me new ones.

What the hell was going on? The girl explained. Since we had last been to Martinique a year ago, someone had kidnapped the wife of the owner of Roger Albert and held her for a million francs ransom. As soon as the ransom had been paid and the woman released, the government had called in all the Martinican francs and exchanged them for French francs. It was a monetary decision that had been made previously, but the kidnapping precipitated the recall action. The gendarmes were waiting for someone to pass the old bills to catch the kidnappers. Only because the young lady at American Express knew Es, had exchanged money for her, and held our mail, were we identified as innocent yachtsmen.

Think about what could have happened for a minute. The guy at the hardware store has me arrested. I protest my innocence. The Martinican gendarmes cable the FBI. Do they have any record of an American citizen named Zane B. Mann?

Oui, mon Dieu! Do they know Zane Mann!

"That dude is a one-man crime wave. Every time he gets on a boat, some woman is kidnapped. Toss him in your deepest dungeon and throw away the key.

Best Regards, FBI"

The whole idea shook me up. We quickly bought some wine and cheese, hurried out to the boat, and set sail for St. Anne and the Martinican Club Méditerranée.

Here Es and George had their day to get even for my previous lechery. The only safe anchorage at the club was off the nude beach. But at this beach there were a hell of a lot more nude men than nude women. Es and George spent the balance of the day peering through binoculars, giggling over the relative merits of the prancing men. It's terrible to see women behave like that!

The permanent ocean currents in the Lesser Antilles flow toward the west between the islands. When reinforced by tidal currents the westward flow can reach two to three knots. At the north end of the islands, the current curls around the top and flows southward. At the bottom of the islands the current pushes north. Off some of the prominent points you may find some severe riptides that may necessitate turning on power to get through. When crossing between islands, set in at least a ten-degree correction and then take frequent bearings. Remember the rule: tidal currents flow toward the moon when it is above the horizon, away from the moon when it is below the horizon.

I mention this because when we crossed to St. Lucia, the breeze was gentle, but the combined currents set us so far west that our easy beam reach turned into a high point. Still, it was a beautiful sail and once we reached the headlands, we got a boot on the tail, riding the south flow almost to Castries.

Port Castries is a deep-water harbor. Big freighters and cruise ships can pull up to the docks at the foot of the city.

Yachtsmen use Vigie Cove; there are slips at the inner cove, but most anchor out at the reef to catch the breezes. It's the only entrance I know where a tall mast is a hazard to low-flying aircraft from the nearby airport. I took the dinghy over to North Wharf at the city to clear customs and was greeted with a ream of paperwork. St. Lucia does not draw a distinction between boats. Yacht skippers fill out the same papers as the captain of a Geest banana ship. And you have to go through the same procedure when you leave. It was a year later at Castries that another peril of being a captain clearing customs was made apparent.

We had met Ann Bronfman and Janie Hart aboard *Meander* several times while cruising the Windwards. Most recently we had shared the cocktail hour with these two lovely and charming persons while tied to the overhanging palms at the Pitons. After a couple of days in that dramatic spot, we left together for Castries, but somehow I arrived at customs first. I was hard at work filling out my ream of forms for the fourth time when I heard Ms. Bronfman say:

"I'm on *Meander*. We've just arrived."

"Your husband will fill out the papers."

The customs man pointed at me.

"I don't have a husband, and I can fill out my own papers." Her normally soft voice rose a little. "Besides, I'm on *Meander*. He's on *Serenity*."

"Well, then, go get the captain on *Meander*," replied the customs man, who obviously had never heard of women's liberation.

"I *am* the captain! *Meander* is my boat!"

Now the voice had an edge that could cut the hawser on a Geest ship. I considered explaining that captain was a unisex word in the U.S., but I decided to keep quiet. When I crept out, her glare included me, the customs officer, and every male in the western hemisphere. Even after several drinks later that evening, Ann still didn't think it was funny.

St. Lucia is my favorite and surely the loveliest of all the Windwards. (Have I said that about every island I've described?) History and geography have combined to give St. Lucia the best of everything. Lush mountains fall off to broad, verdant valleys that are cultivated and maintained to produce a healthy economy. The French heritage and native industriousness have produced islanders who are both proud and independent and yet polite and friendly. Unlike other islands, here the children never beg or try to hustle the tourist; they are curious and interested in visiting with you. The many anchorages are easily the most unusual to be found on any island. The government is the most stable and least divisive of any of the Lesser Antilles, and this fact is reflected in the progress being made in industrial and economic development. It must be added that St. Lucia police officers are the most helpful, amicable, and polite anywhere.

The calmness of the current government is in contrast to the turbulent history of the island. Since the first Europeans arrived, control of the island has changed hands fourteen times, seesawing between the French and the English. First one side won in battle, and then the other won by treaty. When the Napoleonic Wars finally wore to a close, the Treaty of Vienna in 1815 assigned St. Lucia once and for all to England. Even though England won the last battle, France left an indelible claim on the culture. The names of the streets, towns, bays, and mountains are French. The predominant religion is Catholic, not Anglican. Despite the fact that English has been the official language for 160 years, the spoken language is a patois blending French, Carib, and African words with a little American slang circa World War II thrown in. It is so rhythmic and lyrical that it is close to singing. A continental Frenchman can understand only a few words of it. An American shouldn't even try.

Castries has been ravaged by fire several times, and very few of the old colonial buildings remain. The business section is modern and busy. Big supermarkets, department stores, and well-stocked hardware stores supply all the yachtsmen's needs.

In the square adjoining the cathedral, there is an outstanding saman tree said to be more than 140 years old. The tree is called the "massav" tree. About forty-five years ago an English tourist asked his guide for the name of the tree. The local guide, who could understand but not speak English, answered "massav," the Creole for "I don't know." The tourist dutifully wrote the answer in a travel guide, and it has been repeated ever since.

We rented a car so that we could see some of the interior, and after a climbing, twisting drive in second gear we reached Morne Fortune. This is a fort violently fought over. It was captured five times by the French, and five times by the English. The French buildings of stone intermingle with the English brick ones. Some buildings are a combination of both, where one side finished the work of the other. The mountains, no longer bloodied slopes, are covered with brilliant polychromatic flowers and the rich greens of the breadfruit trees. One is saddened by the thought that all this beauty was the setting for angry men killing one another.

On the other side of the pass, you enter the valleys of "green gold." Here waves of sparkling green banana leaves stretch to the distant, hazy sky. The bananas that represent 80 percent of St. Lucia's exports are grown on huge plantations owned by Geest Industries Ltd., and on thousands of individually owned plots. Even the smallest planter is protected by a cooperative marketing association and is guaranteed the same price per stem as the owners of an estate having hundreds of acres. The banana grows on a strange plant. It is really not a tree, but a huge herb. The fruit itself grows upside down from the way it used to hang in the corner grocery store. (You see how old I am. I remember corner grocery stores—whatever happened to them?) The stem of the still-green bananas ready for picking is wrapped in a blue plastic bag to protect the fruit from insects. Once the stem is harvested, the plant is cut down, and suckers at the base grow into mature plants that are ready for fruiting in ten to fifteen months.

One of the things that impressed me so about St. Lucia was the cleanliness of the countryside. Despite the activities connected with the harvest, the fields were raked, the debris burned, and the roadsides picked up by hand. Even the yards of the workers' homes were raked and filled with decorative plants; there were no bottles and tin cans in their front yards as in Antigua.

We crossed over the center of the island and down the windward coast to Vieux Fort. Here the land is flat enough for Lucia's jumbo jet airfield, which was built on the site of a U.S. World War II base. Most of the arrivals take an air shuttle from here to the small field at Vigie Cove. The village of Vieux Fort is the second largest in St. Lucia, but nevertheless it is small and peaceful. It is also a port of entry, and yachtsmen approaching from St. Vincent might consider entering here before proceeding up the coast to Castries.

Leaving the south coast, we climbed out of the dry flatlands into the green foothills through groves of copra, cocoa, and ancient gnarled coffee trees that scented the air.

Off the main highway the road twists down into a crater-like basin that is a collapsed volcanic formation, where steam and gases are vented from deep in the earth. Except for the sunlight, it could be part of Dante's Hades. Black water ponds hiss and boil. Ocher pools, from which a pillar of steaming mud occasionally explodes, burp and plop. Yellow green crystals of sulfur coat the lower rocks, and the air reeks with the swirling corrosive gases that have denuded the surrounding hills. The area would seem to be an ideal place for a thermoelectric plant in power-short St. Lucia, but I would hate to see them ruin this unique sight with something so practical.

Next on the road is the fishing village of Soufrière. Half

the buildings in the little town are very old homes and shops built in an architectural style that dates back to the French occupations; the other half were newly built after a fire in 1955. Es and George found a restaurant on the main street, while I loaded my cameras and went down to the waterfront to watch the fishermen at work. The people here have developed a cooperative method for sharing the work and the catch. The day I was there, the bay was alive with albacores leaping and splashing, streaks of silver and blue in the sun. Small boys rowing outside of the school slapped the water with their oars to herd the fish toward the beach. On a signal from a wizened old man, longboats were launched, loaded to the gunwales with a folded net and five or six men. One by one the nets were connected to form a long arc enclosing the school of fish. Lines were brought ashore from either end of the net, and the people on shore pulled on the lines as they walked toward one another, until the net almost closed to a circle. The men in the boats slapped the water and shouted as the frenzied fish began jumping over the net toward the sea. Some of the big tuna landed in the boats full of men. It seemed to me that more fish escaped than were caught, but at the end there was a great pile of flopping blue fish on the beach. I don't know the system of distribution. Some headed for home carrying a four-foot fish by the tail, slung over their shoulder. Others got half of a fish that had been whacked in two by a swish of the cutlass. Others received a third, and a few kids carried off just the head. After the division, the balance of the fish were boxed for the market in Castries. Everybody works and everybody eats.

As I watched, I got a lot of glowers because of my cameras. I promised not to photograph the women—at least not when anybody was nearby.

All the natives from Haiti to South America dislike having their pictures taken while doing their everyday chores. A woman walking home with a can of water balanced on her head or pulling at the end of a fish net may seem picturesque to you, but she will strongly resent it if you photograph her. The guidebook says it is against their religion, voodoo. Bunk! How would you like to be hanging up the wash in your back-yard, with your hair in curlers and no make-up, clad in a torn wraparound, when some guy, a West Indian at that, leaps over the fence and starts clicking away with a camera? You'd be pretty picturesque, too, and so would your language when you threw him out.

I always tried to ask permission before I shot—it was sel-dom granted—or I shot at a distance with a long telescopic lens. At least that way I didn't knowingly embarrass anyone.

At the extreme north end of St. Lucia is a land development operation called Cap Estates. The two thousand acres include beaches, a golf course, and large home sites; some elaborate residences and a lovely hotel have already been constructed. Unlike many islands, the St. Lucian government has passed tax laws that make home ownership by aliens feasible. The land, however, is not inexpensive and the cost of construction is out of sight.

The real reason for our trip was to visit Pigeon Island and Fort Rodney, from which the British launched their final attack on the French fleet at the Saints. A half-mile causeway has been built out of dredgings to connect the island with the mainland. The climb to the top of the fort only emphasized my advancing age, but the view made it worth the climb. A thunderstorm had rolled over the mountains, and a black curtain of rain obscured the south. To the north, Martinique shone like an emerald displayed on an azure velvet pad. When the storm moved out to sea, St. Lucia sparkled in the reappearing sun, her green slopes decorated with a million diamonds.

Gros Inlet Bay below us was to be the scene of a memorable trial for *Serenity*. A year or so later we spent several days anchored between Pigeon Island and the causeway. The water there is murky and the bottom is loose sand from the recent dredging. (I pride myself in my skill at anchoring. In our three and a half years I have never dragged an anchor once; in fact, I don't understand why this rather simple procedure causes so many problems.) When we prepared for an early start for Martinique, I confidently went through our normal procedure. Es slowly motored up on the anchor as I pointed from the bow and took in the scope. When the rode was straight down, I cleated off the line and signaled Es to gun the engine to dig out the anchor. It didn't dig out. The bow dipped, and we moved forward a few feet, but I couldn't raise the anchor even with my newly acquired mechanical windlass. We repeated the maneuver. I picked up a little slack in the line but no anchor.

Exhausted from tugging on the taut line, I gave up and dove overboard. Following the rode down in ten feet of sand-obscured water, I felt a chunk of brain coral about five feet in diameter. Another dive determined that not only were the anchor flukes hooked under the coral, but the shank of the anchor was wedged in a crevice in the head. Repeated dives would not release the shank. Dripping and panting, I climbed into the cockpit. The choice was obvious. Either we would spend the rest of our lives tied securely to a coral head in this lovely spot, or we had to disconnect the shackle, leave the anchor, and move on. Es, with visions of Fort-de-France boutiques dancing in her head, voted to give up the anchor. While I debated the alternatives, James Griffin, Her Majesty's Royal Navy, ret., from the yacht *Northern Lights,* came by.

"I say, I hesitate to intrude, but you appear to be in a spot of trouble."

"You have succinctly stated the situation. Come aboard."

I explained the problem. We were hooked to a coral head. Every time we powered forward on the anchor, we were dragging the head into shallower water but were not able to free ourselves. We dared not tow the coral head any closer for fear of running aground, and we could not release the anchor underwater.

"I say, old chap, don't be so bloody discouraged, I feel certain something can be done."

I took him forward to inspect my work. He tut-tutted a lot when he saw that I used a ¾-inch nylon line for an anchor rode. The British believe in chain—big chain.

"Would it be possible to free the bitter end? There's a good chap."

I climbed into the forepeak, untied the end of the line from its post, and fed sixty fathoms of ¾-inch nylon up through the deck fitting.

"Now, set another anchor," he instructed. "You do have another anchor, dear boy?"

Yes, I had another anchor. My main one was a thirty-five pound, high-tensile Danforth that had served well up till now. But I had a spare heavy plow carried in the forepeak with its own rode and a big Herreshoff yachtsman carried in chocks on the stern.

I dropped the plow as my new friend put the other line into his dinghy. He rowed over to *Northern Lights* with my line while I set the plow. I lowered my dinghy into the water and went over to see what he was doing.

Now I have to tell you about most English cruising boats. They are big, heavy, and strong. Their standing rigging is thick enough to build bridges. Their running rigging roves through blocks as big as your head. Their spars are timbers that could be milled into enough lumber to build a house. And they are so safe and well constructed that they could be used for ice breaking in Antarctica. Such a yacht was *Northern Lights,* and I shall be forever grateful for it. She had a windlass forward about the size of an oil drum that, given a purchase, could have raised the thirty-five-ton vessel out of the water by itself.

Jim and his wife Ann threw a wrap of my anchor rode

around their windlass and, each on a crank, began to take in the slack. *Northern Lights* drew over to my coral head, and the line came in, creaking and groaning, until the twelve-foot chain at the end fouled on the anchor chock in the bow. Jim rigged blocks and tackle with several purchases, and after much heaving, the anchor broke water still holding the large chunk of coral. We futilely beat on the coral with a sledgehammer until Ann got the idea to reverse the anchor's position. The coral slid off the same way it slid on, and the anchor was finally freed.

The whole operation took several sweaty hours and could never have been accomplished without the Griffins and the heavy gear on *Northern Lights*. Where they signed our guest log that day, it reads:

> Yacht *Northern Lights* of England at Pigeon Island St. Lucia—we helped remove an otherwise permanent memorial to the U.S. in the B.W.I.

In the course of our struggles, Jim told me, "In the Royal Navy we say that seamanship is the art of moving heavy objects." That definition makes Jim Griffin one of the great seaman of all time.

There must be at least twenty good anchorages on the east coast of St. Lucia, but two of them rank with the most beautiful in the Antilles. Marigot Bay is first of all a good hurricane hole, but the lovely bay is also an ideal place to spend a few days doing absolutely nothing. It's a little hard to find when sailing down the coast. In fact, the British fleet once hid in the bay by tying palm fronds to the masts, and the French never noticed them. There is shoal water to the north, but a deep channel runs along the cliffs to the south and then leads around a spit of sand marked by a grove of palm trees into the inner lagoon and peace. The steep hills that surround the bay are covered with trees, and the sweet scent of ripe mangoes drifted through *Serenity's* hatches. Along the cliffs of the outer bay there is a different kind of coral formation. Instead of the shallow reef garden, the coral grows among the rocks of an underwater precipice that drops fifty feet straight down. The mouth of the bay was swarming with fish, and dinner was only a few minutes work.

Even after seeing the Pitons from a distance, you cannot appreciate the drama of the setting until you sail into L'Anse de Pitons yourself. Two volcanic spires, 2,500 feet high, rise vertically from the sea on either side of the bay. A mile-long semicircular beach rims the saddle in between, and acres of rustling coconut palms climb up the slopes from the inland valley.

Unfortunately, many yachtsmen motor in, take a look, and head for a safer anchorage because there seems to be no bottom in the cove. After three visits to this scenic spot I think I have the technique worked out. We motored in very slowly. I cleated off about forty feet of line on the yachtsman anchor and threw it off the stern to trail behind. Then we cut the engine and drifted toward the shoreline. When the dangling anchor caught in the rocks, I dove over the bow and swam like crazy with a line that I made fast on a palm tree. When I took up slack on the stern anchor, we were secure in the most spectacular anchorage in the Caribbean. The bow was fifteen feet from the beach, and looping the painter on the dinghy over the bow line made a dandy system for ferrying back and forth.

I built a fire of dried coconut husks, and we cooked ashore. When the fire died to a red glow, we lay on our backs in the sand. The Pitons funneled all the stars in the heavens to our upturned eyes. Falling stars streaked through the indigo night toward *Serenity's* mast. The night breezes stirred the palm fronds, and the waves whispered to the rocks. It was heady business. I drifted off to sleep, not envying any creature on earth.

13 *St. Vincent and the Sailor's Island, Bequia*

The Spanish sailors who were the first European explorers in the Caribbean described the islands from Puerto Rico west to Central America as *sotavento* (leeward) and the rest, those that we now call the Lesser Antilles, were *barlovento* (windward)—a logical name to anyone who has beat into the trade winds to get to them. But the English, also a nation of sailors, screwed it all up when they applied these traditional and picturesque names to two administrative political groups of their former possessions. Antigua, Barbuda, Montserrat, and Nevis-St. Kitts-Anguilla were named Leewards; the rest to south, Windwards. Since these islands lie in an arc across the winds, some of the Leeward islands are to windward of the Windwards. Confused? Wait.

The Dutch use the names as well. St. Eustatius, Saba, and the Dutch half of St. Martin are the Windward group of the Netherlands Antilles. The ABC islands—Aruba, Bonaire, and Curaçao—are the Leeward group. This makes sense if you look at the islands' relationship to one another on a chart, but it puts the Dutch Windwards in the middle of the British Leewards. All of this confusion is the reason that Leeward is pronounced as it is spelled, and not "looward" as in nautical language, since the terms no longer have anything to do with seamanship.

To further confuse the issue, the English consider Dominica to be part of the Windwards, while the U.S. Naval Oceanographic Office sailing directions list Martinique as the northernmost of the group. The French also have an Îsles du Vent (windward) group that includes Tahiti in the Society Islands in the Pacific, so I won't even mention it.

St. Vincent lies SSW of the Pitons on St. Lucia. Once into the channel, the wind pulled to the ENE, and we had a grand ride until blanketed by the 4,000-foot peak of Soufrière, the volcano that looms over the northern coast of St. Vincent. It's only twenty-five miles across the channel, but it is almost fifty miles from the Pitons to Kingstown in the southwestern corner of St. Vincent, and it was slow going down the lee coast. The west coast is steep-to with no unseen dangers except a series of riptides wherein the waves seem to be going in all directions at once. A succession of rain squalls poured down the mountains, and when we reached the rip, off Chateaubelair, I turned on the engine and motor sailed the rest of the way.

I should have done it sooner. It was after 1700 when we anchored in a corner of the harbor near the deep water wharf. Since I was already soaked, rowing ashore in a blinding rainstorm was no additional discomfort, but the five-dollar overtime charge at the harbor master's and the ten-dollar charge at customs ruined my day. It was too late to move, so we spent an uncomfortable night rocking in a continuous pour. The wind reached thirty knots in what was, by any definition, a well-protected harbor.

The next morning was bright and warm. The way clean, colorful Kingstown was arranged around the bay on steep hills made the last night's wind seem impossible.

The channel between Young Island and the mainland is the most popular anchorage at St. Vincent for private yachts and charter boats. Sooner or later you will meet all your cruising friends there. The anchorage is swept by a reversing current, and a safe mooring requires two well-dug-in anchors. With all the activity in this well-known spot, even if you do a good job of anchoring, someone else is sure to underestimate the current, break loose, and come swinging into you.

Since Es was planning a trip to the States, I passed up Young Island for a more permanent anchorage in Blue Lagoon. The lagoon is home base for Caribbean Sailing Yachts and Stevens Yachts, both very successful bare boat charterers with large fleets. The basin is enclosed within a breaking reef that has two narrow entrances, and it is well protected in all kinds of weather. The entrance from the west is marked by painted stakes. The chart shows seven feet, but we touched bottom a couple of times motoring in. Once inside, I set out two anchors in a V and tied the stern line to a tree on the beach. *Serenity* was settled in for a stay. I checked Es and George in and out with Immigration, and Es left for Chicago. George was to go to Antigua to see her boyfriend. I returned to *Serenity* to catch up with my chores.

One of the questions people ask me most frequently is, "What do you do all day? Don't you go crazy just sitting around and doing nothing?"

I can safely say that there was not one day on St. Vincent that I didn't have at least one project that needed attention. After weeks of cruising, there were all manner of chores to be done. All the bedding, towels, and mattresses were hauled up on deck for drying and airing. Everything below decks was scrubbed and sprayed with diluted bleach to stop mildew and remove musty odors. All the lockers were emptied and clothing hung in the sun. All thru-hull fittings were checked and greased. The water pressure system was inspected and all connections checked. So-called stainless hose clamps are forever corroding apart, and I always tried to replace them before trouble could start.

In the engine compartment, the batteries needed cleaning and water. The engine water and oil were topped off, and all the filters changed. The fuel lines were checked, and all the valves opened and closed so they wouldn't freeze when I needed them. Everything was taken out of the forepeak and restowed so that I could find things in a hurry. All the tools were wiped off and oiled. All the sails were hauled on shore, spread out, and checked inch by inch for torn seams or minute tears; then they were refolded and packed so they wouldn't take up so much room. Canned goods had to be rotated and inspected for rust. A little preventive maintenance kept the Primus stove trouble-free.

On deck the teak was cleaned and oiled. The sunscreen was always chafing through and tearing so that was reinforced and resewn. While the sewing kit was out, I repatched the patches on my shorts. All the winches were dismantled and greased. *Serenity* had running backstays operated by levers near the cockpit, and I was constantly rerigging them with pulleys and lines so that they could be used without leaving the cockpit. I never really worked out a good system.

But to answer the question, "Don't you get bored doing nothing?" There were never enough hours in the day.

If you have to have a crew, may I strongly advise a female. Women are every bit as good sailors as men, and they don't take up as much room psychologically. I'm serious. Women are much more adaptable to the close quarters on a boat than men are. They aren't forever passing on unneeded advice, and when directed to do something, they don't feel compelled to hold a discussion on its merits. What minor shortcomings they may have in the physical effort of sailing is more than made up for by their interest in helping run a shipshape yacht.

George overcame her lack of physical strength quite simply. We weren't in Blue Lagoon twenty-four hours when two young huskies rowed over to see if they could help her. In a week, every male under thirty within twenty miles came by to volunteer. George had her army scrubbing, cleaning, diving, rowing for ice, and taking her to town for shopping and obediently hauling groceries back. I had muscle to crank me up the mast, to cut the rusted bolts on the old windlass, and to get a new one in place. Best of all, George had a date every night, so I was left alone to enjoy my reading in peace. I must say it was awfully quiet around *Serenity* after she flew back to Antigua.

While I was alone, I picked up reports on Hurricane Gertrude, forming off to the southeast. I ran some more lines ashore and waited it out. As Gertrude came closer, the lagoon filled with local workboats and yachts. At the peak there were over fifty boats in the small anchorage. For twenty-four hours Barbados was completely boarded up: no schools, businesses or services were operating, but Gertrude veered away from the island and caused little damage. From inside the lagoon on St. Vincent, our only indication of the passing storm was the buildup of enormous seas that broke on our protecting reef. When things calmed down, I stood guard on *Serenity* with a boat hook to fend off all the transient boats while they untangled themselves and left.

By the time Es returned, *Serenity* was sparkling clean and neat. I was pleasantly surprised at how happy Es was to be back. In the three weeks she had been in the States, she had solved several of our business problems that had come up since we had left two years before, rushed around visiting her mother and sister, and generally wore herself out. *Serenity* bobbing gently in the quiet bay looked awfully good to her after Chicago.

We celebrated her return with dinner at the Sugar Mill Hotel. Ross, the son of the owners, joined us and filled us in on the sights to see on the island. I had been in St. Vincent for a month and except for a few shopping trips to Kingstown, I hadn't left Blue Lagoon. This time our trip around St. Vincent would serve a purpose other than just sight-seeing. Since Desmond Nicholson had aroused our interest in the Arawak Indians, we had located and photographed the Carib stones at St. Kitts and Guadeloupe. Ross told us that there were more of these strange drawings on St. Vincent than anywhere else, and we decided to make them the object of our visit.

There is evidence that early Indians inhabited the area we call the Caribbean as long as four thousand years ago. The Arawaks left their original homeland in the greater Orinoco Basin over two thousand years ago and began a northward migration during which they settled most of the islands in the chain that extended to San Salvador in the Bahamas, where Columbus first met them. Almost three million of these peace-loving people were victims of a Spanish-led genocide. The fierce Caribs are a more recent tribe who apparently did not settle much farther north than Dominica, though their raiding parties to capture Arawak women and food supplies did extend to many islands beyond Dominica.

To us the most fascinating artifacts of the ancient Arawak culture are the misnamed Carib stones, or petroglyphs. On huge boulders the Arawaks carved or incised strange designs that just now are becoming a study for anthropologists.

Ross marked up a map for us and found us a taxi driver named Ken, who knew where some of the stones were. For the next week we crisscrossed the island. We ran up a terrible cab bill, but at least Ken now knows where every Carib stone on St. Vincent is located.

Our standard procedure was to take the cab to the general location. We would then ask the young people in the area about the Indian carvings, and invariably six or seven would lead a parade across a field, down a valley, or up a river to the hidden rock. Why these petroglyphs were always in the remotest locations, far away from where the early artists could reasonably be expected to live, was never explained. Since the incised lines of the drawings were not deep enough for good photographs, the children would have a great time retracing the lines with sandstone pebbles.

Appropriately, the easiest one to find was on Indian Point,

near the anchorage at Mariner's Inn. We walked barefoot along the rocks at the base of the point, climbed the face of the cliff, and found that, sadly, this beautiful example of pre-Columbian art had been defaced with spray-painted graffiti. The one in St. Kitts was similarily ruined.

The most impressive stone was located beyond the village of Layou. In a lovely leafy grotto by the side of a pool stood a rock fifteen feet wide and twenty feet high. The sloping sides of this free-standing pyramid were covered with fanciful designs dominated by the grotesque face of the Arawak god Yocahu.

High in the hills of Barrouallie, we photographed an intricately carved stone that scientists have described as the Arawak sun god. Interestingly, the unusual designs of the base seemed to repeat the male and female symbols of the Cro-Magnon caves in France.

Our most difficult trip was deep in the valley of the Yambou River, where we found two widely separated stones. The first was covered with childlike drawings that Es decided is a wedding scene; the happy bride, the terrified groom, the proud bride's family, and the disgruntled groom's. Nothing much has changed in two thousand years. The second stone had an unusual ray-crowned deity and a cobralike design that is unexplainable in the West Indies.

My favorite was found over a mile inland from an eastern beach on the face of a high cliff. Here, early European settlers had carved a niche wherein a statue of Our Lady of Lourdes was enshrined. Years later, an obscure petroglyph, consisting of four crudely drawn heads, was discovered on the nearby cliff face. How did it happen that two widely separate cultures chose this inaccessible spot to consecrate with religious symbols?

Our travels gave us a good chance to see the voluptuous countryside. Mountainous though it is, St. Vincent may be the most heavily cultivated of all the islands. Because of the terrain, the plantation system never fully developed here. Instead, thousands of small plots have been terraced into the hillside. Yams are grown in rows cut into slopes so precipitous that they seem impossible to reach, let alone to plant and harvest. The Mesopotamia Valley on the southeastern mountain slope is particularly fertile. Swept by tropical rains and warmed by tropical sun, everything grows here, even the fences. Boundaries of the individual plots are marked with sticks that take root and grow leaves in a few weeks!

The farms are an exotic mixture of colors and aromas. Tomatoes, peppers, casavas, cucumbers, pineapples, dasheen, and squash grow side by side. The larger land areas grow arrowroot and bananas, the staple export crops. Clinging to the upper heights are avocado, calabash, soursop, and mango trees. And everywhere one finds the life-sustaining breadfruit trees whose fruit lies hidden among the intricately formed dark green leaves. Autumn is called "turn de pot time," meaning there is so much to be eaten that there is no need to cook.

A St. Vincent treat is the locally grown and roasted peanuts sold in used Heineken bottles. The Bee Wee word for them is "cutters," when served as an appetizer with drinks.

Ross organized an expedition to climb the west side of Soufrière, a volcanic peak that is almost four thousand feet high. It's another towering beauty with a history. In 1902, one day before Montagne Pelée's rampage in Martinique, La Soufrière violently exploded, killing two thousand people. In 1971 the volcano rumbled a bit and tossed up a six-hundred-foot island in the center of the crater lake within its summit.

Es and I and Bob and Lloyd, two young sailors who needed diversion while they pined away for George's return, loaded into Ross's ancient Morris Minor. The poor old car was barely able to climb the heights of the serpentine road that led us northward along the rocky coast. It tottered past the arrowroot factory and Cumberland and Chateaubelair, two bays in which we were to anchor later, until the highway stopped at the dry river at Wallilabou.

We should have known that making it that far in our wheezing vehicle was enough adventure for one day, but after a picnic lunch, I gave Bob my camera bag and Lloyd the knapsack of cold beer, and we headed up the river of lava flow.

We followed the lava river to an elevation of about one thousand feet and then turned off to the north on a path that zigzagged among the trees toward the cloud-covered peak hovering above us. Up the trail we struggled. I took some solace in the panting efforts of my three young companions, but not much. Es dragged behind, and that gave everyone a chance to rest until she caught up. What was really discouraging was the fact that the locals breezed by us up the path. They climbed by with a cheerful greeting, picked up a burlap bag full of avocado or calabash somewhere in the heights above us, and came back down with their load while we had toiled a hundred yards farther up the mountain. At three-thirty, we paused for a pick-me-up of avocado and warm beer. I was secretly pleased when Ross, our leader, announced that he didn't think we would make it to the summit and return by nightfall. At the rate we were going, I didn't think we could make it in three days. And so the expedition ended in failure.

If you want to swim in the crater lake of Mt. Soufrière, I recommend that you start early and try the east side—the way every other sensible person does. You can drive about halfway up, and if you are young, vigorous, and dedicated, you will enjoy one of the most spectacular experiences imaginable. You couldn't prove it by me. With my luck the cloud cover would erupt, and it would rain all the way up and all the way down.

George returned from Antigua, Ken picked her up and brought her to the lagoon for free, and *Serenity* again became the center of social activity on St. Vincent. Mariner's Inn did a rushing business, and the steel band took on a louder beat.

On one of our trips to Kingstown to reprovision *Serenity* for the next leg of our journey, we stopped at the Botanical Gardens. Every flower, every tree, and every plant native to the Windwards can be found in its twenty manicured acres. The gardens were established in 1765, and they shelter a bit of living history: one of the original breadfruit trees grown from the 544 plants that Captain Bligh ultimately brought to the island from Tahiti. The descendants of these plants have spread to the extremes of the islands and provide the most common staple of the islander's diet.

Before we leave St. Vincent, I should give you a word of warning. Vincentians love to steal outboard motors from rich yachtsmen. (A rich yachtsman is defined as anyone who owns an outboard when an islander doesn't.) In order to steal an outboard, it is first necessary to steal a dinghy. One friend of mine, a charter boat captain knowledgeable in the ways of thieves, shackled his dinghy to his stern with a steel cable. It was found drifting up the west coast minus his forty-horsepower Johnson. The stainless painter had been severed with cable cutters. When I interviewed a police officer regarding the problem, he didn't seem to be very disturbed. The thievery was overstated, he said. "They steal only one a week."

If you anchor at Young Island, Cumberland, or Chateaubelair, I suggest that you have someone sleep on deck or take your dinghy and motor aboard.

I was lucky. I had long since thrown away my two-horsepower Johnson. It was taken apart for repairs more often than it was operated. I bought a small English Seagull, a hand-cranked, ugly little motor unchanged from the 1920s. It was built for salt water, and I think it will work forever. The natives didn't think it was worth stealing.

When we left Blue Lagoon, Bob and Lloyd couldn't bear to lose George, so they asked to sail with us at least to Bequia to keep our most famous crew member happy. I agreed.

It's only about eight miles from St. Vincent to the harbor at Bequia, and that certainly isn't much of a trip—until you try it. The seas and the wind have swept across the Atlantic for three thousand miles until they compress into the narrow, shallow channel between the two small islands, and so they kick up a fuss. If the trip over is wild, the trip back is worse. I once took seven hours to sail from Admiralty Bay off Bequia to Blue Lagoon. The current set me so far north, I probably sailed twenty-five miles that day. The first time over was rough, and I couldn't help but wonder about the schooner that does it every day loaded with pigs, goats, vegetables, and the poor passengers it ferries back and forth.

Bequia is an island settled by sailors, and the difference is noticeable. Of course, St. Vincent and all the others are islands, but Bequia is different. There is no airport, and no cruise boats call. Everyone and everything on Bequia go there and back by small boat. The population are descendants of Carib Indians, slaves escaping from Barbados and later, whalers from New Bedford, all of whom arrived in small boats. They understand the call of the sea and the brotherhood of sailors.

Islands, after all, are the ultimate goal of the sailor. Tahiti, Bali, Bermuda, Bequia—these are the destinations of sailors. However long you sail Long Island Sound, Cape Cod, Laguna Beach, or the English Channel, it is a distant tropical island that beckons.

It may seem strange to consider St. Vincent the mainland, but that's how it is. From its earliest days Bequia men have made their living from the sea. They are the most sought-after as crewmen, and they are the best fishermen. The last true whalers are Bequian. And most important, a fellow seaman is welcomed. From the youngest child paddling out on his raft to the oldest woman, whose face is worn from endless days of searching the horizon for her man, everyone on Bequia understands the caprice of the seaman.

During our first visit to Bequia, we spent two weeks wandering around and really got to know the place. In the little town of Port Elizabeth, the pace of life was unhurried, and the people were as friendly as could be. Seamen gathered to talk everywhere. Under the leafy awning of almond trees on the waterfront, there were boats in various stages of completion or repair. On the beach an interisland schooner lay careened while her bottom was scraped and repainted. Nearby was a one-room bakery. We put our order in a day ahead of time and at two o'clock the next afternoon we picked up our piping hot, fresh bread.

The young kids around the waterfront were agents for every service. They picked up and delivered laundry for their mothers and delivered ice, limes, produce, and even eggs to the boats. At night they organized a calypso band and paddled out to serenade us. What they lacked in musical talent, they made up for by the ingeniousness of their instruments.

One cottage industry we discovered was model making. In the backyard of a house near the harbor, some young men had set up a woodworking shop, and I had a model of *Serenity* made. They copied my original drawings with the skill of their shipbuilding elders. The completely rigged and painted model was almost four feet long and was built for thirty-five dollars.

Perched high on a hill about a mile from the beach, in a most unlikely spot for a marine store, is "Lully's." We found a good supply of fishing and diving gear there as well as fine English boat fittings, a lovely collection of oil lamps, and a fair stock of British Admiralty and U.S.H.O. charts. Best of all, they had a complete selection of courtesy flags for the islands. Locating them elsewhere can be expensive and troublesome.

Admiralty Bay is the standard first-day stop or turnaround point for bare boats and charter boats operating in the Grenadines. Usually they are in the anchorage just overnight. The more permanent residents of the harbor are a surprisingly large number of live-aboards, who have dug in moorings and stay in Bequia for months, and cruising types like ourselves, who fall in love with the bay and settle in for several weeks. By the time we reached this point in our cruising, we knew everyone on the boats, and almost every cocktail hour or dinner was shared with others.

Our meeting place in the heat of the afternoon was the Whalebone Inn. The bar is made from a whale jawbone and the bar stools, from the whale's vertebrae. The beer is cold, and there is a bulletin board to check for messages from friends who have been there and left.

At sundown, the guests on the charter boats, the crews on the bare boats, and the cruising types gathered at the bar at the Frangipani Hotel or at the Sunny Caribee. The latter resort has a freshwater pool and showers in the beach bar, and if they buy an occasional drink or dinner, the manager doesn't mind if sailing crews use them.

On a typical evening, we'd pick up another cruising couple and row over to the resort dock. After we were shown to our table, someone else would arrive, and we'd drag over another table. More arrivals and more tables soon added to the confusion. By the time dinner was served, all the tables in the dining room were pushed together, and the waiters no longer knew who had ordered what. George and her growing group of admirers seemed to be able to find a steel band to dance to almost every night.

The familiarity among yachtsmen causes a minor problem for new arrivals. Because you know you will be observed by all the cruising fraternity, it is considered mandatory to sail into the harbor. A real show-off will pick his spot and drop the hook without turning on the engine. This is easier said than done. When coming from the south, you are on a humming beam reach but as you round the West Cay about four miles from the anchorage, you point dead into the wind, and as you draw close, the wind is blanketed by the high ground behind Port Elizabeth. It takes lots of tacks and lots of patience.

One afternoon, a year or so after our first visit to Bequia, Es and I were settling down in the cockpit for our sundown tot when *Doki,* a Morgan Out-Island 41, rounded the far point. Her owner, Hank Strauss, spent thousands of dollars making *Doki* a safe, comfortable cruiser. But a sailing boat, she ain't. Watching her slow sail in, we counted twenty tacks. On a few of them her progress was nil, and I suspect Hank was turning on the engine to bring her about. The sun had set by the time *Doki* drew alongside and anchored. Es and I stood and applauded the tenacious feat of seamanship. On board doing all the sail work was an exhausted Doug Terman, skipper of the charter boat *Encantada.* Doug, Hank, and I had raced together most of the past spring, and we called them over to refresh themselves with our special rum punch. When we ran out of ice on *Serenity,* the party moved over to *Doki,* where we were joined by Bill Mills from *Toroa.* I don't remember eating dinner, and at midnight, I gave up and returned to my bunk.

To give you an idea of how carefully and thoroughly cruises are planned in the islands, we were awakened three hours later by the group on *Doki*—they were leaving. In the course of the evening's story telling, Doug Terman had mentioned a glider that was for sale in Martinique. After we left and before Hank ran out of ice, it was decided that they all should go up to Fort-de-France and see the glider. By the light of Sirius and Orion, *Doki* and *Toroa* sailed out of Admiralty Bay on their urgent mission.

We came very close to staying in Bequia. Over the hills to the north of town, we found a famous old plantation that has been subdivided for a housing development. The former manor house had been remodeled into the Spring Hotel. Clinging to the cliff overlooking the hotel was a strange house called "Hawksnest." It consisted of three rooms stacked one on top of the other. The seaward side of the three floors was open so that from each balcony we could see the Grenadines rising in the distance from a lacy turquoise sea. But water was supplied from a house up the road, and there was no electricity. One edge of the bottom room was anchored onto a winding road, and the other edge was propped up on twenty-foot stilts. Everytime the wind blew, Hawksnest threatened to topple onto the hotel, three hundred feet below. I checked on the cost of having a proper foundation and water cistern built under the rooms, and the price was about double the cost of the house.

The south side of the island is the home of the whalers of Bequia. For one hundred years preceding the turn of the century, schooners from New Bedford sailed into Admiralty Bay and picked up crews to handle the whaleboats. At the end of the season, they dropped off the Bequians and returned to New England with the rendered oil. Some of the wiser Yankees decided the trip to the freezing North wasn't all that attractive and stayed behind. This accounts for the color and accents of many of the islanders.

Commercial whaling today is a totally unnecessary slaughter conducted by giant floating factories belonging to the Japanese and the Russians. Its sole purpose is to collect an oil that the world can get along without just fine. There is *nothing* to recommend it.

The Bequians hunt for food, not profit. During the season a constant watch for migrating whales is kept high in the southern hills. If a whale is spotted, a signal fire is lit and the whalers launch their beautiful little boats. They pursue the whale under sail, the harpooner braced on the bow. If a whale is struck, its mouth is bound shut to maintain buoyancy, and the huge mammal is towed back to Petit Nevis where it is butchered and the meat divided among the islanders. The first time we were there, they had not seen a whale all season. The next year two whales were captured. The strange monopoly of the whaling nations is such that the rendered oil of the Bequians is unsalable. Man is an endangered species, as well.

We had seen several whales on our journey, particularly in the passages between the southern islands. Having read the accounts of whales attacking sailboats off the west coast of South America, we were frightened when we first saw the giant creatures breaching, rolling, and spouting in the open sea. But they were fascinating to watch, and our fear soon turned to admiration for their grace and the enormity of their size. Once, when we were in the Dominican Channel, we sailed after a pod to photograph them. The pictures look like big logs floating in a small pond.

The south coast of Bequia is also the home of the isolated French community called Pagent Farms. The inhabitants are not farmers at all, but boat builders and fishermen. Although they have lived on this scenic peninsula for generations, they have not mingled with the more gregarious Bequians. The day we wandered through the village, we found a class of school-children gathered beneath the palm tree on the beach. Their teacher was seated on an oil barrel, the blackboard propped on his knees, and goats grazed among the attentive students. I cannot verify the quality of the education, but those who learn here, surrounded by the sea, the beauty of nature, and the gentle encouragement of the trade wind, must grow to adults satisfied with themselves and at peace with their neighbors.

As I write this, I cannot help but wonder if "Hawksnest" is still for sale. When any sailor leaves the sea, he should be granted a place on Bequia.

14 Serenity *Sails the Grenadines*

The group of islands between St. Vincent and Grenada are known collectively as the Grenadines. There are five large islands and at least fifty small ones, if you include some that are little more than large rocks. Unlike their mountainous neighbors, they are relatively low and thus do not generate enough rainfall to make them green and productive. Their arid landscape is similar to the Virgins, but they have one marked advantage; while the Virgins lie west to east, the Grenadines stretch north to south and sailing is always a beam reach. The distance from Bequia to Carriocou is less than forty-five miles, and you can find a chain of interesting anchorages no more than three hours apart. There are two excellent cruising guides to the area, Julius Wilensky's *Yachtsman's Guide to the Windward Islands,* and *Yachting Guide to the Grenadines* by Donald (Squeaky) Street, Jr. We had our charts marked by Paul Squire, the charter captain on *Stranger,* who has sailed this chain for years and knows every rock worth looking at.

This brings up a good point. If you plan to go sailing, don't be brave and don't be bashful. Ask for information. Those charter boat skippers who consider their knowledge business secrets won't help you. Ignore them—they're the bad guys. Most charter boat captains are generous with their advice. Certainly all cruising people will help you. They will show you the best anchorages, point out any dangers, and frequently tell you about unusual places they have discovered that are not mentioned in the guides. You can tell a cruising skipper by his frayed shorts, the length of his hair, and the can of beer in his hand. The last point I haven't figured out. I never drank a can of beer in my life until I went sailing.

We covered the Grenadines on three different trips, and it would be boring to report each anchorage on each island. They all have a special character of their own. You pick your places depending on whim, the weather, and the need for isolation or companionship. Next to the Virgin Islands, the Grenadines have to be one of the busiest cruising grounds in the Western Hemisphere. Many times you will head for a favorite spot only to find the cove filled, but since there are plenty of other places nearby, everyone can do his own thing.

The first of the larger islands south of Bequia is Mustique. The only good anchorage is at Grand Bay, and that has a reputation for being rolly. During our stay it was still as glass, which proves only that things change from day to day and that you have to check it out for yourself.

If a sand beach slopes gently up from the water, it usually marks a calm bay. A ridge that is a foot or so deep running along the waterline indicates the sand has been eroded by swells. Such an area is usually an uncomfortable place to set the hook. The size and direction of the swells are governed by distant storms and winds, and they change, too, so that what was a bad anchorage a week ago can be calm and peaceful today.

Mustique is owned by Colin Tennant, a wealthy British businessman who has spent a fortune building a waterworks, electrical generation system, air strip, roads, and housing for the workers. Land has been sold to very, very weathy people, including Princess Margaret, whose homes look as if they were all designed for *Town and Country* magazine. The cattle and horses grazing in the shade of the fine old trees create a pastoral scene more English than West Indian. While we were there, we learned of plans to dredge a salt pond at the southern end of the island in order to build a big marina. Lots of activity and lots of money are being devoted to this once-deserted island.

In the channel between Pillory Rocks we saw the rusted hulk of the *Antilles,* a cruise ship that ran aground and caught fire in January 1971. The passengers and crew were saved through the efforts of the fishermen on Bequia and people on the charter boats working in the Grenadines at the time. I would think twice about taking *Serenity* through that cut, and what the cruise ship was doing there, I can't imagine.

After we had toured Mustique and had our sundown tot on board *Serenity,* Es and George continued their marathon word game that had been driving me crazy for weeks. The game consists of picking twenty-six letters at random, writing them opposite the letters of the alphabet, and within a five-minute time limit, listing famous personages having the initials that result. A simple game for simple people? You would think so, but you are forgetting the generation gap. The problem was that Es's idea of famous people were NFL football players and 1960 politicians. George's tastes ran to English rock musicians and obscure French movie stars. It was as if they were playing the game in two different languages.

"Do you have a J. P.?"

"Jethro Pugh."

"What in bloody hell is a Jethro Pugh? Do you mean Jethro Tull?"

"Who is Jethro Tull?"

"What do you have for L. Z.?"

"Led Zeppelin."

"George, the object of the game is to name a person, not an airplane."

"J. D.?"

"Joe DiMaggio."

"Who?"

"Have you been living in a cave in Scotland? Joe DiMaggio is the most beautiful man in the whole world!—J. B.?"

"Jacques Bergerac."

"Who? I've got Jack Benny."

"Who? I'm going to quit, you cheat."

This went on for hours. As the official referee, I needed the wisdom of Solomon, and I had to lie a lot.

Canouan is a dry and barren island. The small population scratches out a meager existence by farming and fishing. Charleston Bay is broad and well protected but quite shallow, and only a few yachts stop. While we were there, the mail boat had to anchor well out into the bay; the passengers and supplies were ferried in by rowboat. Walking through the small settlement, we were approached by a timid young boy.

"You want bugs, Mon?" he meant lobsters.

"Sure. How big are they?"

He held his hands apart.

"I'll take two. How much?"

"A dollah."

"OK. Are they fresh?"

"Plenty fresh."

He disappeared, and by the time I was back at the dinghy, he had returned with two friends, neither of them more than twelve years old, but no lobster. The three of them got into my dinghy.

"Me show you," said the leader.

It seems I had made a deal for me to do the diving while they sat in the boat and pointed to the water. At least they rowed. They took me to a reef at the mouth of the bay, and I slipped over the side. There were plenty of lobster, but they were all less than a foot long.

"Too small. You shouldn't pick bugs out that small."

The kids couldn't have cared less about my ecology advice. On the way back to *Serenity* they promised to come back the next morning and show me where the really big ones were.

I was a little nervous when my young guides directed me to move *Serenity* around the southern point and inside an exposed reef. Waves crashed on the reef, and foam filled the narrow inlet behind. I got the anchor down and hooked in good, donned my flippers and mask, and swam out to the wave-swept reef. It was loaded with big lobster. I snared two hiding in stag coral and returned proudly to my crew.

"See, I tol' you. Anytime you want bugs, you ast me."

I gave my enterprising young guide a dollar. Es packed up a bag of canned meat, beans, and fruit and told the boys to give the food to their mothers. I rowed them ashore, but before I got back to *Serenity* the kids had opened the cans and were having a private picnic on the beach.

The most-written-about, photographed "pièce de résistance" in the Grenadines is the Tobago Cays. Even though I still think the best diving is in the Bahamas, I won't try to be blasé about the cays. I've never been able to get near them without spending several days there.

The name Tobago Cays applies to four tiny islands—Petit Rameau, Petit Bateau, Baradal, and Jamesby—that are embraced by Horseshoe Reef. To windward, giant swells destroy themselves on Worlds End Reef. The turbulent waters modulate on Horseshoe's inner atoll, leaving the islands windswept but the anchorages tenable. A husky current runs through the channel between Rameau and Bateau, where nearly everyone anchors. Great care should be taken in setting your hook there, and let out plenty of scope. But if you promise not to tell anyone else, the best place to anchor is just off the little beach on Baradal.

The cays can be a place of peace and contemplation. One day, Es asked to be dropped off at Jamesby on my way out to the reef. When I returned hours later, I found her propped against a rock on the miniature beach, staring out at the varied blues of the sea and sky. What each of us sees out there among the billowing clouds and the tossing white caps is very private.

Our seclusion was broken by the arrival of a fleet of bare boats. If I have sounded condescending toward bareboaters, I apologize here and now. I have rented bare boats several times and will again. Nevertheless, they are a source of amusement and concern for cruising people.

The easiest way to spot bareboaters is that they always forget to take in their boarding ladder. It's true. They go charging out of an anchorage with the boarding ladder banging on the topsides. Another telltale habit is towing a dinghy with the motor down. They are also a little deficient in knot-tying skills. There are a hell of a lot of dinghies floating around the Caribbean because somebody's hitch on the stern cleat didn't meet Ashley's standards. A surprising number of locals have been accused of stealing a dinghy that just drifted off. Since the owners of the bare boats are also aware of this, the deposit they require on dinghies and motors is a substantial percentage of the cost of the charter.

The most serious difficulty bareboaters get into is anchoring. Experienced sailors come to the Caribbean and forget the basic rules they learned long ago. The wind blows and the current sets hard here. You must always dive on your anchor and make sure it's dug in. If it is not, don't be lazy. Pull it up and do it again. Then let out plenty of scope: 5 to 1 is minimum, 7 to 1 is better. That's why they give you all that rope! Americans traditionally use nylon rode with ten inches of chain shackled to the anchor. Europeans use heavy chain, and they have an understandable reluctance to crank in any more than is necessary. Most bare boats can be identified by an anchor rode that drops straight down from the bow. It's no wonder so many are awakened in the middle of the night as the current drags them out the channel.

But they may be forgiven for these mental lapses. Bareboaters are out to have a good time, and they are always the happiest, most fun-loving sailors in the harbor. If they themselves have a complaint, it is that they try to do too much on a short cruise. It is not necessary to set an international distance record in twelve days. Cruising people learn that it is better to stop and really see a few places than wear out the crew and see nothing.

An example of what can be missed if you are moving too fast is Mayero, a tiny island just across from Tobago Cays. It doesn't look like much, but on a later cruise, Es and I spent over a week just poking around that two-mile island. We had Saline Bay all to ourselves and made the most of it by swimming back and forth to our private half-mile beach. Everyone likes diving on a wreck, and there is a good one to try just off the northern point. A Royal Navy gunboat, *Puruna,* ripped her bottom out and sank beyond the reef during World War I. Snorkeling over her—there is about twelve feet of water over the bridge deck—is a good reminder not to go sailing around the Grenadines at night.

Ashore there is a fairly steep hill of about 350 feet and near its top, a picturesque old church. From the peak, we had a panoramic view of the burnt green islands and the parade of white sails that swept among them.

We were joined by two couples who had sailed up from Trinidad in a little trimaran. In return for showing them the location of *Puruna,* they invited us to a fish fry on the beach. The men shot a whole bag full of fish swimming in the eroded remains of the gunboat. One thing nice about a trimaran— if you want to go to the beach, you sail it up on the beach and step out; if you want to dive on a reef, you sail up to the reef, drop the hook, and roll over the side.

The most beautiful gunk hole in the Grenadines is on the northern end of Mayero. If you happen to be reading this some cold northern night and fantasizing an image of your own boat in your own beach-fringed cove, where the warm breeze rustles the palm trees and tropical fish play in the shadow of your keel, Salt Whistle Bay is the place you are imagining.

Half of the small, oval-shaped cove is taken up with two coral gardens. Near the beach in the center there is room for no more than three boats, and they had better be good friends. A short walk across the spit separating the windward side is a long beach that is one of the best for shelling. The offshore reef calms the water lying over the azure-tinted sand. As you float in the afternoon sun, the water is actually hot. It is interesting to me that there is better snorkeling, better fishing, and more engaging anchorages at Mayero than at the much more famous Tobago Cays, 1½ miles away.

I first met John Caldwell in the pages of his book, *Desperate Voyage,* the story of his attempt to sail from Panama to Australia in a small boat right after World War II. An inexperienced sailor, John saw no other way to return home to his bride. The voyage ended when he was shipwrecked in Fiji, but later John and Mary built another boat and sailed it two-thirds of the way around the world to the Caribbean. During the many years that they chartered *Outward Bound,* John became known as the Johnny Appleseed, or more properly Johnny Coconut, of the islands for his efforts in planting coconuts on the beaches in order to make them more beautiful.

Now *Outward Bound* is anchored off the resort the Caldwells have built on Prune Island, now renamed, naturally, Palm Island. The hotel is casual and low key and would be a great place for a get-away-from-it-all vacation. Johnny, their son, runs a first rate scuba operation. He takes divers to the surrounding reefs and rents gear to qualified do-it-yourselfers.

The customs officer at Clifton Harbour on Union Island is a mandatory stop for yachts heading south to Grenada and north to the St. Vincent islands. The Customs House stands alone at the foot of the government dock, and clearance during office hours is quick and painless. Entry into the reef-encircled harbor is a little tricky, but once in, the anchorage is a secure one. Nevertheless, most cruisers get their official business done and move on to a more famous spot, thereby missing one of the most unusual scenes in the Grenadines.

One morning, as an enormous orange sun cleared the hills of Palm Island, we watched brightly painted fishing sloops race into Clifton Harbour as each crew tried to be first to weigh in their day's catch. Arguments over the supposedly crooked scales and the fishermen's vocal contempt for the skimpiness of their rivals' catches would have awakened even the soundest sleepers. Later, the conch divers arrived with plastic trays of cleaned meat. All of this activity took place at André Beaufrand's establishment, which is known in all the cruising guides as a new hotel, but is actually his private residence and place of business. M. Beaufrand sells fuel, water, and block ice at his dock and operates a marine railway that can hold up to fifty feet at the cheapest rates in the Caribbean. An airstrip has recently been completed, and the fresh seafood is flown to Martinique, Beaufrand's former home.

Later in the morning we dinghied ashore. As Es climbed the dock, she let out a scream that could be heard in Bequia. Lying on the dock were two 8-foot sharks and several smaller ones. Fishermen were butchering two more on the seawall. We watched as the belly of a big blue shark was slit, and out popped about ten fully formed miniature sharks encased in transparent sacs like little gift-wrapped toys.

The seawall formed an irregular-shaped pool about 100 feet long, and in it were five more sharks swimming in ominous, lazy circles. When the day's catch was more than was needed, the live sharks were dumped into the pool to be kept for a less fortunate day.

It turned out that one of Beaufrand's businesses was supplying shark meat to the gourmets of Martinique. The shark fishermen were Venezuelans rather than locals, and after a conversation that went from English to French to Spanish, I received permission to accompany the men on the next day's trip. At sunset, they left the harbor in an outboard-driven wooden skiff to set their nets. These gill nets were made of tough nylon cordage with openings about six inches square. They were floated above one of the many reefs that make sailing in this area such a careful process.

Well before dawn, the fishermen were knocking on *Serenity's* topsides and, shivering in my foul weather gear and loaded with cameras, I joined the hunt. Once on the reef, they began to haul in their nets, armed only with homemade gaff hooks set in weighted pipe handles.

As each shark was pulled in, it would be disengaged from the net by hand and tossed, flopping and grunting, into the bilge of the skiff. By this time I had climbed to the farthermost peak of the bow—supposedly to get a better camera angle. As they continued to pull in the catch, the boat settled lower in the water, and I tried to get smaller and smaller on my perch. I, too, have heard of sharks attacking their captors even aboard a boat. My new friends were nonchalant. The leader called to his helper, *"¡Ay estúpido, te metiste la pata en la quijada!"*—rough translation, "Hey, dummy, you've got your foot in his jaws!"

We ended up with eight sharks, and admittedly the largest was only five feet long, but you can carry this macho thing too far.

We motored in with what was considered only a nominal day's catch, and later in the day, I was presented with the jaw of the largest shark as a reward for keeping out of their way. I cleaned the remaining flesh from the jaw and fastened it to a ventilator to bleach in the sun for the next few weeks.

While I worked on my toothy prize, *Naraina* came in the bay to clear customs. *Naraina* is a very special charter boat and Richard and Barbara Weinman, her owners, are very special people. Richard is a graduate of the French Naval Academy and Barbara, an American graduate of Smith. We met most of the chartering couples when they came over to *Serenity* to leave their guests alone for a bit, or more probably to escape the endless chatter. Richard and Barbara have maintained their enthusiasm and good humor for more than fifteen years; theirs is one of the most heavily booked charter boats in the business.

That afternoon they brought their big whaler over to say hello and drop off a welcome gift. They had served several huge lobsters for lunch, and there was too much for the guests. Barbara gave us an enormous bowl of lobster antennae and feet (spiny lobsters have no claws)—the sweetest, most delicate parts. That evening we made a mess in the cockpit, but we dined on chilled lobster parts, hot sauce, and cool wine. I hope *Naraina's* guests ate as well as we did.

When given a choice, it's usually wise to clear customs and immigration at a small town instead of a capital city. For example, enter St. Vincent at Union or Bequia instead of Kingstown; enter the Bahamas at Cat Cay or Bimini instead of Nassau. Officers in the main city are usually impressed with the prerogatives of their office and are uncommonly overbearing.

But don't go through customs at Hillsborough unless you really want to stay at Carriacou. The police station is right on the beach, but you will probably have to take a cab to the airport to find the customs man. When you have finished all the paperwork, you still haven't done anything but enter Carriacou. You have to do it all over again when you enter Grenada. If you are only pausing in Tyrell Bay, leave up the Q flag and don't go ashore. When you have collected your nerve to cross Kick'em Jenny, leave without officially entering.

The island *is* worth a stop, however. The largest of the Grenadines, Carriacou was settled at various times by the English, French, and Scots. The Scots left a continuing heritage of boat building, and Carriacou schooners are the best of the interisland freight haulers. The French left an amazing number of good roads. Back when the French were trying to defend the island from the English fleet, they decided it was cheaper to build roads than get more artillery. Whenever the English would approach, the French would haul their guns across the hills and arrange them around the heights over-looking the bay. The English assumed the entire island was heavily fortified. There are a lot of old cannon strewn around Carriacou. The English contribution is a new airport, but it hasn't changed things much. The arrival of the mail boat twice a week is still a major social event.

Why the main town wasn't built on Tyrell Bay instead of the roadstead at Hillsborough, I don't know. Tyrell Bay, also known as Harvey Vale, is a first-rate anchorage. We took a dinghy ride up a wide creek that enters the harbor from the north. Once over a sand bar at the mouth, the creek winds about a mile inland. There is no shoreline, just interwoven mangroves, and not a breath of air stirs. The murky water is supposed to be at least twelve feet deep, and it is the best hurricane hole in the Grenadines. The one time the eye of a hurricane actually passed over the island, the creek was filled with boats. They all survived just fine, but the storm filled in the sand bar at the mouth, and the sailors had to dredge themselves out.

If you have an unexpected visitor after dark, don't be fright-ened or turn on any lights. He will be the retail salesman for the local smugglers. After a little bargaining, you should get a very good buy in Bajan rum or Scotch whiskey. The residents of Carriacou haven't been building all those schooners for one hundred years for nothing.

Es cons us in to Fort-de-France on the island of Martinique.

Diamond Rock, off the coast of Martinique. In 1804, British troops scaled its sheer sides and threatened French vessels from their lofty aerie.

Salaamat, *the charter boat we ran for Curtain Bluff Hotel.*

Lunch for our guests aboard Salaamat.

The coral reef — an ever-changing theater we urged our guests to view.

Landing a captive 'cuda in the boat is a much more satisfying experience than meeting one underwater. But always remember that barracuda eat fish, not people.

Lobster for lunch. Though it lacks the succulent claws of its cousin from Maine, the spiny lobster provides a delicious, ample meal.

The fishing families of Soufrière on St. Lucia. Everyone gets a share of the catch, though how much for what I was unable to determine.

The spectacular Pitons of St. Lucia. A mile-long beach sweeps from one of the twin volcanic spires to the other.

This hefty piece of brain coral that captured Serenity's *anchor would have kept her at Gros Inlet Bay forever if it hadn't been for a sturdy English yacht and her skipper's expert seamanship.*

An Arawak petroglyph deep in the valley of the Yambou River on St. Vincent.

The Botanical Gardens in Kingstown, St. Vincent, where a breadfruit tree that Captain Bligh brought from Tahiti resides in ancient dignity.

Cumberland Bay, one of our anchorages off the lush island of St. Vincent. Everything grows here, even the fences.

No harbor delights the eye like St. George's on Grenada.

The shark fishermen on Union Island at work. When they took me along on an expedition, I had a hard time keeping the camera steady as the sharks tumbled to the bottom of the skiff.

Evening comes to Spice Island.

Los Testigos, off the coast of Venezuela. All is peaceful, silent, and unspoiled.

The windward beach on Los Testigos.

Cindy, one of the Waffa trio, who took us on their Venezuelan cruise.

Es and Cindy find a perch for some serious conversation.

Doug Terman checks the starcut during the Trinidad-Grenada Race.

Anguilla's deserted beaches provided a peaceful week for homeward-bound sailors.

"Fair winds, Serenity.*"*

15 We More-or-Less Settle on Spice Island

The three most infamous, most discussed passages in the Caribbean are the Mona, the Anegada, and Kick'em Jenny. The first two had proved a breeze for us, but Es decided our luck couldn't hold, and it took an extra day of preparation before she was ready to brave the passage. It's only thirty miles from Tyrell Bay to St. George's, harbor to harbor, and just sixteen miles of open water between Grenada and Carriacou. They are reported to be the sixteen roughest miles in sailing. In the center is a group of islands—Île de Ronde, Les Tantes Caille, Diamond Isle, and, if you have time for sight-seeing, London Bridge, a narrow island that the force of wind and sea has worn a hole clear through.

The appellation of Kick'em Jenny is applied both to Diamond Isle and the rips north of it. Intellectuals say the name is a corruption of the French "Caye qui gêne," the island that discomforts. I prefer the explanation that it was named by a sailor who owned a bellicose donkey named Jenny that kicked like hell. Its fame arises from a healthy trade wind and a very confused current that makes the sea behave as if it's being stirred in a mixmaster. It is anticlimatic to report that in spite of our trepidation, our first passage was relatively easy. On a later trip through the caldron, however, it was a different story. *Serenity* bucked and leaped, dove and heeled like a wild mare with a burr under her saddle and a spur in her flank.

On our way down we had heard bad stories and warnings about Grenada. That past winter, the island had been granted full independence from Great Britain. Various factions that opposed the government of Premier Eric Gairy staged several demonstrations and forced the new nation into an island-wide strike. The government overreacted, the police brutalized the strikers, and riots and passions flared. Before the chaos ended, one man was killed, several were injured, and part of the business section was wrecked and looted. Water and electricity were turned off, and the island's commerce ground to a halt.

Cruising yachts and charter boats pulled out for St. Vincent, taking loads of fearful tourists with them. Americans and Canadians who had homes on the island fled, and the resort hotels emptied. The rumors that reached us up-island made it sound like a Black Power uprising against the whites. In fact, the uprising had nothing to do with race or tourism. The confrontation was between black citizens and Gairy, their black premier.

It will take years for Grenada to get over it, and that is unfortunate. It is a memorable island with no overt racial antagonisms. By the time we arrived in November, hostilities had cooled. Many of the yachts had returned although some, like Stevens Yachts, had moved their base to St. Vincent, never to return. The resort hotels were empty during the entire winter. The ironic result of the whole affair was that we were made to feel more than welcome at the previously crowded stores, restaurants, and beaches.

My mother used to make pomanders and sachets out of small silk bags, which she embroidered with flowers, filled with dried flowers or spices, and gave as gifts. The whole island of Grenada smelled like those remembered gifts. A third of the world's supply of nutmeg comes from Grenada. A bonus is mace, a red membrane wrapped around the ripened nut. But that's not all. The fertile valleys nourish cinnamon, cloves, ginger, thyme, saffron, and cocoa. The year-round aroma of Spice Island is intoxicating.

This is a magic island. Green mountains rise amid corrugated valleys from white and black lava beaches into voluptuous clouds. St. George's is a pastel rainbow of red-roofed houses and gingerbread churches, through which the soft air carries a scent of spice and the sound of bells. Grenada is an island so favored by the sea that the sailor may choose among twenty safe anchorages and find delight in each.

Since we planned to settle in this delightful spot for the winter, we stayed at L'Anse aux Épines (pronounced "Lan Supeen" by the locals), or Prickly Bay. Spice Island Charters maintained a small, parklike boatyard there, and we decided for the first time in our travels to tie up to the dock and relax for a few months. It's only five miles to St. George's, and there always seemed to be someone going into town with whom we could share a ride.

The harbor at St. George's is a sunken volcanic crater with one lip collapsed to form the entrance. The carenage is a deepwater bay surrounded on three sides by a sea wall. Native interisland boats tied to the quay load and unload goods directly across the street to the nineteenth-century shops and warehouses lining the bay.

The other half of the harbor is a shallow bay called the Lagoon, the anchorage for the gold-plated charter boats and cruising boats. There are several long finger piers, a fuel dock, two lifts that can take anything up to a small freighter, a ship chandlery, showers, and a waterfront bar and restaurant. The whole complex is called Grenada Yacht Service, or GYS for short. It is the center of yachting for the Windwards. By the time winter was over, some of the most magnificent yachts in the world had paid a call.

I usually can't stand to go shopping. I dream up all kinds of projects that *must* be done or the boat will sink so that Es will go to town alone. Not so in Grenada. I enjoyed the pleasant pace of life on the carenage. While Es worked her way through the stores, I bummed around the waterfront, talking to anyone who would visit with me. You could waste an afternoon walking down one pier visiting with friends.

Behind the waterfront, pastel houses spaced among the breadfruit and flamboyant trees climb the hills. On the cliff to the north, the entrance is guarded by Fort George, built by the French in 1710 but renamed by the English. Across its entrance is a bronze replica of the underwater statue, *Christ of the Deeps.*

The whole scene—the harbors, the Georgian buildings, the yachts, and the tumble of homes on the hillsides—looks as if it were designed by an artist to appear on a picture postcard. No other harbor delights the eye like St. George's.

While we were based in Grenada, we made a couple of trips to Petit St. Vincent, a small island off the northeast coast of Carriacou that is completely given over to a spectacular resort. When we went up there for something called Agents' Week, the small, reef-enclosed harbor was crowded with sailing vessels. There were three-masters, schooners, sleek sloops, yawls, and a brigantine. Banners snapped in the trade winds, while smartly uniformed sailors polished brass and scrubbed teak.

It could have been Rodney's fleet preparing an attack on the French squadrons of de Grasse. But it wasn't. The French tricolor was already there. So, too, were the Stars and Stripes, the Canadian maple leaf, the ubiquitous Panamanian flag, and the British red ensign. The greater part of the Caribbean charter fleet was preparing to stand inspection by U.S. charter agents.

Among the million dollars' worth of yachts, there was one to satisfy almost any taste: the handsome 112-foot *Ring Andersen,* out of Vancouver and skippered by Jan deGroot; *Dana,* an 82-foot Baltic trader converted to a luxury charter yacht; Jean Yves Terlain's 128-foot *Vendredi Treize* (Friday the thirteenth), a strange, black tri-master built originally for the single-handed trans-Atlantic race; *Good Hope,* a newly outfitted 60-foot sloop out of Boston; and thirty-five more, all sparkling bright, awaiting the beginning of the charter season.

In case you've never chartered a boat and are thinking about a vacation cruise, maybe I can give you some advice. First of all, you'll need a good agent to get into Paradise. There are just a fixed number of boats, and almost any agent can arrange a booking on almost any boat. It's like multiple listings in real estate.

Choosing an agent is your first important task. Unfortunately, anyone with a typewriter, some postage stamps, and the price of an ad in the yellow pages can call himself a charter agent. Some have never been to sea in their lives; others have never seen the boats they are chartering or would not know a good crew from a bad one. Since the agent's commission is paid by the yacht and is included in the charter fee, it costs you no more to have the best. The dangers are real. An agent can go bankrupt while holding your 50 percent deposit. An inexperienced agent can double book, and after your long flight to Grenada, you're left on the dock while your dream boat sails off into the sunset. Many an expensive vacation has been ruined by the wrong choice of agent.

I was impressed by the nine charter agents who had flown at their own expense to Petit St. Vincent and who spent three days inspecting the yachts, interviewing the crews, and discussing the coming season with the skippers. From there they flew to Antigua, and later the Virgin Islands, for similar reviews. Yachts, owners, and cooks change from season to season. The queen of the fleet two years ago can be this year's rusty bucket.

Because a good agent's primary job is to match the guests with the proper yacht, he needs an intimate, current knowledge of the boat and crew to begin with. The next step is up to you. You must frankly and explicitly tell your agent what you expect of your trip. Most agents will send you a check-list to be filled out before a yacht is chosen. Will this be your first ocean cruise? Do you want to cover a large area even if it means hard, wet sails? Do you want the peace and quiet of secluded anchorages or would you rather dance all night to a steel band at a native jump-up? Will you expect to go ashore for local souvenir shopping? Dine out at local resorts? Are you a snorkeler, a licensed scuba diver, a sheller, or a fisherman? What foods do you like? Dislike? Your agent will advise you and tell you what's possible and what is not. But it's your money and your vacation. It's up to you to state your desires clearly.

Since charter boats come in all sizes and accommodations, the next decision is equally difficult. Who is to sail with you? Will it be a second honeymoon for just the two of you or a trip with your best friends? Or, more dangerous still, three couples? It always surprises novice sailors to find out how fast friendships can dissolve when they are cooped up on a sixty-foot boat for two weeks. And then, too, do you share the same interests? While you're at the wheel, beating down St. Lucia Channel, salt spray in your face, a glorious sun tanning your bikinied wife, will your favorite bridge partner be below, head in the head, trying desperately to end it all? Don't wait until you're two thousand miles from home to find out. On the other hand, there have been cruises with as many as fourteen people that were a total delight.

Once you have settled the details and a first choice of a yacht is made, your agent will check with schedule-clearing agents in the normal cruising grounds of the yacht and the dates can be confirmed. At that time you will be required to pay a 50 percent deposit, which should be placed in a proper escrow account. The balance is payable prior to boarding.

A word of caution. Make certain you know exactly what you are paying for. The price quoted should be all-inclusive, with no hidden extras leading to unpleasantness at the last moment. Liquor, wine, and mix are sometimes included in the weekly rate, sometimes not. Get a clear idea of how this substantial item is to be paid.

And finally, in the Caribbean at least, getting there is not half the fun. Your agent should be as knowledgeable about air travel as about boats. It's part of the adventure, of course, but you're apt to be on several airlines from super jets to small feeder planes until you arrive tired and hot in your city clothes at your waiting yacht. Take your agent's advice on what to bring along. Even then you will bring too many clothes and not enough film or sunscreen lotion. If you want to really impress your skipper, don't bring aboard any hard luggage or hard-soled shoes.

If all this sounds like a chore, it isn't meant to be. It is only to warn you to be careful and thoughtful in your decisions. It's all worth it. A properly arranged cruise will be a vacation of such sensuous pleasure that it cannot be compared to a land-bound stay at a resort hotel or the regimentation of a cruise ship.

Less than a half mile to the south of Petit St. Vincent is Petit Martinique, the home of five hundred citizens who are purported to be among the wealthiest per capita in the West Indies. They don't make it farming. Even flowers won't grow on this small, barren rock. All the men on the island are mariners. To illustrate their source of income, cigarettes and whiskey cost less on Petit Martinique than Haze Richardson, manager of the resort on PSV, can buy them wholesale from the distributors in St. Vincent. Since Petit Martinique is a dependency of Grenada, in theory you are supposed to clear out of Petit St. Vincent and into Carriacou before making the half-mile dinghy ride, but customs officials have long ago given up trying to regulate the go-to-hell attitude of the hardy sailors of Petit Martinique.

In search of a carton of American filter cigarettes as a respite from the English brands I had been smoking, I climbed from the dock up a crumbling precipice to the home of my purveyor. All the homes are little, weather-beaten saltboxes with gingerbread trim that would look more appropriate in Nantucket.

While we negotiated the price, the proprietor offered me a drink of jackiron, the local mountain dew rum. He half-filled a jelly jar with a clear liquid having the consistency of motor oil (I'd say, "and the taste," but I've never tasted motor oil). It is liquid dynamite. My drink was warm, of course, but Haze tells me that ice cubes won't float in jackiron. He says dropping an ice cube in that thick liquid and watching it sink to the bottom of the glass startles the consumer more than the effects of the drink.

The trip back to Grenada was a memorable one. Jan deGroot invited us to sail on *Ring Andersen. Ring* is a sea-going classic, painstakingly built in Denmark by the famous naval architect whose name she bears. With ninety-five feet on deck and a twenty-one-foot beam, she has cabins the size of an ocean liner's and a saloon that you would like to have in your home. You can always tell when *Ring* is entering a harbor— her three-cylinder diesel goes karumph, pause, karumph, pause, karumph; her cruising rpm is 100.

The crew on *Ring* had arranged an impromptu race back with *Dana* with a case of beer as the prize. *Dana,* too, was built by Ring Andersen in Denmark. Rigged as a brigantine, she is 82 feet long and has a 21-foot beam. We karumphed out into the light air, and the race was on—but not very fast. As we rounded the northern end of Carriacou, we met *Harvey Gamage* coming up the other way. *Harvey Gamage* is a 110-foot, gaff-rigged topsail schooner. Because of the slight breeze, she had everything including the tablecloth hung up.

Here, within a hundred yards of one another, were three of the few remaining great tall sailing ships. An acre of white sails spread across a brilliant blue sea. It was a sight not to be repeated soon again.

We yelled over to Simon Bridger to bring *Harvey Gamage* about and join the race, but he had a schedule to keep and couldn't accept the challenge. *Harvey Gamage* has an unusual arrangement for a charter boat. Simon picks up guests at the Holiday Inn in Grenada, spends ten days cruising the islands, and drops off at the Holiday Inn at St. Lucia, where he picks up another load and sails down to Grenada to repeat the process. Simon says it is a little like driving a bus.

I would like to report on the thrilling race, but by the time we reached Kick 'em Jenny, it was dead calm and the engines were turned on by mutual agreement. Still, the two ships motor sailing into St. George's harbor side by side stopped traffic on the carenage.

If the Grenada Yacht Service in St. George's was an upper crust gathering of charter boat guests and crews on their best behavior, Prickly Bay, where *Serenity* had settled in, was a society of cruising people and charter boat crews on their off-time. Ours was the more relaxed, honest relationship. Because *Serenity* had the first slip on the dock next to the marine railway, we had a front row seat to check everyone who was hauled out. Proximity, however, has some disadvantages.

The best-known sailor in the Caribbean has to be Don (Squeaky) Street. Much of his fame comes from his excellent cruising guides and articles in *Sail,* apart from the fact that he has been sailing in these waters for almost twenty years. As he says, "I know most of the reefs because at one time or another I and *Iolaire* have bounced off practically every shoal spot in the Lesser Antilles." He is also justly famed as a skilled seaman. With Don at the helm, *Supercilious* swept every race at Antigua Race Week one year.

His heavy old yawl *Iolaire,* built in 1900, is equally famous. Some years ago Don got mad and threw the engine overboard. With her bright red topsides, she is a familiar sight tacking into each anchorage.

While we were in Grenada, *Iolaire* was pulled up on the

ways in order to prepare her for a voyage to Newport, from where she would leave for an impromptu race to England and then a race for old wooden sailboats. Famous though she may be, *Iolaire* is not exactly the best-equipped boat I ever saw. Once or twice a day, Don walked over to our conveniently located boat and in his squeaky voice called,

"*Serenity,* do you have a one-inch wood chisel?"

"Sure."

"Do you have any 2½-inch bronze screws?"

"Sure."

"Do you have an 11/16 box end wrench?"

"Sure."

"Do you have a caulking iron?"

"No. Some bastard borrowed it and sailed away with it."

"Do you have any epoxy?"

"Sure."

"Is it fresh?"

"Sure."

And as the natives say, "T'ing an t'ing," which means, etc., etc.

One evening we were sitting down to dinner when there was a knock on the side. It was Squeaky.

"My wife wants to go out to a restaurant. Can I borrow a pair of shoes?"

"Jees, Don, I'm twice your size. I wear a twelve."

"She's going to be awfully mad if I don't get some shoes."

We found a pair of Es's sandals that fit him, and he dutifully took his wife to dinner.

We were beginning to get a little antsy sitting still. We had planned to go to Trinidad, but we wanted to wait for Carnival and that was four months away. When we had a good-bye party for the Morgans on *Rosa Solis,* who were leaving for Brazil, we began seriously discussing Venezuela, lying some one hundred miles over the southern horizon.

16 Cruising with a South American Flavor

There must be a commonly held belief among cruising yachtsmen that Grenada sits on the end of the world and that traveling any farther south carries the threat of sailing off the edge into the waiting jaws of the sea monsters. Nearly everyone reaches Grenada and turns around and heads north. I'm not prepared to advance any radical theories about the world being round, but I can testify that the many islands along the rugged coastline of Venezuela are a wonderful, seldom-visited area. When we met the Waffas of *Ilene Too,* our decision to sail there was reinforced.

The Waffas—Ted, Ilene, and step-daughter Cindy—spent three years building their forty-five-foot ferrocement ketch in Long Beach, California. They sailed her down the coast of Central America, through the canal, across Colombia, the ABC Islands, and Venezuela, to Grenada. She was tied up across the dock from us at L'Anse aux Épines. *Ilene Too* is a rugged, beautifully finished example of what can be built of ferrocement; she is beamy, well-equipped, and comfortable. We listened to the stories of their cruise, and when we were invited to join them for their return trip to Venezuela, it was easy to sign on. We stowed all the loose gear in a locker on shore, arranged to have our neighbors look after *Serenity,* and headed south aboard *Ilene Too.*

During the bright moonlit night, heavy trades and a powerful following sea pushed us along at a steady seven knots. By dawn, the brilliant cobalt blue of the Caribbean was gone, and rising out of the lumpy jade of the Atlantic were the islands of Los Testigos. By 1000 we were anchored in a quiet cove at Testigo Grande.

These islands, like most of those we were to visit, remind one of the uninhabited islands in the British Virgins. Hilly, barren, and dry, they are covered wth cacti, aloe, sea grape, and manchineel trees. A few divi-divi trees cling to the rocky peaks. But unlike the Virgins, all is peaceful, silent, and unspoiled. As I have said, it is very hard to find a place to hide in the Caribbean these days. With the growth of the bare boat business and the increasing number of charter and cruising boats, even the remotest anchorages must be shared. In season, there are up to thirty-five yachts tangled together at the Tobago Cays. If cruising means to you the remoteness and solitude of an empty harbor, you had better plan to follow us southward.

Los Testigos is the home of a very few fishermen who exchange their catches for supplies brought over from the mainland. If you don't care to do your own diving, fresh fish or lobster can be purchased for pennies. While snorkeling on the reefs, we were able to shoot enough fish for dinner in minutes. The windward side of the island has a two-mile long beach where the winds have piled the sugarlike sand into dunes fifty feet high. Great combers roll in to crash against the rock outcroppings that divide the beaches. Thick veins of multicolored quartz slice the black rocks like bands of jewelry. We spent several days hiking in the rugged hills and diving in the still waters of the leeward shore.

When it was time to leave, another all-night downhill sail brought us to Margarita, a completely different island. Entry at Pampatar was time consuming and once it was accomplished, we moved around to the major city on the island,

Porlamar. The island is large, forty by twenty miles at its widest, and mountainous.

Margarita is a favorite vacation spot for Venezuelans, and the city of Porlamar is a strange combination of Tijuana and Miami Beach. Hundreds of duty-free shops hustle everything from French perfume, Japanese hi-fi sets, and Scotch whiskey to Insty-print T-shirts. Local pearls are hawked on the streets at bargain prices. Since I don't know a good pearl from a bad one, we passed. It was Christmas week, and the streets were crowded with people hurrying to buy gifts before returning to the mainland. The beach is lined with new high-rise hotels and apartment condominiums. The few breaks in the skyline are filling up with more new construction. Giant cranes rise above the partially completed structures like so many modernistic mosques. The bay is filled with large power yachts from La Guiara, and huge ferryboats thrash back and forth from Puerto la Cruz. It's all a bit much for the cruising types, but there are compensations. We took on 450 gallons of diesel at eleven cents a gallon, U.S., cigarettes were less than three dollars a carton, and a delicious seafood dinner complete with cold, dry martinis cost about five dollars.

It is outside of the city that one sees the true beauty of Margarita. The island occupies 350 square miles, ringed with beaches and quiet lagoons. Nearly every village has the ruins of an old fort or castillo, and everywhere there are graceful old churches honored in the long history of this island. The village of Juan Griego on a sweeping bahía filled with fishing craft is particularly picturesque. At Laguna de la Restinga, oysters can be picked off the roots of mangrove trees, and this is one of the few places in the world that the scarlet ibis can be seen in its natural habitat.

Here I must interrupt for a personal aside in the hope that it will be an object lesson for newcomers to the cruising world. During my many months of cruising I seldom wore shoes, but during our trips around Margarita I wore a pair of sandals and soon developed a small blister on each instep. Then I waded ashore in front of the local fish market to secure our dinghy (I would hate to describe the stuff I waded through) and walked around some more in the seldom-used sandals. I'm too tough to worry about a couple of little blisters, right? Wrong. In two days the blisters had quadrupled in size, my normally size-twelve feet had swollen to twice their ample size, and red lines were climbing the inside of my leg. If I didn't panic, Es, a registered nurse, did. She dinghied ashore to find a doctor and was back in a few minutes with the ski boat from the Bella Vista Hotel. The room clerk had called the emergency room, and soon I was speeding to the hospital accompanied by the room clerk to translate my pain and suffering into Spanish.

Within an hour the infection was cut out, scraped, cleaned, and dressed, and I had had a giant tetanus shot. All without benefit of anesthesia. I ain't *never* gonna do that again.

The object lesson: there are little wiggly things down here that your body and the antibiotics you carry on your boat have never seen before. If you get any blisters, cuts, or sores, don't be brave. Check with the nearest doctor and let him prescribe the local remedy. Because of my foolishness, I spent the rest of the trip changing bandages and hobbling around, my diving and hiking at an end. Later I was entertained in one of Caracas's finest restaurants, dressed in my fanciest and only suit, barefoot.

We spent a quiet New Year's Eve on Isla Cubagua near the site of the first settlement in South America. This island was discovered by Columbus in 1498, and hundreds of European adventurers have fought over the pearl beds that surround the island. The city of Nuevo Cadiz, founded in 1500, soon became the center of the pearl trade in the New World. In 1541 a tidal wave destroyed the settlement, and part of the ruins can still be seen on the barren spit of land near our anchorage. Snorkelers can find the rest of the ruins in the clear water nearby. The local fishermen claim that you can hear the chimes of old cathedral bells immersed in the shallow water, but though we celebrated the New Year with several bottles of tax-free champagne, we didn't hear any bells.

For days we had seen the great dusty rose mountain ranges of northern Venezuela climb eight thousand feet above the sheer coastline. The next sunset found us in the lee of another beautiful adobe fort at Araya and after a short sail the next morning, Cumaná.

This fine old city looked the way I had expected a South American city to look. Carefully tended squares with their equestrian statues of early patriots interrupt winding narrow streets. Lovely old colonial architecture has lots of grillwork and balconies and massive doors with wrought iron hardware.

Cumaná is the center of a very successful shrimp industry, and the port is busy with the coming and goings of brightly painted shrimp boats. The harbor is dirty with an aromatic mixture of dead fish and diesel. Staying there very long is quite a strain, but we did buy fresh iced shrimp for one bolívar per kilo (translation: twenty-five cents for two pounds).

The rest of the trip to Puerto la Cruz traversed some of the most unusual cruising grounds we had ever seen. We spent two weeks covering the next fifty miles. A hundred-foot wall of sea-eroded cliffs tumbled into thirty fathoms. We sailed the coastline within twenty-five yards of the pounding waves until it seemed our spreaders would scrape the multicolored rocks. Great gashes in the cliffs, which were sometimes no more than a few yards wide, led to deep water inland. Picture a tropical Norwegian fjord.

At Mochima the fjord is five miles long and at least ten fathoms deep all the way in. It is about a half mile at its widest, and little wooded islands thrust up out of the still water. As you wind around the bends, the steep walls give way to an occasional tiny palm-fringed beach. And all of this in a calm, windless silence. Motoring out the next day, we interrupted a school of albacore, and after three quick strikes on our trailing line, we had fresh fish for dinner.

Just off the coast there are two groups of about a dozen islands, Caraca and Chimana. Each island is indented with good anchorages, some of which are the steep-walled, bottle-shaped bays we had grown used to, but others have curving sweeps of pink sand, where sandpipers dance with the waves.

In one channel we watched a graceful whale breaching and playing for more than an hour. Several times porpoises tumbled in and showed off for us. The women went shelling every day, and we finally insisted that they pick out the perfect ones and throw the rest back for fear that they would sink the boat with their daily hauls. We spent lazy days moving from one lovely cove to the next and swimming, sunning, and reading. We watched the pelicans dive-bombing the shoals where the green water yellowed on the coralheads. Except for an occasional fisherman we didn't see another boat. All of this was within sight of the evening loom of Puerto la Cruz. Tell me about the good cruising in the Virgins!

The only annoyance in cruising this area is the Venezuelan bureaucrats' love of paperwork. First, everyone on board must have a visa or travel letter. These are good for thirty days and can be renewed. They are obtainable from any Venezuelan consulate (there is one in Grenada). Next, upon your arrival at your first port of entry, you request a *zarpe,* or cruising permit, from the port captain who will also want several copies of your crew list. Then the customs officials will want to fill out forms concerning your ship's stores and some more crew lists. Immigration will want to see your visas, passports, and more crew lists, and finally the local National Guard will want a description of your yacht and some crew lists. In all you'll need ten or twelve, but wait until they are asked for. If you volunteer, the first guy will take them all, and you will have to go back to the boat and type up some more. Also, be sure that your zarpe shows all the intermediate stops in and out, or you will have to request a new one in every port you enter. It's a good idea to present yourself to each port captain and show him your zarpe. This will help maintain good Latin American relations. All of this is naturally conducted in Spanish, and it's a lot of bother, but it doesn't cost anything. There are very few foreign yachts cruising here, so they tend to treat you like a freighter or cruise ship.

Puerto la Cruz, population 100,000, is brand new. The entire city has been built in the last thirty years. Its broad highways, tall apartment buildings, and shops are filled with busy people. The city has grown so fast that it's impossible to get a telephone, and they still haven't gotten around to building an airport. We restocked the boat at 1960 U.S. prices in a modern supermarket and went crazy buying supplies in the new Sears store.

We anchored opposite the Sinclair Yacht Club at El Chaure. The hills surrounding the bay are covered with huge oil storage tanks, and at the mouth of the bay there are two pumping stations that can serve four giant tankers at a time. If you have never seen one of these monsters empty, it is hard to believe. They tower seventy-five feet in the air. With their bulbous bow and the curve of their bilge out of the water, they look as if the slightest puff of wind would capsize them. Watching these behemoths maneuvering in and out every day gives you some small idea of Venezuela's wealth.

Es and I called friends in Caracas whom we had met at Curtain Bluff. They urged us to come visit them, so we set out by bus for the capital. The dry hills of the east gave way to cocoa and copra plantations. Rushing rivers irrigated broad vistas of grazing land filled with cattle. Large stands of bamboo cackled in the wind. The twisting highway climbed the green mountains until we drove over a high saddle and there, in a valley 3,500 feet above sea level, was the city of Perpetual Spring.

Surely Caracas is one of the most dramatic cities in the

world. Ringed by mountains, this city can only build up, and up it has built. Its population has doubled and tripled in recent years to reach 2.5 million. All of the residents seem to have automobiles, and all of them are in a hurry. We saw traffic jams on the *autopostas* that made the Los Angeles freeways seem like the wide open spaces. The architecture is modern, unrepetitive, and inventive. The shopping centers are more elaborate than anything I've seen in the States. The restaurants would do credit to New York City and at half the prices.

Our charming friends, Mirtha and Nico Becks, couldn't have been more accommodating. They wined and dined us, drove us everywhere for a week, advised us, and interpreted for us. They own a weekend home in an area called Río Chico, some one hundred miles from the city. In this unique development seventy-five miles of rivers and interconnecting canals lead to the ocean. There are so few homes there presently, that as we roared around the maze of waterways in Nico's power boat, we flushed great blue herons and startled white egrets. It must be like Fort Lauderdale was fifty years ago.

The Sunday we were in Río Chico was Super Bowl IX (the Minnesota Vikings vs. Pittsburgh), and it was being relayed by satellite to Caracas. After what Miami had done to the Vikings the previous year, I was certain this was *our* year. When did the Steelers learn how to play football? The Becks didn't understand why it was so important, but they had a neighbor with an antenna big enough to receive Caracas and arranged for Es and me to see the game. First of all, the game was broadcast in Spanish. Secondly, the Venezulans didn't know a damned thing about football, so the game was interrupted every few minutes by a group of soccer players at the local studio trying to explain the fine points of the game. Since the Vikings forgot everything they ever knew about football, maybe they should have listened to the soccer players. It wasn't one of my favorite football games.

With an interest in checking out the local yachting scene,

we crossed over the mountain range to La Guaira, Venezuela's busiest seaport. Many of the goods and materials needed to support the burgeoning economy funnel through this relatively small port. When we were there, the warehouses were filled and crates were piled high along the waterfront. The streets were clogged with trucks. There were fifteen freighters anchored out waiting their turn at the crowded docks. This would be a good place for the visiting yachtsman to avoid. The customs and port officials are months behind in their work, and interrupting them with a private clearance could only lead to a hassle for the yachtsman.

A few miles east there are two marinas. The first is part of the Macuto Sheraton Hotel complex and next to it is the Carabelleda Golf and Yacht Club. Both are filled with large power boats and elaborate sports fishermen. Both managers extend a welcome to U.S. yachtsmen, and to the extent that slips are open, the courtesies of the clubs are available. They are as fancy and complete as the finest marinas in southern Florida. The favorite cruising and fishing grounds for the local yachtsmen, however, is Los Roques, a group of about forty coral cays fifty miles north of La Guaira.

The last real city we had been in was San Juan and that had been three years ago, so we walked the city streets, wide-eyed like a couple of rubes from Minnesota. We even went to two movies in one night. Every Venezuelan we met went out of his way to help us with our struggling Spanish. They all professed their affection for the United States, but they were a little confused about our politics. Finally, the noise, the air pollution, and the endless rushing around reminded us that we were boat people, and we headed for Puerto la Cruz and *Ilene Too* to prepare for the hard sail back. Getting back isn't as simple as coming down.

The trick seems to be to head eastward along the coast of Peninsula de Paria until you can get a decent cut at the winter northeast trades. This sometimes means going all the way to

Trinidad. We motor sailed into the two-knot coastal current and stopped each night in a protected bay until the wind gradually shifted toward the east.

At 1830 one evening off Cabo Tres Puntas we swung northward and headed for Grenada. Now the strong current was abeam, but huge swells had built up and were rolling straight into us. Fortunately, the winds remained light, or we could have been in a real mess. A series of rain squalls and a thin moon robbed the sea of all its light. The next day hardly dawned at all as the rain continued. Visibility was limited from one 25-foot roller to the next, and in the deep troughs our world was a small oval of angry gray water.

The motion got to some of our crew; Es, Cindy, and Ted were pretty sick and spent the day in their bunks. Ilene, unperturbed, read in the saloon. When it grew darker still, my very green-looking wife came up to take the wheel so I could get my meal. There was none of this canned beans and sandwiches nonsense on *Ilene Too*. Dinner at anchor or in the middle of the ocean was several courses with tossed salad and dessert. While I was wolfing down my food, a glass rolled off the galley counter and smashed on the stove. While the boat pitched and rolled, Ilene took out a full-size upright vacuum cleaner and calmly cleaned up the mess. Now *that's* what I call a fully-equipped cruising yacht.

We plowed uncomfortably under sail and motor until late that night when we located the brilliantly lit cross overlooking St. George's harbor and finally Point Saline Light. It took us thirty-one long hours to cover the ninety miles. Wet and tired, we slid into L'Anse aux Épines where *Serenity* awaited us, safe but lonely.

The tough passages are soon forgotten, to be recalled in exaggeration much later where sailors gather and sea tales are told. The good days—the sun-filled quiet anchorages, the pleasures of a new country, and the warmth and good humor of its people—these were the new memories we brought back.

17 The Trinidad-Grenada Race and Our Cruise Ends

Much to our surprise, *Rosa Solis* came sailing into Prickly Bay one day. The Morgans hadn't gone to Brazil after all. They had made it to Trinidad easily enough, but when they reached the coast of Guyana, the combination of the southeast trades, which they hadn't expected so soon, and the south equatorial current setting against them at the rate of three knots proved to be too much. After several uncomfortable days of no progress they turned around, cruised Trinidad and Tobago, and returned to Grenada.

Howard Morgan is still determined to reach Brazil, where he served as a naval officer in World War II, but his new plan will require some time. He recently bought *Encantada* and sailed her to Fort Lauderdale. From there he will cross to England, sail down to the Canary Islands, follow the coast of Africa, and then go across to Brazil. It's a lot longer that way, but with the wind and the current with them and with their courage and determination, I'm certain the Morgans will complete their voyage.

If I have a thing about seeing other people's boats, Es has one about other people's homes, especially here in the tropics where architectural imagination is freed. A big overhanging roof for protection from the sun and rain and a minimum number of walls to provide privacy are the only limitations. Most of the houses are wide open to the breeze and the view.

Carl Schuster has a large modern house on Mt. Hardman Bay in Grenada. It has only one bedroom. "To discourage longtime guests," he explained. We all spent many hours sitting on his veranda listening to Carl tell stories about his early days cruising in the West Indies. One of his interesting theories is that Columbus's landfall was not San Salvador. Following the Columbus journal and explorer's descriptions, Carl has resailed the approaches and is convinced that Columbus could have landed only on Caicos.

Carl is a remarkable man. In 1961, he started the successful Nutmeg Restaurant in St. George's and later sold it. Now he devotes his time to racing his pride and joy, *Zig-Zag,* in any competition he can find, and he must be at least seventy. During one of our pleasant evening tots, he asked Doug Terman and me to join his crew as navigator and helmsman for the Trinidad-Grenada Race.

Zig-Zag is a Pearson 43, and she has won a lot of races. In fact, she has won the Trinidad-Grenada Race in the past, but with the never-ending rule changes and newer racing machine designs, she is beginning to show her age. Carl wanted to get his crew used to working together and toughen them up a bit, so every Thursday afternoon we entered the Grenada Yacht Club races to practice. We needed it. *Zig-Zag* flew an enormous spinnaker and a newly purchased star-cut that we managed to wrap around the forestay about half the time. But slowly we worked into shape. In addition to Doug and me, Carl had his longtime first mate Joe, a Grenadian; Billy, a super-tough cockney sailor who was also the arm wrestling champion of the Grenada Yacht Service; and Maggie Britter, who would be covering the race for *Yachting* as I would for *Sail.*

First we had to get to Trinidad. We were the only entry from Grenada with any real chance of bringing the trophy back, and there was a crowd of well-wishers gathered on the dock to see us off. Carl arrived leading a piglet on a leash. The pig was squealing like crazy when he was passed aboard and started skating around the fiberglass cockpit with his sharp little feet.

"I'm not going sailing with any goddamn pig," Doug whispered through clenched teeth. It was not simply that Doug disliked pigs; as our navigator, he considered the pig a personal affront. The use of pigs as an aid to navigation is well known in the island. Schooners loaded with goods from Barbados would sometimes miss their home island because of errant winds or currents. The pig was thrown into the water and, in theory, started to swim toward its home. The helmsman took up the new course, and the pig was hauled aboard. To further emphasize the piglet's role, Carl named him Prince Henry the Navigator. Terman was still disgruntled when we cast off our lines, waved to our well-wishers, and set sail for Trinidad.

One of the pleasures of a new pickup crew is that everyone has a new audience. The hours pass rapidly as each watch swaps stories about previous races and previous voyages. As *Zig-Zag* reached across the southern end of the Caribbean, stories flowed freely as the crew settled into the easy companionship that comes with shared experiences. The night passed with only a few sail changes ordered mainly to give the foredeck crew a chance to practice in the dark at sea.

By morning we were off Boca de Monos (Mouth of the Monkeys). This narrow strait is formed by a group of high rocky islands and to the east, the cliffs of Trinidad's north coast. Carl had sailed the strait many times and pointed out the swirls of current and the lack of consistent direction to the blanketed wind. His lecture on expecting the unexpected in the Bocas was to prove valuable later.

We cleared customs and anchored in Chaguaramas Bay, the new home of the Trinidad Yachting Association, which had organized the thirteenth running of the race.

Doug had spent a lot of time in Port of Spain when he outfitted *Jacinta* many years before, and he showed me the town on my short visit. The city is a real potpourri of ethnic groups: East Indians, Africans, Chinese, British, Spanish, Lebanese, and Syrians; and it is a happy blend that lives in bustling harmony. The architecture reflects the diverse backgrounds of the inhabitants. I saw East Indian bazaars, a Lebanese rug merchant, an American-style supermarket, and a French hi-fi store doing business side by side on a busy street. Doug knew a special Oriental restaurant, and that night I had the best Chinese meal I ever had (that includes a year I spent in China, where the food was lousy).

The next morning we practiced for our start inside the bay and checked out the competition. There were nineteen racing boats and a separate class of four multihulls entered. Based upon handicaps, ours was the scratch boat in the fleet. There were two new Hughes 38s entered. One of them, *Domani,* was sailed by Sidney Knox, commodore of the Trinidad yacht club, and it was clearly the boat to beat.

The race started at 1600. During the tense pre-start maneuvering we tacked about with the small jib and made a pass at the line and then wheeled about again. Doug came hurrying back to the cockpit and stepped on the pig. The pig started squealing, and Doug started yelling, "I'm going to kill that pig," as he reached for a winch handle.

"Later, I'll help you," I said. "Now what's happening?"

A little calmer, Doug answered, "If we start at the top of the line, it'll be a beam reach. I think we can fly the star-cut."

"We'll never maneuver with it, can you apes pop it at the line?"

"You watch us." He took another swipe at the pig. "You sheet it in—hard!"

"Have Joe pass up the stays'l. We might as well go whole hog."

Doug stared at the pig and climbed forward.

Some of the other boats caught the wind change and were putting up their big jennies. Under cover of the cockpit combing, I rigged the mizzen stays'l but left it in the bag. Forward, the star-cut spinnaker bag was lashed to the pulpit, and the halyard, guy, and sheet were made fast. While we worked our way upwind, the rest of the fleet watched us as if we had gone crazy. Then we all wheeled and headed for the line.

"Fifteen, fourteen, thirteen, twelve," Maggie counted.

The other boats drew ahead of us.

Carl yelled, "Put it up!"

"Ten, nine, eight . . . ."

Billy pulled hand over hand on the halyard. The red, white, and blue spinnaker blossomed like a giant flower. Joe cranked the halyard winch, and I bent over the sheet winch cranking like a maniac. The gun boomed. *Zig-Zag* leapt forward.

"Ease the guy, ease the guy!"

I climbed to the high side and inched out the guy.

"Enough. Sheet it, sheet it!"

Back I went to the sheet winch, the boiling water a foot from my head. The sheet hummed like a violin string. I cleated it off and looked around. I had planned to photograph the start, but that was forgotten. We had twenty-five yards on the whole fleet and were pulling away.

"Keep clear, I'm putting up the stays'l."

I quickly raised the mizzen stays'l. Joe sheeted it on the end of the mizzen boom. The light sail fitted the gap between the mizzen and the main, and it was the first time I ever got a stays'l up without a tangle. *Zig-Zag* heeled to her work. Carl, at the wheel, was grinning like a seven-year-old.

"Beautiful, beautiful."

The first mark was an offshore island where the course turned and ran parallel to the coast. We were well ahead by now. Doug came back; he was grinning, too.

"How do you like the apes, now?" he asked.

"Don't retire yet. It's going to be a dead run after the mark. Are you going to change to the big spinnaker?"

"It will cost more time than it's worth. Let's play with what we have."

"OK, but you better stand by for a jibe."

We rounded the island and headed straight downwind. Behind us big multicolored chutes unfurled, and the leaders began to close the gap. There is no sensation quite like running before the wind and current. The air seems still, and the water alongside doesn't seem to move, yet the islands sweep by. The only feeling of motion is the yawing of the bow and the creaking of the sheets through the blocks. It's a handful for the helmsman, but everyone else can enjoy the unusual experience.

By the time we reached the Bocas, five other boats had closed with us. The rest of the fleet was strung out behind. But it didn't make any difference who got there first. Once into the channel, we found a dead calm. The current, Carl had assured us, always flowed north through the Bocas. But this afternoon it was flowing in circles, actually forming whirlpools on the calm surface.

Sails slatted, windless. The racing boats lost steerage and drifted in every direction—some stern first, some sideways. One or two made 360-degree circles in the whirling water. Crews were kept busy fending off competitors. A catamaran almost straddled *Zig-Zag's* bow. Slowly, inexorably, the fleet drifted toward the exit. I could have swum the distance in less time. As the sun disappeared, we found ourselves sliding into the ocean through no skill on our part, upwind from most of the fleet. Sails drawing again, we set off for Grenada.

All through the night I sat hunched over the wheel. Every time I shifted to brace my foot on the cockpit seat, I stepped on the sleeping pig. I waited for Carl to go below to get some sleep so that I could throw Henry the Navigator overboard. Carl, Doug, and Billy perched on the high side, discussing strategy. The lights of the other competitors were behind and downwind of us. Every so often Doug would go below, and in the pale red light do things with his slide rule and radio direction finder. He announced that we had made up our handicap and were on course.

Then the rain squalls hit. Foul weather gear was passed up. Down came the big jenny; the mizzen was doused. We boomed along with a reefed main and a small jib. From where I sat, I could see only the dancing numbers in the compass and forward, the eerie hooded figures in yellow and orange, lit by the green running light. Very spooky. The squalls quit. Up with the mizzen, up with the jenny, out with the reef. The mast lights of the trailing fleet sunk lower on the horizon. Within minutes of Doug's prediction, there was Point Saline Light. Blink, blink, blink—pause fifteen seconds—blink, blink, blink. Right on course.

By dawn we were off Point Saline. Es and the whole crowd from Prickly Bay were lining the cliff at the base of the light. I could see Es raise one finger and point with the other hand. We were number one. And we were in our own ball park, now. Carl had sailed from Point Saline to St. George's a thousand times. He knew every eddy, every puff. Except there was none. Dead calm again.

Doug lay on his back at the forestay, looking up at the telltales on the jib.

"Come up—up—fall off—come up." He played every whiff of air.

Billy and Joe worked the sheets, trying to keep the sails filled. It was tantalizing. Carl decided to stay as far offshore as we dared to seek the wind. The committee boat and the finish line buoy were half a mile away in the fresh sunlight.

Behind us the other leaders charged up in the free air. Once around Saline Point, they, too, glided to a stop, except for *Domani,* which made a big mistake and hugged Grand Anse Beach. At least we thought it was a mistake until we saw the light morning air that drifted down the hills fill her sails. She moved forward, a bare thin wake trailing behind. After the longest thirty minutes on record, we drifted across the finish line. The crowds onshore shouted and waved the new Grenada national flag, but we knew better. *Domani* coasted over the line, easily beating us on corrected time.

At the victory banquet at the yacht club the next night, I told Carl that if he were a real gentleman, he would invite the crew to a piglet barbeque, but he didn't think I was funny. Henry the Navigator still lives on Carl's estate in Grenada. He'll never know how close he came to a very, very long swim.

We continued to race the balance of the season with considerably more success. Prince Henry was replaced by vote of the crew with Hank Strauss, an honor he could hardly refuse. And while I enjoyed the excitement and the physical effort, I must admit here and now that I'm not impressed with sailboat racing. It is, I concede, a firmly fixed prejudice. I love to compete and have participated in several sports, both team and individual. I have raced sports cars, motorcycles, inland scows, and snowmobiles, but I think sailboat racing is a nonproductive sport.

During many years of auto racing, great contributions have been made to the speed and safety of automobiles. Disc brakes, independent suspension, fuel injection, and more efficient engines are just a few of the improvements that have found their way into today's car after testing and development on the racetrack. What has today's insane yacht racing rules developed? Fragile, under-rigged, under-sailed, uncomfortable, unsafe Clorox bottles. And the advertising agencies have the chutzpah to call last year's losers in the Southern Ocean Racing Conference cruising boats. The rule makers have set sailboat construction and design back fifty years.

I will admit that one-class racers don't cheat any more or less than race car mechanics, and at least the sport purports to pit one man's skill as a sailor against another's. (In car racing the saying is that the only thing that beats cubic inches is cubic dollars.) And yet I cannot find anything that the America's Cup, Olympic one-class, or multi-class ocean racing have developed that would benefit the average run of deep-sea cruisers. I believe that length for length, sail for sail, with no phony rules to interfere, *Serenity* at thirty years old could beat a modern racing machine on a long race. Even if I'm wrong, the crew would be a hell of a lot safer and more comfortable on *Serenity* when the race was over.

One last harangue. Many of the gentlemen sailboat skippers I have met would sink your boat if they thought that they could get away with rounding a mark ahead of you. Race car drivers are not gentlemen. They have dirty fingernails and they swear a lot, but once on a proper line for a corner, they will let you through without a challenge. The implied code of ethics among drivers is far more gentlemanly than anything I've ever seen among racing sailors. A protest filed on an auto racecourse is a rare and expensive occurrence. But in the average hometown yacht club race, the red protest flag pops out like measles. As I have said, I'm not impressed with sailboat racers and their boats.

By careful planning and attention to our tasks, we managed to screw away the winter without accomplishing anything meaningful. It was a delightful time.

The first of April we hauled *Serenity* for a bottom job. I hired a couple of local young men, and we repainted the topsides, installed a new knotmeter, painted the bottom, and were ready for the water in three days. Dodd, the yard manager, eased the railway cradle down the ways, and at the end of the cable we were still six inches from floating. Dodd cranked us back up a few feet to wait for high tide the next day. There is nothing so ignominious as a sailboat tilted half in and half out of the water. Friends came by to encourage us.

"You're going to have to go a lot faster if you plan to fly."

"What's the matter, Zane, miss your slip?"

"If you plant it, she'll make a lovely flower box."

Finally someone passed over a long board, and we crossed over to the dock, leaving poor *Serenity* on her strange perch for the night. It was the only time in her life she looked unlady-like.

The trip up-island was slow and easy, as we called at familiar anchorages to see old friends again. On every island there were goodbyes to be said. The highlight of that cruise was the peaceful week we spent on Anguilla, enjoying its lovely deserted beaches, and quiet, friendly people.

And then it was over. By October we were back in Fort Lauderdale. It was 3½ years since we had left Connecticut as two inexperienced, apprehensive sailors. Leaner, tanner, and wiser, we were now more certain of our identity and our relationship with each other and our world. In retrospect, I can truly say that I never had a bad day—not one. I've heard Es say, "While we were out in the middle of nowhere being tossed around like a cork, I couldn't wait for it to end. As soon as it was over, I couldn't wait to start again."

18 Some Reflections on Boats and Things

Back during the days when I was daydreaming about the possibility of sailing off into the sunset and leaving all my problems behind, I read every book I could find by others who had taken an extended cruise. I did this not so much to share their adventure vicariously, as to learn what I could about boats, equipment, and expenses—information that would help me plan my own voyage. This chapter is reserved, then, for others who may be thinking about following us, but whose experience may be as limited as ours was.

It is not that I expect anyone to take my advice as gospel. I am, as you have learned, a man of strong personal opinions. Rather, I hope that you will use the information gleaned from our experiences to weigh against your own knowledge and the advice of others.

Remember the Hungarian instructions for making chicken paprika? First steal a chicken. Voyages start with a boat—the boat. I never got over our good fortune in lucking into *Serenity*. She proved to be close to perfect for our needs. Your needs, of course, may be different. What I know about cruising boats I learned by inspecting every boat I could get aboard, and they numbered in the hundreds.

There is little good to say about American mass-produced fiberglass boats. Despite what the salesman may claim to the contrary, very few of them were ever intended for long-distance, open water cruising. They are cheap and easy to maintain, and there is a wide choice of sizes and styles, but I'd hate to be caught in a full gale in any of them. I've seen the seam between the deck and hull peeled back like a sardine can, hatch covers blown completely off, chain plates ripped out as if they had been set in butter, winches flung overboard when the fastenings pulled through the deck, engines wrenched loose from their beds, and a mast driven through the step into the keel. A famous make of this sort once arrived in Antigua with every bulkhead pulled away from the hull. Usually fiberglass boats are so light and tender that they rock if someone turns over in his bunk.

There are mass-produced boats that cruise successfully, but in every case the owner has completely reworked them. Everything on the boat has been reinforced, and the rigging and the gear upgraded at the expense of considerable time and money. But at least they are safe.

American and English manufacturers do make good, sound fiberglass cruising boats that are not out-of-date racing boats with extra berths squeezed in. They are normally of limited production and heavily constructed with pride and concern. No attempt has been made to save pennies on every fastening and fitting. The rigging is stout and the gear oversized. They are expensive, and they look it. If you are fortunate enough to be able to afford one, you will have the rarest of all boats— a safe, secure yacht with the minimum possible maintenance.

I don't know why mass-produced boats have to be so dangerous. Maybe we should all pitch in and buy Ralph Nader a yacht. I firmly believe that there are too many damned laws now, but I also believe that airplanes are a lot safer than boats because of those laws. Everything to do with the construction of an airplane—the design, engine, air frame, fittings and accessories, and even the mechanic—has to be approved by the FAA. If airplanes were built like boats, we'd still be taking the bus to San Francisco.

Wooden boats aren't the complete answer either, and it is true that when you buy an old wooden boat, you're also buying someone else's old problems. But wood yachts tend to be built with less concern for cost cutting, and the fittings are much heavier. I recently raced on a forty-one-foot plastic boat. The lifeline on *Serenity* had a larger diameter than its main shrouds, and the turnbuckle on my jumper strut was bigger than its forestay turnbuckle. I had lots of trouble with a working garboard strake and a poorly executed mast step on *Serenity,* but I never had a fitting break. The common fear of teredo worms and dry rot on wooden boats is grossly overstated. Careful regular maintenance will control both problems. Besides, if you're going to live on a boat, what will you do all day if you haven't got something to take care of?

I've been on only one aluminum boat, but I've been on several steel ones and have been very impressed. The standard bugaboo, electrolysis, wouldn't bother me on a cruising yacht. Cruisers are seldom plugged into shore power and rarely in a crowded marina. When I look for another boat, I will look first for a steel one.

On the subject of size, an old rule is the best. Get the biggest boat you can afford and can sail alone. Never mind your family or crew. They won't be around when you need them most. What can you handle? In my case, I think forty-five feet with the required sails and ground tackle was my upper limit. You may be stronger or younger and can handle more, but remember that dockage fees, haul out charges, taxes, licenses, and insurance rates are usually based on footage. The bigger the boat, the more expensive it will be in more ways than initial cost. But on the other hand, a small boat gets too small very fast, especially with guests.

Before a naval architect gets a job, he should be forced to sleep in a V berth at sea for a month. Maybe then they would quit calling that leaping, bucking torture rack in the forecastle the owner's stateroom. V berths originated in the days when paid hands were to be separated from the captain and it was improper to mix. I married my paid hand, and mixing is the name of the game.

One way to tell the experience of the designer is to check the berths on the boat. If there are more than four berths on a thirty-five-foot boat, forget it. It was designed by an advertising agency, not a sailor. If there is one quarter berth and one pilot berth both on the same side—say, starboard—get off the boat quick. It's liable to sink. It was designed by an architect who has never been to sea, since it was built to sail on a port tack forever. If you ever get on a starboard tack, the only place to sleep is on the cabin sole.

Serenity didn't have a double berth below, and for 3½ years I didn't hear the end of it. Accordingly and reluctantly, I will concede that only at anchor in a dead calm bay, with a big opening hatch overhead, is a V berth better than no double accommodations at all. If you are romantic enough to go sailing, you are romantic enough to share a double berth.

If you are planning to cruise anywhere from Virginia south, the cockpit is the most important area on the boat. It should be large enough to set up a table for meals, and the seats should be large enough to sleep on. *Serenity* had a bridge deck in the cockpit, and I rigged a plank to make a double bed. We spent most of our nights sleeping under the stars.

You are going to spend hours—days—hanging on to the wheel. Look around to make sure there is some place to sit down. You will be amazed at the number of naval architects who design cockpits with no comfortable place for the helmsman. These boats are best used as background for photographs advertising men's after-shave.

The common saloon arrangement of a dinette on one side and a pullman kitchen running down the other side belongs in a ticky-tacky tract house, not a boat. Yes, I know I said kitchen. I wouldn't dignify that dangerous scheme by calling it a galley. If you want anything to eat while at sea, the galley must be designed to brace the cook from the motion, and protect him or her from boiling soup, flying cans, sliding dishes, and spilling dishwater.

If the only seating in your saloon is the dinette (even the name isn't nautical), you can plan on eating half your meals on your lap because the table is usable (if at all) on only one tack. The idea of lowering the table to form a berth is as ridiculous as asking your guests to sleep on the dining room table at home.

One well-designed head is enough for any normal cruising boat. However long you like to sit and think each morning, nobody is hurrying off to school or to catch the 8:15 to the city. Scheduling the use of the head works itself out. The space for the second head is too valuable for the few minutes it will be used each day. Twice I have sailed other boats with two heads; both times the second head was used to stack cases of canned goods.

One head is all a human being with normal mechanical skill can keep operating anyway. Industrial designers and corporate executives must take pleasure in laughing at all us aesthetes, poets, and noble dreamers crouched in the tiny room, water and spare parts sloshing back and forth, while we try to repair one of the damned things. Unless you suffer from terminal constipation, never ever get on a boat with an electric head. If you can't keep a manual one operating for a month straight, think about an electric one. At worst, you will have to go over the side and that may be the best idea of all.

And while we're on that subject, may I say that holding tanks are an expensive joke. In my day I have helped finance maybe a quarter of the sewage treatment plants in the Midwest, and I have some knowledge of the subject. One paper mill dumps more high biochemical oxygen demand wastes in a day than all the cruising yachts in the world combined. The ocean is completely and endlessly capable of assimilating the human wastes from long-distance cruises. It's just that yachtsmen are all extremely visible and "rich." Congress would rather tackle us than the industrial polluters who have caused our waterways to stink so. In a marina with restricted tidal flow, you use the heads and showers onshore; that's what they are there for. But don't ask anyone where the waste water disappears to.

Nine-tenths of your garbage is also biodegradable and, as long as it's not in plastic bags, can be tossed overboard in the middle of a passage. That selection of garbage includes tin cans, but definitely does not include plastic or glass containers. Tin cans will be eaten up by salt water in a matter of days. I've dived on hundreds of reefs and I've never seen a can, but I've seen plenty of whiskey bottles. Plastic and glass must be taken ashore for disposal.

The only piece of equipment that worked constantly for three years was my Zippo lighter. It was also the only piece of equipment that didn't cost double its normal price because it was made for marine use.

My submersible bilge pump quit when the seal leaked. The pump was ingeniously designed to be sealed against any possibility of being taken apart and repaired, but not sealed enough to keep out water. I wrote an angry letter to the famous manufacturer, and they sent me a rebuilt pump which I paid for, including postage and import duty. Once installed, it lasted ten minutes. The trick in keeping a marine submersible pump working is not to submerse it.

My other bilge pump was made of bronze and had a hard rubber impeller. But the machine screw that held the impeller to the stainless shaft was common steel, and it corroded through. The cost accountant who replaced the stainless screw with a common steel one and saved $.0012 didn't realize that I was going to pump salt water. Half of the rusted screw was still threaded into the shaft. If you have never spent a day drilling a ¼-inch hole in the end of a stainless motor shaft with an egg-beater-type hand drill and then tapping new threads to replace a two-cent screw, you have missed one of the great character-building experiences. It is guaranteed to build blisters, biceps, fortitude, and a much larger vocabulary.

I kept remembering the famous line, "The best bilge pump in the world is a frightened man with a bucket."

I took my marine VHF transceiver in for repairs and the radio man who looked it over said, "My God, it's all corroded. Have you had this thing out on the ocean?"

It always comes as a surprise to these people that you actually try to use the marine gear on the ocean.

Anything electronic baffles me. I have no idea of how a radio works, and I don't believe TV is even possible. The only good advice I ever got on repairing electrical devices came from Les Glickman, who was a computer designer and builder before he bought *Karina,* and sailed into the dawn.

"Spray it with CRC, hit it sharply with the palm of your hand, and if it still doesn't work, throw it overboard."

Serenity had a Perkins 4.107 diesel, and it worked fine. I carried spare fan belts, gasket sets, filters, impellers, fuel injectors, and even a spare alternator. The major maintenance job on the engine was disassembling and flushing the freshwater heat exchanger that periodically clogged up with gunk. I learned how to do this from a complete engine shop manual we carried. I had repair manuals for every device on the boat bound in plastic sheets in two notebooks that I couldn't have lived without.

I wouldn't get on a yacht with a gasoline engine. In fact, I didn't allow any volatile liquids below decks. We carried our outboard fuel lashed to a deck fitting where it could only spill overboard.

Our expensive safety harnesses were made of Dacron with stainless buckles and snap shackles, but the spring in the shackle was ordinary steel, and it rusted out. The harnesses weren't so safe after that.

The firing pin in the flare gun corroded despite the fact

that it was sealed in a plastic box and periodically oiled.

It was not just my gear. Every time I would be sitting on a dock cleaning, oiling, or scraping, a neighbor would stop by and report that something on his boat had just rusted into uselessness. Most of this stuff was manufactured by well-known corporations, advertised in the best yachting magazines, and sold in responsible marine stores. And it's junk—all junk.

Ralph Nader, oh where are you now when we need you?

I don't believe I've overstated anything. Your primary concern must be a safe, strong boat and a healthy reserve of money for maintenance and repairs. And only after that, think about fancy equipment. When you pick out a boat, look at it with a critical eye. Imagine, if you can, the ultimate storm and then check it over again. Disaster can happen to anyone.

One bright clear day in Grenada, I helped cast off lines for a professional delivery crew who were taking a relatively new forty-foot fiberglass sloop up to St. Lucia, a trip they had made many times before. A sudden blast capsized them within sight of the Pitons, and in seconds the boat sunk. The two men made it to the dinghy with emergency supplies, but no one on St. Lucia saw them. The wind and current swept them offshore, and they drifted for twelve days until they were picked up near the Central American coast.

When we first got to English Harbour, a group of young Californians were completing the refurbishing of an eighty-foot three-masted schooner, *Santa Cruz*. I have never seen a more hard-working, dedicated crew. I photographed her first sail on completion, and she was a well-founded, heavily rigged traditional beauty. Three years later she was making a routine passage from Dominica to Antigua when, twelve miles southeast of Montserrat, she was hit by a squall of such ferocity that she rolled over and trapped one of her owners, Korky Gill, below. Her four surviving crew members were tossed into the loneliness and terror of the night. Luckily, two Sunfish lashed to the deck broke free and shot to the surface, and the four paddled eight hours to reach Montserrat and safety.

That is a very big ocean out there, and it's very deep. You're going out in the middle of it, and you are taking your crew with you. It is not a decision to be taken lightly. Safety at sea not only requires a sound, sturdy boat, but also decent food and rest. No sailor can function without all three. If you are lost at sea, the chairman of the board of the conglomerate that built your boat, the production line foreman, the itinerant worker, and the advertising copywriter won't lift an eyebrow. The final, ultimate responsibility is yours alone.

The most valuable things on *Serenity* were my collection of tools. I had one big toolbox filled with mechanic's tools left over from my racing days, so I had only to add a few pieces to make it complete. I bought a second carpenter's box and filled it with every woodworking hand tool I could think of. I did have some electric tools—a drill, two sanders, and two saws. They were useful mainly in boat yards, but emergency repairs seldom wait for boat yards. I also carried a wide assortment of fastenings, both bronze and stainless; nuts and bolts; grommets; and snap fastenings. A tap-and-die set and a staple gun with stainless staples are necessities. You will also need a soldering iron that can be heated on the stove, a good assortment of electrical squeeze connectors, and several rolls of insulated wire of various gauges.

I wouldn't have made it without two-part epoxy in resealable cans. There are different types—liquid, paste, underwater—I had them all. The list of things you can do with epoxy is really endless. You can patch sails, waterproof electrical splices, repair pipes, and reset screws. The spark plug blew out of my single-cylinder outboard motor, and I glued it back in with epoxy. Despite the heat and the compression, it worked for two months until I could drill it out and fit an adapter plug into the hole. Carry as much wet and dry sandpaper, paint, varnish, and brushes as you can stow. You can buy food and drink any place you go, but tools and fastenings are frequently impossible to find.

Even if you start out not knowing which end of the screwdriver to put in your mouth, you will have become a shipwright, engine mechanic, sailmaker, electrician, plumber, rigger, and probably an authority on busted fingernails and skinned knuckles by the time you return from an extended cruise. When you come across something that you don't know about or have never fixed before, ask somebody. There are an amazing number of skilled mechanics sailing around on boats, and all are generous with their help and advice. If you don't possess any particular talents to swap, keep a good supply of beer on board.

Other than electronics, there are few things on a boat that you can't take apart if you just sit and stare at it for a few minutes. I always reminded myself that the damned thing was put together by an ordinary mortal and I'm as smart as he is, so I must be able to fix it, given enough time. It is true that I sometimes ran out of time, but I usually got it fixed. The next owner of *Serenity* is going to find some pretty strange repair jobs, but almost everything works.

Unless you are very rich, you will be forced into doing much of your repair and maintenance work yourself. About half of the boat yards will let you do your own work at haul-out time. The other half have local laborers available at far less than stateside wages. You can always find local workers who can sand, paint, and varnish. Here again, ask another yachtsman to recommend somebody; some of the local workmen are better talkers than they are workers. Your fellow cruiser will also tell you the prevailing wages and customs. Skilled labor —machinists, welders, and sailmakers—are relatively expensive and not terribly reliable.

There are exceptions. When we reached Tortola, I was very worried about my wet exhaust system. It hadn't corroded through yet, but when it did, it could ruin my engine. Through another yachtsman I found Ashton McCall, the diesel mechanic for Caribbean Sailing Yachts. On his own time, he designed, welded, and installed a standpipe exhaust system that is safer and stronger than my original one. The parts, labor, and Ashton's good company cost $120.

My advice is worth repeating. When you get into trouble, ask for help from someone who has been cruising in the area longer than you have.

Repairs bring us to the subject of money. Our boat and everything on it were paid for. We did not carry any boat insurance because the premiums were exorbitant for the protection they offered. Even so, our 3½-year trip cost us one-third more than we had planned. Our expenses ran four hundred dollars a month, excluding a few items. Our monthly expense average does include all haul outs and normal maintenance, but does not include a yard bill for the replacement of both garboard strakes and the rebuilding of our mast step. I consider this an extraordinary repair, but extraordinary repairs do happen, and you have to be prepared for them. Too many couples spend too much for their boat and when a major breakdown occurs, they are stuck in a distant harbor far from home, waiting for God knows what to rescue them.

We did spend more money than many live-aboard cruisers on car rentals and taxis because we enjoyed exploring every island and considered it very much a part of our experiences. We also ate ashore more than some, but in many cases it cost little more to eat in a local restaurant than to cook for two people. That's a matter of your own feelings. Other than the noted exceptions, I imagine our expenses were about average among cruising couples. Cruising is the most expensive way in the world to travel third class.

Earning money while cruising is pretty tough. I did sell several articles to yachting magazines, but the payment was not always worth the effort. Only a very few writers or photographers can make a living while cruising. We did spend a season day-chartering at Curtain Bluff Hotel, but the best that can be said is that it didn't cost anything. Sometimes breaking even is not a bad thing.

It is improbable that you can depend on making any meaningful contribution to your income and still cruise. Long-term chartering is an undependable racket for the full-time professionals with experience and a reputation. If you are an artist, craftsman, or designer, you may be able to peddle some of your work, but don't count on it. There are many more good divers than there are diving jobs, and most of them are willing to dive just for the fun of it. If you are a welder, engine mechanic, teacher, or doctor whose skills or training would be useful on the islands, you have two choices—get a work permit or bootleg. It is next to impossible for an American to get a work permit on the islands, even for desperately needed skills. Es is an R.N. and trained nurses are rarer than doctors, but she could never get a work permit. Bootlegging, working without a work permit, is both dangerous and temporary. Sooner or later someone will blow the whistle. At best, you will be kicked off the island; at worst, you will pay a fine or have your boat confiscated and then be kicked off the island. I knew two sailors, one a welder and the other an outstanding ship's cabinetmaker, who were both in great demand. Both were apprehended and got into serious difficulties. We met a charming young guy who knew how to weave great hats out of palm fronds, which he sold to tourists on the beach. He lasted two weeks until the locals nailed him. Smuggling or interisland freighting is reserved for the locals, and they aren't going to let you have a piece of the action. I don't have to tell you that smuggling dope is a hard way to go. Just stop by and take a look at any island jail.

A British sailor might be able to get a work permit on a British island, and a Frenchman might get a work permit on a French island. An American can't get a work permit anywhere.

American Express and Visa credit cards are valuable in the islands. There is usually a bank affiliate that will honor them and issue local currency against them. Personal checks are cashed only after clearance, and that can take a lifetime. All money exchange is unreasonably expensive. You can plan on a shrinkage of 5 to 10 percent on all forms of exchange. I was once paid 'for a diving job with a check drawn on an Antiguan Bank. When I cashed it in the bank's branch in Grenada, the long-distance calls and various charges came to 15 percent of the check. I screamed like a wounded eagle.

"Do you realize that if every check used in payment for every commercial transaction in the world were discounted by 15 percent, it would take 16 2/3 days before the entire currency float of every nation would be in the hands of the international bankers?"

The banker was unimpressed. Cool, suave, and unperturbed, like every banker the world over, he calmly explained,

"You just don't understand our problems, sir."

"I don't understand? I was a professor of international economics for twenty years at Harvard!" (That was a bald-faced, unmitigated lie. I've never even seen Harvard.)

Placated, head held high, I marched out of the bank—minus 15 percent of my check.

Our cruise was really made possible by a fortuitous happening. Our attorney, Barry Lazarus, thought it was romantic and exciting that two of his straight clients were taking off. He volunteered to handle our stateside business, which meant that he paid all our credit card charges and handled our money and taxes. I don't think he still thinks it's so romantic, but nevertheless he did take care of everything while we were gone. It will take somebody like Barry—a lawyer, an accountant, or a member of your family—to handle your affairs for you. If you are to enjoy your cruise, you will be moving around enough to make normal communication and normal business relationships impossible. Without someone to take charge for you, a long-distance, time-consuming cruise is difficult to arrange and manage.

Imagine, for example, an interview with a credit manager. You tell him that you have no permanent address, no job, and no belongings other than those you carry with you on a boat and that you don't know where you'll pick up your next mail. Just before he throws you out of his office, he may give you an award for the best story of the year.

Be warned, however, that whomever you choose—friend or attorney—you will have to sign scores of documents and a power of attorney. Barry once told me that he was authorized to divorce Es without any complaint from me. He chose not to because there was never enough money in our bank account to make it worthwhile.

When we chartered boats before, they were vacations. When the vacation was over, we returned to the real (or is it unreal?) world to settle our own affairs. Cruising is not an endless vacation. There are serious problems to be faced every day. Your floating home needs constant attention. There are daily physical demands. Your mental processes must be adaptable to new demands and stresses. Mundane matters of finance, things you take for granted in your present life, become serious concerns. There is nothing that can't be solved, but they do require your attention.

What is remarkable is how quickly you can adapt to the island way of life. Other than the maintenance of your boat, everything else solves itself mañana (someday). If you are neat, orderly, and compulsively efficient, forget it. You are not suited for a life of freedom and formlessness, a life of daydreams come true. To the rest of you, I wish only fair winds and far places.

Index